PSYCHOLOGY OF PERSUASION

PSYCHOLOGY OF EMOTIONS, MOTIVATIONS AND ACTIONS

Psychology of Expectations
Pablo León and Nino Tamez (Editors)
2010. ISBN: 978-1-60876-832-5

**Cognitive and Neuroscientific
Aspects of Human Love: A Guide
for Marriage and Couples Counseling**
*Wiiliam A. Lambos and William G.
Emener*
2010. ISBN: 978-1-61668-281-1

Psychology of Intuition
*Bartoli Ruelas and Vanessa Briseño
(Editors)*
2010. ISBN: 978-1-60876-899-8

**Extraverted and Energized: Review
and Tests of Stress Moderation
and Mediation**
Dave Korotkov
2010. ISBN: 978-1-61668-325-2
2010. ISBN: 978-1-61668-703-8 (E-book)

**Emotion's Effects on Attention and
Memory: Relevance to Posttraumatic
Stress Disorder**
*Katherine Mickley Steinmetz
and Elizabeth Kensinger*
2010. ISBN: 978-1-61668-239-2
2010. ISBN: 978-1-61668-532-4(E-book)

**Friendships: Types, Cultural,
Psychological and Social Aspects**
Joan C. Tolle (Editor)
2010. ISBN: 978-1-61668-008-4
2010. ISBN: 978-1-61668-386-3 (E-book)

**Reputation and the Evolution of
Generous Behavior**
Pat Barclay
2010. ISBN: 978-1-61668-153-1
2010. ISBN: 978-1-61668-402-0 (E-book)

Smoking as a Risk Factor for Suicide
Maurizio Pompili
2010. ISBN: 978-1-61668-507-2
2010. ISBN: 978-1-61668-817-2(E-book)

**Creativity: Fostering, Measuring
and Contexts**
Alessandra M. Corrigan (Editor)
2010. ISBN: 978-1-61668-807-3
2010. ISBN: 978-1-61728-067-2 (E-book)

**Personality Traits: Classifications,
Effects and Changes**
John Paul Villanueva (Editor)
2010. ISBN: 978-1-61668-619-2

PSYCHOLOGY OF PERSUASION

JANOS CSAPÓ
AND
ANDOR MAGYAR
EDITORS

Nova Science Publishers, Inc.
New York

For permission to use material from this book please contact us:
Telephone 631-231-7269; Fax 631-231-8175
Web Site: http://www.novapublishers.com

NOTICE TO THE READER

The Publisher has taken reasonable care in the preparation of this book, but makes no expressed or implied warranty of any kind and assumes no responsibility for any errors or omissions. No liability is assumed for incidental or consequential damages in connection with or arising out of information contained in this book. The Publisher shall not be liable for any special, consequential, or exemplary damages resulting, in whole or in part, from the readers' use of, or reliance upon, this material. Any parts of this book based on government reports are so indicated and copyright is claimed for those parts to the extent applicable to compilations of such works.

Independent verification should be sought for any data, advice or recommendations contained in this book. In addition, no responsibility is assumed by the publisher for any injury and/or damage to persons or property arising from any methods, products, instructions, ideas or otherwise contained in this publication.

This publication is designed to provide accurate and authoritative information with regard to the subject matter covered herein. It is sold with the clear understanding that the Publisher is not engaged in rendering legal or any other professional services. If legal or any other expert assistance is required, the services of a competent person should be sought. FROM A DECLARATION OF PARTICIPANTS JOINTLY ADOPTED BY A COMMITTEE OF THE AMERICAN BAR ASSOCIATION AND A COMMITTEE OF PUBLISHERS.

LIBRARY OF CONGRESS CATALOGING-IN-PUBLICATION DATA

Psychology of persuasion / editors, Janos Csapó and Andor Magyar.
    p. cm.
  Includes index.
  ISBN 978-1-60876-590-4 (hbk.)
  1. Persuasion (Psychology) I. Csapó, Janos. II. Magyar, Andor.
  BF637.P4P74 2009
  153.8'52--dc22
                        2009043038

Published by Nova Science Publishers, Inc. ✦ New York

CONTENTS

PREFACE

Persuasion is the activity of demonstrating and trying to modify the behavior of at least one person through symbolic interaction. This book surveys formal models of persuasion dialog that are now widely used in argumentation and artificial intelligence as tools for the identification, analysis and evaluation of arguments. Within the sports arena, coaches and athletes routinely look for ways to improve performance. While most of these attempts tend to focus on physical practice, the role of the mind, and psychological factors such as self-efficacy, has become increasingly important. The research and theory within this area are explored and the authors make recommendations with regards to the content and delivery of pep talks. Furthermore, it is well-known that most advertising persuades by argument and most of those arguments are logical. The authors apply Gilbert's Multimodal Argumentation Model to a series of advertisements. In addition, a peculiar kind of persuasive communication is discussed: the fictitious argument between a human being and personified death. As the choice of German-speaking texts examined here exemplifies, the dialogic and rhetorically structured way of dealing with the mortal threat has been living on well into Modern times. Other chapters explore current research on regulatory fit and persuasion into the larger contexts of elaboration likelihood and transportation likelihood. Current research on how regulatory fit affects persuasion through advocacy messages and through narratives is looked at as well.

Chapter 1 - The theory of argumentation is a rich, interdisciplinary area of research straddling philosophy, communication studies, linguistics, psychology and artificial intelligence (Bench-Capon and Dunne, 2007). Argumentation can be abstractly defined as the interaction of different arguments for and against some conclusion. Argumentation has developed context-sensitive practical methods used to help a user identify, analyze and evaluate arguments, especially common ones of the kind often found in everyday discourse, legal argumentation, and in other contexts of use. In argumentation theory, types of dialog are used as normative models that provide standards for analyzing a given argument as used in a conversational setting in a given case. So far, most of the work has concentrated on what is called persuasion dialog, a type of conversational setting in which one arguer uses arguments to try to persuade another arguer to accept some view that the first arguer holds.

This paper surveys formal models of persuasion dialog that are now widely used in argumentation and artificial intelligence as tools for the identification, analysis and evaluation of arguments (Greenwood, Bench-Capon and McBurney, 2003; Leenes, 2001; Lodder, 1999; Prakken, 2006). A very simple system that has formed the basis of many other formal systems of persuasion dialog is chosen to show how such models can be applied them to a number of examples that represent interesting problems or phenomena of persuasion. Persuasion dialog can now be considered a specific term used in computing and argumentation studies to refer to a specific type of rule-governed procedure with a specific goal of resolving a difference of opinions by means of arguments put forward and questioned Prakken, 2006).

Many examples of persuasion dialogs can be found in ordinary conversation. However, the rules of rational argumentation governing such dialogs are often problematic to determine and apply, because such conversations often tend to wander, cease abruptly, use subterfuge, degenerate into verbal quarrels, and so forth. For this reason, in this article the authors will take our examples from argumentation that takes place in a particular type of persuasion dialog, a familiar type of legal dialog in a trial setting, in which two opposed parties try to persuade a third party, a judge (trier of fact). Our model will abstract from many of the details on what goes on in such exchanges, and only tries to model how examples of an argument put forward by one side or reacted to by the other side fall into certain common patterns.

Chapter 2 - In the era of quality in interactive communications, persuasion is an implicit attribute in the human-computer interaction process and the human-computer interface design. Persuasion avails itself of the new technologies to modify the behaviour of the potential users of the on-line and off-line interactive systems. In our case, the authors will focus on its presence in the on-line systems aimed at university education. The authors think of education as being one of the cornerstones of any society, just the same as health care therefore, it is important to discover how persuasion underlies in some environments which can seriously damage the potential users, multimedia content generators, interactive systems designers, etc. Consequently, the authors present a series of techniques and heuristic methods to unveil the persuasion practiced on-line for the last eight years in a European university context. Through it, it will be possible to analyze and understand each one of the variable components that foster or destroy the validity of on-line information through persuasion. Through the obtained results a heuristic guide is presented in order to detect the presence of persuasion with advice as to how to avoid it in the case that there is no intention to have an influence on behaviour. Simultaneously the power of persuasion in the virtual community of students and teachers will be analyzed, with examples where credibility fades into disappearance in some cases. A linguistic and semiotic analysis will make it possible to establish a series of isotopies along time to discover in our case of study those links in which persuasion can be linked with manipulation and even with destructive behaviours such as bullying, mobbing, bossing about, stalking, etc. all of them very well disguised in the construction of e-mail messages, for instance.

Chapter 3 - This chapter puts current research on regulatory fit and persuasion into the larger contexts of elaboration likelihood and transportation likelihood (the likelihood of becoming experientially engaged with a narrative). I lay groundwork by describing regulatory fit with prevention focus and promotion focus, how regulatory fit is operationally defined, and how it can affect judgments through feelings-as-information, metacognitive, and other processes. Then I review current research on how regulatory fit affects persuasion through advocacy messages and through narratives, noting where interpretational ambiguities exist. Finally I speculate about how effects of regulatory fit on persuasion might differ according to elaboration or transportation likelihood and according to whether the regulatory-fit experience results from an initial event unrelated to the communication or from engagement with the communication itself.

Chapter 4 - This chapter deals with a peculiar kind of persuasive communication: the fictitious argument between a human being and personified death. This old literary motif shows a person who is about to die arguing with an anthropomorphic death figure. As the choice of German-speaking texts discussed here exemplifies, the dialogic and rhetorically structured way of dealing with the mortal threat has been living on well into Modern times. Various classical strategies of persuasion have been adapted to this particular scenario, trying to give the respective conceptions of life and death a vivid and convincing voice.

Chapter 5 - Within the sports arena, coaches and athletes routinely look for ways to improve performance. While most of these attempts tend to focus on physical practice, the roles of the mind, and psychological factors such as self-efficacy, have become increasingly important. Self-efficacy has long been a strong predictor of athletic performance (Feltz, 1988, 1994) and may perhaps be one of the keys to enhanced competitive performance. While verbal persuasion is a source of self-efficacy, one often overlooked aspect of this efficacy source is the pep talk. The pep talk is the coach's final opportunity to help set athletes up for success prior to competition. It is possible that an effective pep talk has the ability to persuade athletes to feel more efficacious (Vargas-Tonsing and Bartholomew, 2006), to appropriately channel facilitative emotions (Vargas-Tonsing, 2009), and to start competition with positive expectations for success (Vargas-Tonsing and Short, 2008). Thus, this overlooked form of verbal persuasion can help create the springboard for a positive cycle of performance. By design, the pep talk leads to feelings of functional emotions and high efficacy which then impacts performance. The improved performance further enhances these positive feelings which should, in turn, continue to enhance performance; thus establishing a positive cycle. It is clear that the pep talk is one small aspect of verbal persuasion with potential for great impact. This chapter will explore the research and theory within this area and make recommendations for the content and delivery of pep talks.

Chapter 6 - As a first step towards development of intelligent system using a virtual agent that proactively interacts with a user and changes user's intension according to the user's circumstances, the authors examine how to react with the user under several emotional situations. The authors set up scenarios that evoked emotional feelings in a user and controlled the agent's reaction in order to evaluate the user's impression of the agent. In this experiment, they made 96 patterns of content, which were a combination of emotional scenarios, facial expressions, and words used by the agent. The test subjects accessed the content and answered a questionnaire on the Web. After discussing the experimental results, the authors derive a rule for the agent's reaction favorable to the user on the basis of facial expressions and words.

Chapter 7 - A half century after Vance Packard's *The Hidden Persuaders* labelled advertising as immoral because of psychological techniques used to get us to buy, we are still seeking ways to determine when an ad crosses an ethical boundary. Most advertising persuades by argument. Michael Gilbert of York University maintains we need to examine three other modes of argumentation as well: emotional, physical, and intuitive. This chapter examines the application of Gilbert's Multimodal Argumentation Model to a series of advertisements, exploring how analyzing in all four modes can help a reader decide whether a particular ad violates his or her ethical principles

Chapter 8 - The advancement of technologies has brought us numerous advantages in our daily lives, however, at the same time, a sedentary lifestyle has caused lack of physical activity and lifestyle-related disease, which is becoming a social problem.

The authors propose to utilize a mirror as a medium that increases awareness of daily walking by facilitating reflection, where motivational elements are embedded into not only presented information, but also its presence.

A mirror acts as a self-focusing stimulus, which facilitates \textit{objective self-awareness}, a state in which an individual is ready for evaluating her current self-conception against an internal standard of correctness. Furthermore, the \textit{objective self-awareness} is enhanced by super-imposing motivational information with the appearance of a person staying in front of a mirror.

In this article, the authors design an augmented mirror with four strategies to reflect on daily walking: 1) pleasurable interaction with information obtained through daily activity, 2) supporting reflection on each day's walking, 3) avoiding negative feelings while providing negative feedback and 4) facilitating inter-personal encouragement. Then, in-house experiments are conducted with 8 participants for 3 to 6 months. A comparative study with other display objects, a digital photo frame and wall, is done to see the effect of a mirror. The result implies that our proposed system supported reflection on a person's daily walking. Positive effects of the four strategies have also been found.

In: Psychology of Persuasion
Editors: J. Csapó and A. Magyar, pp.1-34

ISBN: 978-1-60876-590-4
© 2010 Nova Science Publishers, Inc.

Chapter 1

ARGUMENTATION MODELS FOR PERSUASION DIALOG

Douglas Walton
University of Windsor, Windsor, Ontario, Canada

The theory of argumentation is a rich, interdisciplinary area of research straddling philosophy, communication studies, linguistics, psychology and artificial intelligence (Bench-Capon and Dunne, 2007). Argumentation can be abstractly defined as the interaction of different arguments for and against some conclusion. Argumentation has developed context-sensitive practical methods used to help a user identify, analyze and evaluate arguments, especially common ones of the kind often found in everyday discourse, legal argumentation, and in other contexts of use. In argumentation theory, types of dialog are used as normative models that provide standards for analyzing a given argument as used in a conversational setting in a given case. So far, most of the work has concentrated on what is called persuasion dialog, a type of conversational setting in which one arguer uses arguments to try to persuade another arguer to accept some view that the first arguer holds.

This paper surveys formal models of persuasion dialog that are now widely used in argumentation and artificial intelligence as tools for the identification, analysis and evaluation of arguments (Greenwood, Bench-Capon and McBurney, 2003; Leenes, 2001; Lodder, 1999; Prakken, 2006). A very simple system that has formed the basis of many other formal systems of persuasion dialog is chosen to show how such models can be applied them to a number of examples that represent interesting problems or phenomena of persuasion. Persuasion dialog can now be considered a specific term used in computing and argumentation studies to refer to a specific type of rule-governed procedure with a specific goal of resolving a difference of opinions by means of arguments put forward and questioned Prakken, 2006).

Many examples of persuasion dialogs can be found in ordinary conversation. However, the rules of rational argumentation governing such dialogs are often problematic to determine and apply, because such conversations often tend to wander, cease abruptly, use subterfuge, degenerate into verbal quarrels, and so forth. For this reason, in this article we will take our examples from argumentation that takes place in a particular type of persuasion dialog, a familiar type of legal dialog in a trial setting, in which two opposed parties try to persuade a third party, a judge (trier of fact). Our model will abstract from many of the details on what goes on in such exchanges, and only tries to model how examples of an argument put forward by one side or reacted to by the other side fall into certain common patterns.

PERSUASION DIALOGS IN MODERN ARGUMENTATION THEORIES

Persuasion dialog is a term commonly used in argumentation studies (see Walton and Krabbe 1995; Walton 1999), artificial intelligence (see Loui 1998; Brewka 2001), and artificial intelligence in law (see Prakken 2001; Bench Capon 1998; Gordon 1994). As clearly stated by Prakken (2006: 1), persuasion dialog can be broadly defined as a dialog in which two or more participants try to resolve a difference of opinion by means of arguments, in order for each party to lead the other participants to change their point of view. On those views, persuasion dialogs do not need to be verbal exchanges, as they are often applied to online disputes (see Godden and Walton 2005; Atkinson et al., 2006), multi-agent systems (see Betahar et al. 2004) , or agents-machine interactions (see Ravenscroft 2009).

Persuasion dialogs are grounded on the interlocutors' (or agents') commitments, namely the speaker's undertaking to a statement he made. The statements of the agents engaged in a persuasion dialog are not analyzed in terms of belief or knowledge, but rather of interpersonal rules of communication or effects on the dialogical situation. Statements bind the speaker to a certain type of dialogical behaviour, obviously relative to the type of communicative setting or type of interaction. For instance, asserting a proposition would reasonably lead the speaker not to deny it in his next move, or to defend it in case it is challenged by the other party. This dialogical perspective was opened by the works of Hamblin (1970; 1971), in which he used the notion of commitment to formalize dialogs and describe fallacies. On his view, formal dialogs are aimed at exchanging information; however (1971: 148) he distinguishes between information-oriented dialog from other systems, in which participants are permitted "to develop an argument by securing assent to individual steps". Those systems are grounded on a rationality principle, meaning that not only is the speaker committed to his statements, but also to their logical consequences. This account became the foundation of Walton's formal dialog games (1984), and the idea of distinguishing different types of dialogs on the grounds of commitment rules and participant's goals was later developed by Walton and Krabbe (1995) in the idea of the persuasion dialog.

Persuasion dialog represents an abstract normative model of how rational argumentation should ideally proceed when two parties have a difference opinion and want to try to resolve the issue by bringing forward their strongest arguments, while at the same time criticizing the argument of the other side. The core notion of rational persuasion in the basic and simplest instance of persuasion dialog can be shown using figure 1 (Walton, 1989: 6).

Each party has a task to perform in the dialog, and the successful carrying out of that task by using rational argumentation is the goal of each party. The proponent's task is to rationally persuade the respondent to come to accept her (the proponent's) thesis. The respondent's task is to rationally persuade the proponent to come to accept his (the respondent's) thesis. Of course, how such an abstract model of rational persuasion can be applied to real examples of persuasion attempts in conversational argumentation raises many interesting questions. In this paper, we apply one of the simplest of the various abstract models to a series of real examples.

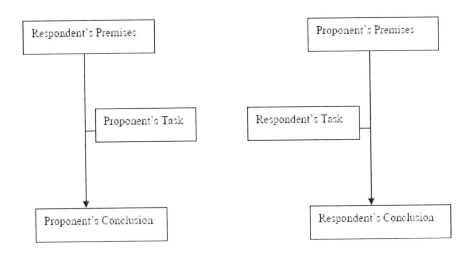

Figure 1. Commitment structure of persuasion dialog.

The abstract model of persuasion dialog set forth in the next section is very simple. There are only two parties, called the proponent and the opponent, and each tries to persuade the other to accept a claim by using arguments to prove it. Persuasion dialogs stem from a conflict of opinion, consisting in the respondent's denial or questioning of the proponent's position, and presuppose that each party has the capacity and freedom of defending its point of view (see Vanderveken 2001). The commitment to incompatible positions (A: Bob stole the milk; B: Bob did not steal the milk), or the interlocutor's refusal to accept the speaker's viewpoint (A: Bob stole the milk; B: Why do you say that?), is the dialogical situation which the dialog is aimed at altering. The interlocutor's goal is to change the other party's commitments, and therefore its evaluation of a situation, which can be a description (Bob stole the milk) or a judgment (Bob is a thief). The instrument to lead the interlocutor to change their position is a chain of arguments following from premises belonging to the knowledge shared by the latter. Arguments in persuasion dialog can be conceived as patterns of reasoning transferring the acceptability of the premises, or rather the strength of the interlocutor's commitment to them, to the conclusion (for the transferring of plausibility from premises to conclusion, see Hahn and Oaksford xxxx (the rationality).

The historical roots of the notion of persuasion dialog can be found in the meaning of the word "persuasion" (Rigotti 1995: 11). This word semantically stems from *pístis*, namely the credit that a speaker obtains by means of his speech, namely the recipient's agreement. On Rigotti's view, "the relation constituted by *pístis* is not only cognitive, but goes though the whole area of the human relationships, both institutionalised and personal" (*ibidem*). In persuasion dialogs, the goal is to achieve the interlocutor's agreement with the speaker's viewpoint, respecting his freedom of choice, in order to modify his or her decision making related to a particular judgment on a state of affairs (see Rigotti and Cigada 2004). The purpose is to change some of the interlocutor's commitments (Walton and Krabbe, 1995) in order to lead him or her to modify his viewpoint.

One of the crucial matters in persuasion dialog is the target of persuasion. Dialogs can be between two parties, or between two parties and a judge who assesses the parties' argument and decides which is the winning party, or which viewpoint is better supported by evidence and reason. In the first case the judge corresponds to the parties themselves, whereas in the second case it coincides with the interlocutor. This distinction between those two types of persuasion dialog was in the tradition identified with one of the differences between dialectics and rhetoric (see Boethii *De Differentiis Topicis* 1206C).

The goal of a persuasion dialog is to reveal the strongest arguments on both sides by pitting one against the other to resolve the initial conflict posed at the opening stage (Walton, 2007). This burden of persuasion, as it is called (Prakken, 2006), is set at the opening stage. In a persuasion dialog the proponent, has a particular thesis to be proved, while the respondent has the role of casting doubt on that thesis or arguing for an opposed thesis. These tasks are set at the opening stage, and remain in place until the closing stage, when one party or the other fulfils its burden of persuasion. The proponent has a burden of persuasion to prove (by a set standard of proof) the proposition that is designated in advance as her ultimate thesis. The respondent's role is to cast doubt on the proponent's attempts to succeed in achieving such proof.

The two crucial aspects of persuasion dialog, as modeled in recent formal systems (see below), is change of the interlocutor's dialogical situation by means of arguments grounded on propositions already accepted by the other party. All these accounts stem from a common conception of dialog game developed by Hamblin, Woods and Walton (1978), Mackenzie (1979), Hintikka (1979) and Barth and Krabbe (1982). Dialogs evolved from the application of logical axioms to propositions which were not considered true or false, but only belonging to the commitment store of the participants. Dialogs were distinguished in (Walton and Krabbe 1995: 66), and later in (Walton 1998), in basic six types, according to the participants' goal, initial situation, and the goal of dialog, shown in table 1.

Table 1. Persuasion dialog as a type of dialog

Type of Dialog	Initial Situation	Participants' Goal	Goal of Dialog
Persuasion	Conflict of opinions	Persuade the other party	Resolve or clarify issue
Inquiry	Need to have proof	Find and verify evidence	Prove (disprove) hypotheses
Negotiation	Conflict of interests	Get what you want most	Reasonable settlement that both can live with
Information-Seeking	Need of information	Acquire or give information	Exchange of information
Deliberation	Dilemma or personal choice	Co-ordinate goals and actions	Decide the best available course of action
Eristic	Personal conflict	Verbally hit out at opponent	Reveal deeper basis of conflict

In this table we can notice how the different dialogs are distinguished from the point of view of the type of interpersonal situation (conflict, need to obtain information or proofs), and the goal that interlocutors share. The identity of the participants' dialogical purpose leads to a dialogical exchange which is characterized by the basic presupposition of their common goal. For instance, in persuasion dialog the proponent and the respondent have the common goal of clarifying an issue that is controversial. Each participant has the individual goal of persuading the other party, but not, for instance, by making inappropriate moves, like threatening the other party instead of giving reason to support a claim.

The type of goal shared by the interlocutors, along with initial situation, determines the type of dialog they are engaged in. The crucial issue in this perspective is to determine what the other party's commitments are in a particular dialog exchange.

A dialog is formally defined as an ordered 3-tuple $<O, A, C>$ where O is the opening stage, A is the argumentation stage, and C is the closing stage (Gordon and Walton, 2009, 5). Dialog rules define what types of moves are allowed (Walton and Krabbe, 1995). At the opening stage, the participants agree to take part in some type of dialog that has a collective goal. A global burden of proof is set at the opening stage. In law, this is called the burden of persuasion. During the argumentation stage there is an evidential burden of proof (often called a burden of producing evidence) for each argument that means that the argument will fail to persuade unless sufficient evidence for it is produced. This evidential burden of proof can shift from one side to the other during the argumentation stage as arguments are put forward and critically questioned. Once the argumentation has reached the closing stage, the outcome is determined by the trier, who determines whether one side or the other has met its burden of persuasion, according the standard of proof set at the opening stage.

Dialogs are constituted by a succession of speech acts. Every dialog has a set of rules, establishing the interlocutors' allowed moves relative to their conversational roles, and the types of argument that are to be considered acceptable. These rules depend on the conversational setting (including the interlocutors' common and shared knowledge), framing a meta-dialogical normative level, to which the interlocutors can appeal in case the dialogical procedure has been infringed.

The types of dialog outlined above are only the most protypical; however, several other types of dialog can be found in ordinary conversation. Some of them, like political debates, can be represented as sharing elements of different types of dialog. In a political debate, the interlocutors try to persuade the public and at the same time to personally attack the other party. This type of dialog, for this reason, has elements in common with eristic and persuasion dialog (see Walton 2000; Jørgensen 1998). However sometimes the interlocutors apparently are committed to a certain type of dialog, but in fact one of them is pursuing a goal different from the purpose of the dialog he is purportedly engaged in. We take up many examples of such interesting phenomena in what follows.

Formal Systems of Persuasion Dialog

Four formal dialog systems were constructed in (Walton, 1984) as structures to model the kinds of moves characteristically made in persuasive argumentation. The four systems start from a minimal one called CB that is similar to the system H of Hamblin (1970) and the system DC of Mackenzie (1981). There are two parties, called the proponent and the respondents. Each has a thesis (proposition) to be proved that is designated at the opening stage, and it devise arguments to prove this proposition using as premises only propositions that are commitments of the other party. CB was designed to study how strategies of proof work in persuasion dialogue in cases that involve basic problems of incurring and retraction of commitments. The idea behind this family of systems was to start with only the most simple and basic systems first, and then add rules onto them in order to work with specific applications. The problem is that the range of applications is so variable (for example in multi-agent systems), if we start with highly complex system, many of the procedural rules are too rigid, and may not be needed anyway, in order to deal with a specific application.

For its rules of inference CB uses only classical propositional calculus, even though many other defeasible rules of inference of the kind now called argumentation schemes can be added. Following Mackenzie (1981), a statement T is said to be an immediate consequence of a set of statements S_0, S_1, ..., S_n if and only if 'S_0, S_1, ..., S_n, therefore T' is a substitution instance of an inference rule in the dialogue system. A statement T is said to be a consequence of a set of statements S_0, S_1, ..., S_n if and only if T is derived by a finite number of immediate-consequence steps from immediate consequences of S_0, S_1, ..., S_n. The set of set of rules for CB below is from (Walton, 1984, pp. 132-135).[1] Hamblin (1970; 1971) required that the commitment-store of each player be a set of public statements, for example a set of sentences written on a blackboard in view of all the dialog participants, and CB follows this convention. There are two participants, α and β.

RULES OF THE DIALOG SYSTEM CB

Locution Rules

(i) Statements: Statement-letters, S, T, U, ... , are permissible locutions, and truth-functional compounds of statement-letters.
(ii) Withdrawals: 'No commitment S' is the locution or withdrawal (retraction) of a statement.
(iii) Questions: The question 'S?' asks 'Is it the case that S is true?'
(iv) Challenges: The challenge 'Why S?' requests some statement that can serve as an argument for S.

Commitment Rules

(i) After a participant makes a statement, S, it is included in his commitment store.
(ii) After the withdrawal of S, the statement S is deleted from the speaker's commitment store.
(iii) 'Why S?' places S is the hearer's commitment store unless it is already there or unless the hearer immediately retracts his commitment to S.

---

1 An example dialog called Republic of Taronga is given in (Walton, 1984, pp. 120-127).

(iv) Every statement that is shown by the speaker to be an immediate consequence of, statements that are commitments of the hearer then becomes a commitment of the hearer's and is included in his commitment store.

(v) No commitment may be withdrawn by the hearer that is shown by the speaker to be an immediate consequence of statements that are previous commitments of the hearer.

Dialog Rules

- (R1) Each speaker takes his turn to move by advancing one locution at each turn. A no-commitment locution, however, may accompany a why-locution as one turn.
- (R2) A question 'S?' must be followed by (i) a statement 'S', (ii) a statement 'Not-S', or (iii) 'No commitment S'.
- (R3) 'Why S?' must be followed by (i) 'No commitment S' or (ii) some statement T, where S is a consequence of T.

Win-Loss Rules

(i) Both players agree in advance that the dialog will terminate after some finite number of moves.

(ii) For every statement S accepted by him as a commitment, a player is awarded one point.

(iii) The first participant to show that his own thesis is an immediate consequence of a set of commitments of the other participant wins the dialog.

(iv) If nobody wins as in (iii) by the agreed termination point, the participant with the greatest number of points wins the dialog, or the dialog is declared a draw.

What sort of strategy does a proponent α need to adopt in CB in order to succeed in his goal of persuading β to accept his thesis T to be proved in CB? α needs to search for premises that β is committed to, and that also imply α's thesis to be proved using argument justified by the rules of inference. However, as a general strategy, β needs to try to avoid committing himself to any statement that could be used as a premise in any argument that concludes in T. So there is a general disinclination to take on new commitments in this type of dialog. That is the reason why win-loss rule is in place. It awards incentives for taking on commitments. If possible, participants should even retract commitments where possible, in order to minimize chances of losing.

We might even consider further simplifying this set of rules by, for example, instead of having a set of rules for propositional calculus, just have one rule, deductive *modus ponens*, now sometimes called strict *modus ponens*. It is the rule: if A then B; A; therefore B. Here the if-then is a strict (material) conditional, meaning that it is false that A is true and B is false. Let's let the symbol $\rightarrow$ stand for the strict conditional. Then strict *modus ponens* has the form: $A \rightarrow B$; A; therefore B. Or we might extend that very simple system by having a rule for defeasible *modus ponens* as well: if A then defeasibly B; A; therefore (defeasibly) B. This rule applies to inferences like 'If Tweety is bird, Tweety flies; Tweety is a bird; therefore Tweety flies. Such an inference is defeasible, meaning that it can fail in some instances. For example, suppose that Tweety is a penguin. In such a case, the premises are acceptable but the conclusion is not. Let's let the symbol => stand for the defeasible conditional. Then defeasible *modus ponens* has the form: $A => B$; A; therefore B.

The most central problem in developing workable systems of persuasion dialog is posed by the phenomenon of retraction (Walton and Krabbe, 1995). To fulfill its goal, either party will often retract a commitment as soon as he realizes that the other party might use them as premises in arguments used to attack his position. In CB, points were given to encourage commitment, but this solution is arbitrary, sometimes problematic, and in general and not very satisfactory. The system CBV is constructed to handle this problem. In CBV, implicit commitments as well as explicit commitments are admitted. CBV is based on the idea that there is an additional set of commitments that are not on public view to them to the participants. Such implicit commitments are called dark side commitments because they are not on view to either party, in contrast with explicit (light side) commitments that are visible to all parties in a dialog. Implicit commitments can however be revealed by being transferred from the dark side to the light side, in accord with commitment rules. For example, suppose a party denies he is committed to a proposition, but then it is found in his set of implicit commitments. This party must immediately resolve the inconsistency, for example by either retracting the implicit commitment or the explicit commitment.

An additional commitment rule RDS govern how propositions are transferred from the dark side to the light side of a player's set of commitments as a dialog proceeds.

(RDS) If a participant states 'No commitment S' and S is in the dark side of his commitment store, then S is immediately transferred into the light side of his commitment-store.

Below the rules for CBV from (Walton, 1984, pp. 252-254) are given.

The Game CBV

Locution Rules

(i) Statements: Statement-letters, S, T, U, . . . , are permissible locutions, and truth-functional compounds of statement-letters.
(ii) Withdrawals: 'No commitment S' is the locution for withdrawal (retraction) of a statement.
(iii) Questions: The question 'S?' asks 'Is it the case that S is true?'
(iv) Challenges: The challenge Why S?' requests some statement that can serve as a basis in proof for S.

Commitment Rules

(i) After a participant makes a statement, S, it is included in his commitment store.
(ii) After the withdrawal of S, the statement S is deleted from the speaker's commitment store.

(iii) 'Why S?' places S in the hearer's commitment store unless it is already there or unless the hearer immediately retracts his commitment to S.

(iv) Every statement that is shown by the speaker to be an immediate consequence of statements that are commitments of the hearer then becomes a commitment of the hearer's and is included in his commitment-store.

(v) No commitment may be withdrawn by the hearer that is shown by the speaker to be an immediate consequence of statements that are previous commitments of the hearer.

(vi) If a participant states 'No commitment S' and S is on the dark side of his commitment store, then S is immediately transferred to the light side of his commitment store.

Dialog Rules

- (Rl) Each participant takes his turn to move by advancing one locution at each turn. A no-commitment locution, however, may accompany a why-locution as one turn.
- (R2) A question 'S?' must be followed by (i) a statement S, (ii) a statement 'Not-S', or (iii) 'No commitment S'.
- (R3) 'Why S?' must be followed by (i) 'No commitment S' or (ii) some statement T, where S is a consequence of T.

Strategic Rules

(i) Both participants agree in advance that the dialog will terminate after some finite number of moves.

(ii) The first participant to show that his own thesis is an immediate consequence of a set of commitments of the other participant wins the game.

(iii) If neither party wins as in (ii) by the agreed termination point, the dialog is declared a draw.

During a successful CBV dialog, more dark side commitments sets of both parties are revealed. Not only does each party come to understand the position of the other party more deeply, but also gains insight into the reasons behind his own views.

To illustrate what sequences of argumentation CBV look like, we present the sample dialog in table 2. R stands for a round, a pair of moves, the first by α and the second by β. Before the dialog in table 2 begins, X is a dark-side commitment of β. α's thesis to be proved in the dialog is U.

At the first move, α asks β whether he accepts S. β replies that he does. Then she asks him whether he accepts (S and T) => U. He replies that he does. Already at round 2 then, it is clear that α successfully persuades β to accept U if he can be persuaded to accept T. It is easy to see that α does this, and thereby proves U, by tracking down the argumentation in the right column representing β's commitments. RDS applies at round 7, making X an explicit commitment of β. X implies V, V implies T, and T is the missing component needed to prove U from (S and T) => U, using defeasible *modus ponens*.

Table 2. A sample dialog of argumentation in CBV

R	Move of α	Move of β	Commitments of α	Commitments of β
1	S?	S		S
2	S and (T => U)?	(S and T) => U		(S and T) => U
3	V => T?	Why V => T?		
4	W; W → (V =>T)	V =>T	W; W → (V =>T)	V =>T
5	V?	No commitment V.		
6	X => V?	X => V		X => V
7	X?	No commitment X.		X

DIALOG GAMES AND DIALOG SHIFTS

Dialogs depend on the purposes of the participants. Sometimes they may be pursuing the objectives of a type of dialog, but they decide to shift to another type of dialog in order to accomplish some goal needed for the prosecution of the previous one. For example, they might need some information in order to continue their persuasion dialog or deliberation. In such cases, the argumentation needs to be seen as relevant to the goal of the prior communicative exchange in which the current dialog is embedded. A clear case of information seeking embedded into persuasion dialog is a criminal trial in which expert witnesses are called to testify in order to provide missing information needed to support or question a party's claim.

A highly significant case in which expert consultation played a crucial role in determining the outcome of the trial was *R v Sally Clark*, EWCA Crim 1020 (2003). In this case a British solicitor, Sally Clark, was prosecuted for the murder of two of her sons, both died within few weeks from their birth. The issue was to determine whether the children died of natural death, fact that would have acquitted the defendant, or whether the cause of their death was not natural, which would have given the prosecution the possibility of providing arguments for the defendant's culpability. In this case, the possibility of the persuasion dialog the two parties were engaged in depended on the outcome of the information-seeking the original dialog shifted to (*R v Sally Clark*, EWCA Crim 1020 (2003) at 17):

Case 1. Information-Seeking Used to Open a Persuasion Dialog

There was no evidence that anyone had noticed any injury to either child during their lives that had given rise to suspicion that either child was being abused. Such evidence as there was suggested that they were babies who were well cared for, loved by their parents and happy and content. Hence this was a case where realistically any finding of guilt was bound to be decided upon the medical evidence relating to each death and particularly upon the evidence of the pathologists.

The information seeking showed that the cause of death was unascertained and therefore the theory of murder could be only one possible explanation to be proved among several other possibilities (*R v Sally Clark*, EWCA Crim 1020 (2003) at 57-61; 93). The function of this information-seeking dialog was to re-open the persuasive dialog. The shift from a persuasion dialog to an information-seeking, however, is often an instrument for the two parties to prove the premises supporting their conclusion. For this reason, an information-seeking dialog can become a battle of the experts, in which the experts' testimony becomes the backing of an argument, and it is used to support a theory or to discredit it. An example can be found in *People v. Orenthal James Simpson* BA 097211 (L.A. Super. Ct. 1995)[2]:

Case 2. Information-Seeking as Backing in Persuasion Dialog

In O.J. Simpson case, O.J. Simpson, former American football star and actor, was brought to trial for the murder of his ex-wife Nicole Brown Simpson and her friend Ronald Goldman. on June 12, 1994, Brown and Goldman were found dead outside Brown's Bundy Drive condominium. Evidence found and collected at the scene led police to suspect that O.J. Simpson was the murderer. The prosecution opened its case by playing a 9-1-1 call which Nicole Brown Simpson had made on January 1, 1989. She expressed fear that Simpson would physically harm her, and he could be heard yelling at her in the background. The prosecution also presented dozens of expert witnesses, on subjects ranging from DNA fingerprinting to blood and shoeprint analysis, to place Simpson at the scene of the crime.

Simpson had hired a team of high-profile lawyers, including F. Lee Bailey, Robert Shapiro, Alan Dershowitz, Robert Kardashian, Gerald Uelmen (a law professor at Santa Clara University), Carl E. Douglas and Johnnie Cochran. Attorneys specializing in DNA evidence, Barry Scheck and Peter Neufeld, were hired to attempt to discredit the prosecution's DNA evidence, and they argued that Simpson was the victim of police fraud and what they termed as sloppy internal procedures that contaminated the DNA evidence

The information-seeking dialogs were aimed at supporting the prosecution's or the defense's arguments. The prosecution called experts to testify that DNA evidence showed that the defendant used the glove found on the scene of the crime, whereas the defense hired scientists to discredit the reliability of DNA tests.

Shifts may occur between several types of dialogs. In trials, persuasion dialog is used to persuade the judge or the jury of the defendant's culpability or innocence, but then the dialog shifts to a deliberation in order to establish the penalty. In its turn, a deliberation dialog may shift to an information-seeking dialog, if the grounds on which the decision has to be made are not sufficient, as in the following case[3]:

Case 3: Shifts Between other Types of Dialog

The jury must determine how much in punitive damages to award the estates of the victims. In California, juries are advised to punish financially without destroying. Discussion of finances are meant to give jurors a guideline.

---

2 http://en.wikipedia.org/wiki/O.J._Simpson_murder_case; Simpson defense to bolster frame-up theory this week. USA Today, 16/10/1996. Retrieved on 07/06/2009 from http://www.usatoday.com/news/index/nns137.htm
3 Lawyer's argue over Simpson's worth. USA Today, 07 February 1997. Retrieved on 07/06/2009 from http://www.usatoday.com/news/index/nns213.htm .

Except for the bottom line, the plaintiffs contested few of the figures submitted by Simpson. But they argued that his fame is a marketable commodity that propels his after-tax net worth to $15.7 million.

Mark Roesler, an expert in marketing celebrities, said Simpson could make up to $3 million a year. He said a pair of Simpson's old tennis shoes recently sold for $805. "There are people out there who are willing to pay a premium for something that was owned by him."

The decision about how much to charge on the defendant was grounded on an information seeking, aimed at establishing the reasonableness of the punitive damages.

In dialog shifts, however, sometimes some features of the new dialog the interlocutors are engaged in can be not respected. In case of expert-witness examination in trials, the shift from persuasion dialog to information seeking contains elements of the persuasion dialog in which it is embedded. Experts are chosen by the parties in order to prove that their claim is convincing; however, if the choice of witnesses can be considered a persuasive element, the dialog itself has to be aimed at determining the truth or plausibility of some information. The case in which an expert witness tries to persuade the jury or the judge of the plausibility of a party's position using arguments exceeding the boundaries of the type of dialog is different. For instance, let's consider the case of a dialog shift that occurred to prove whether some information is true or not. The information-seeking dialog has the goal of obtaining this information, and experts are consulted for this purpose. However, sometimes the expert witness infringes on the limits of this type of dialog by disguising a persuasion move under the purpose of providing information.

An interesting case ca be the following (*R v Sally Clark*, EWCA Crim 1020 (2003) at 17). In the abovementioned case 1, an expert witness, Professor Meadow, was asked by the prosecution about some statistical information as to the happening of two cot deaths within the same family. The expert replied as follows (*R v Sally Clark*, EWCA Crim 1020 (2003) at 99).:

Case 4: Different Goals in Dialog Shifts

"This is why you take what's happened to all the children into account, and that is why you end up saying the chance of the children dying naturally in these circumstances is very, very long odds indeed one in 73 million."

This opinion was not aimed at providing information about the elements of the deaths, but to lead the jury to draw a specific conclusion independently of the data and figures provided by the other witnesses. This evidence, was "contended may well have had an unfair impact upon the jury's considerations" (*R v Sally Clark*, EWCA Crim 1020 (2003) at 94), and was contested as follows (*R v Sally Clark* at 105):

The areas of attack were threefold. First, evidence was called to show that the statistics were misleading; second, it was said that the evidence was led without regard to the guidance given by this Court in R v Doheny and Adams [1997] Cr App R 369; and third it was contended that the prosecution utilised the statistics in a way that gave rise to the "prosecutor's fallacy" identified in relation to DNA statistical evidence in R v Deen, The Times 10 January 1994.

This evidence was admitted, but was irrelevant to determine the facts of the case, and had an impact on the jury influencing their verdict.

The conflict between the goal of the dialog and the purpose of the participants can lead to potential manipulations of the dialogical setting. The participant is supposed to be pursuing a determinate aim, while in fact his intentions are incompatible with it. The participant conceals in those cases a dialog shift, like it frequently happens in cross-examination (for the goals and the admitted questions in cross-examination, see Friedman 2000). Cross-examination is a dialog aimed at assessing the reliability of a testimony through bringing to the light possible witness' inconsistencies or contradictions (see *Whorton v. Bockting*, 549 U.S. 406 (2006), pp. 4; 6). However, the dialog may shift to a persuasion dialog, in which the examiner tries to persuade the court that the witness is unreliable, by presenting his version of the facts or leading the third party to draw some conclusions from the answers of the witness. The purpose of evaluating the statements is not respected by the party, who actually wants to persuade the court.

A clear example can be found in the cross examination drawn from the OJ Simpson case. Mr Bailey, representing the defence, is cross examining detective Fuhrman. The goal of the defence was to show that the evidence found on the scene of the crime, a bloody glove apparently belonging to the killer, was actually implanted by the detective himself. Mr Bailey wanted to show how the detective acted on the basis of racial hate against the defendant, and tried to show a previous history of racial accuses against him. After Fuhrman's denial of having uttered some racial slurs against black people , Mr Bailey wanted to persuade the jury that his answers were made up (14 March 1995, PM, at 0055):

Case 5: Persuasion in Cross-Examination

Q. Okay. You still don't know what their objective was in doing this, is that right?

A. Well, I assumed it was preparation.

Q. Preparation for what?

A. Cross-examination.

Q. About Kathleen Bell?

A. Yes.

Q. About certain language that some find offensive?

A. Yes.

Q. You are concerned about that, then, is that led to this tripartite simulated cross-examination; correct?

MS. CLARK: Objection.

THE COURT: Sustained. Calls for facts not in evidence, and speculation.

Mr. Bailey tried to persuade the jury of the unreliability of Fuhrman's statements, implying that he wanted to train through a simulated cross-examination on that specific subject to lie at the hearing. Instead of showing particular contradictions, the questioner is actually trying to lead the jury to his own conclusion.

The dialog shifts presented above clearly show how the goal of the dialog and the participants' goals are crucial to determine whether a move should be considered admissible or not in a dialog. Some moves clearly show a strategy different from the proper goal set for the type of dialog, and for this reason, they are signs of an implicit dialog shift.

DIALOG SHIFTS AS MANIPULATIONS OF THE COMMUNICATIVE SITUATION

The types of dialog, as seen above, depend on the parties' communicative goals that stem from the collective goal of the dialog. Shifts frequently occur in dialogs. However, the admissibility of such shifts depends on the interlocutors' communicative purpose. When a shift occurs because an issue related to the current dialog has to be resolved in order for the dialog to proceed, it is usually relevant and admissible. However, some shifts show a disagreement on dialogical goals. For instance, during a persuasion dialog a participant may threaten the other party in order to lead it to agree with a particular position, or personally attack it. In this case, the basic goal of the dialog, to resolve a difference of opinions, is not being expedited, as the participant only intended to get the most favorable outcome from the dialog, say by humiliating the interlocutor.

Some fallacies can be explained as illicit dialog shifts, in which one of the participants alters the dialog goal. A clear example can be the following excerpt from the Nazi process against the conspirators 20 of July 1944[4]. Here the judge, Roland Freisler, interrogates the defendant, William count Schwerin von Schwanenfeld:

Case 6: Ad Hominem Arguments in Persuasion Dialog

Schwerin: Mr. President, what I have done by way of political experiences, has had some difficulties for me as a consequence, because I have truly worked very long for all things German in Poland, and from this time, I have experienced a great deal insofar as our position vis-a-vis the Poles goes. That is a---

Freisler: A great deal, that you are blaming National Socialism for?

Schwerin: I thought of the many murders…

Freisler: (screaming): Murders?

Schwerin: Domestically and abroad--

Freisler: You are just a two-bit crook, a common thieving lowlife! Are you breaking apart?

Schwerin: Mr. President!

Freisler: Yes or no? A clear answer!

Schwerin: No.

Freisler: You can't break down any further, you are just a little wretched pile, that doesn't even have any regard for himself anymore.

In this example, a direct *ad hominem* (Walton, 1998, p. 249), that is, a direct attack to the interlocutor, has been committed. The judge, instead of evaluating the defendant's argument, stops the persuasion dialog and prevents Schwerin from defending himself. The personal

---

4 The video can be found at the webpage http://video.aol.com/video-detail/judge-roland-freisler-aka-raving-roland/1580908353. Transcripts are available at http://www.spiritus-temporis.com/roland-freisler/.

attack distorts the goal of the whole dialog, turning a process into a public condemnation. The attack infringes the two basic presuppositions of a persuasion dialog, namely the conflict of opinion, and the freedom of the interlocutors to defend their point of views. The goal becomes to overcome the defendant, to win the discussion and discredit him. In trials personal attacks usually against the other party are not so explicit, but are however common improper tactics (see Saltzburg 2007: 119).

Implicit attacks can be also improper persuasive means used in cross-examination to lead the jury to draw a specific conclusion from the witness' behaviour (14 March 1995, AM, at 0062):

Case 7: Ad Hominem Attacks in Information Seeking

Q. Okay. Do you have any memory of even one of these ten questions?
A. No.
Q. Not a single one?
A. No.
Q. This happened when, Detective Fuhrman?
A. I believe it was two or three weeks ago.
Q. Two or three weeks ago?
A. Yes.
Q. Now you have been exhibiting a startling memory for a crime that was eight months ago; have you not?

This circumstantial *ad hominem* is based only on pointing out a feature of the witness' behaviour; however, it is a persuasive move, leading the third party to draw a conclusion about his credibility. Persuasive moves in a context of dialog in which only the information provided by the witness is relevant to the dialogical purpose, those types of persuasive moves are inadmissible.

Argument from consequences are commonly used in trials, especially when discussing the reasonableness of the interpretation of a certain legal provision. In an argument from consequences (see Walton 1995: 155) the reasonableness (or unreasonableness) of the conclusion follows from the reasonableness (or unreasonableness) of its consequences. A clear example can be the following *Muscarello v. United States*, 524 U.S. 125 (1998) at 132-133 (for a similar case, see also *Garner v Burr*, 1 KB 31(1951) at 33). In this case, the interpretation of the word 'to carry' is argued on the grounds of the acceptability of its legal consequences. The term 'to carry' can be in fact ambiguous (Solan 2007: 407): it can mean "to move while supporting" or "to wear, bear, or carry them upon the person or in the clothing or in a pocket, for the purpose of use, or for the purpose of being armed and ready for offensive or defensive action in case of a conflict with another person":

Case 8. Acceptable Arguments from Consequences

From the perspective of any such purpose (persuading a criminal "to leave his gun at home") what sense would it make for this statute to penalize one who walks with a gun in a bag to the site of a drug sale, but to ignore a similar individual who, like defendant Gray-Santana, travels to a similar site with a similar gun in a similar bag, but instead of walking, drives there with the gun in his car? How persuasive is a punishment that is without effect until a drug dealer who has brought his gun to a sale (indeed has it available for use) actually takes it from the trunk (or unlocks the glove compartment) of his car? It is difficult to say that, considered as a class, those who prepare, say, to sell drugs by placing guns in their cars are less dangerous, or less deserving of punishment, than those who carry handguns on their person.

This sequence of argumentation is reasonable in a context of dialog in which the goal is to resolve a conflict of opinions, for a value judgment on a thesis is drawn from a value judgment on its consequences. This reasoning is used to evaluate the reasonableness of a position or the fairness of a judgment (see for instance *McMillian v. State*, 502 So. 2d 510 (Fla 1987)). However, sometimes argument from consequences is used to lead the interlocutor or the third party in a persuasion dialog to a specific course of action.

For instance, (see Walton 2009: 65), a participant in a critical discussion can force the interlocutor to accept his point of view, threatening him of bad consequences in case of disagreement. This type of move, commonly called *ad baculum* or argument from threat, shifts a persuasion dialog to a negotiation, in which the goal is to get the interlocutor to the wanted course of action. Instead of reaching an agreement, the speaker wants to influence the interlocutor's actions. In *People v. Kipp* 187 Cal.App.3d 748 (1986), the jury was to determine whether an insane acquittee, a mentally disordered offender, should be released. However, the Appellee instructed the jury that their decision would determine whether he appellant should be hospitalized or released on parole. This argument was aimed at threatening the jury of a possible negative consequences of their decision (*People v. Kipp* 187 Cal.App.3d 748 (1986) at 751):

Case 9: Threats as Improper Consequences in Persuasion Dialog

Kipp held it is error to advise the jury in an [***9] NGI extension proceeding that their verdict will decide whether the petitioner should be released or continue to be confined for involuntary treatment. Such an instruction is likely to distort the verdict because the jury could fear his release and be more inclined to rule against the NGI committee regardless of the evidence

This instruction was likely to promote fear of the appellant's release, and therefore lead the jury to shift the type of dialog to a negotiation instead of a persuasion dialog in which the evidence was to be assessed. For this reason, the court determined that such instruction was an error (see also *People v. Collins* 10 Cal.App.4th (1992) at 690, 695).

The purpose of the dialog is the principle used to determine the reasonableness of dialogical moves. For instance, appeals to emotions are arguments commonly classified as fallacious by logical textbooks (see Walton 1997); however, they can be relevant argument in certain contexts of dialog. An example of their reasonableness can be the following appellate court decision (*People v. Ryan*, 327 N.Y.S.2d 207 (N.Y.App. Div.1971)). The court was to decide about the seriousness of an offence, in order to proceed with determining the punishment; the counsel for the defendant pointed out the disgraceful situation of the latter:

Case 10: Appeals to Emotions as Reasonable Arguments in Persuasion Dialog

> in view of the completeness of the defendant's disgrace, his discharge from the department, [***7] his loss of pension, and the piteous spectacle of his stricken wife and handicapped children, all utterly reliant on his presence, his sentence can presently be mitigated without detriment to the needs and protection of society; and that the fulfillment of his jail sentence would add more to the immedicable woe of his family than it would punish him

The court, in this case, found that "when an appellate court is confronted with a plea ad misericordiam, it must take a broader view of all the facts and circumstances, measuring justice and the rights of society, punishment and the avoidance of cruelty. And mercy, in its proper place, is an attribute of an appellate court" (*People v. Ryan*, 321 N.Y.S.2d 207 (N.Y.App. Div.1971))). In a decision making dialog, the assessment of the defendant's situation sometimes necessarily involves the use of representations and images arising the interlocutor's emotions. Another clear case can be *United States v. Moussaoui* (333 F.3d. 509, 517 (4th Cir. 2003)), in which the al-Quaeda plotter was proven guilty of 9-11 attacks. In this case, the jurors had to decide whether condemn the defendant to death sentence or life term imprisonment. At this stage of the dialog, the prosecution was allowed to present evidence showing pictures of the terrorist attack and recordings from the jet hijacked.

Emotions, as shown in (Damasio 2000: 281-282; Solomon 2003), are cognitive instruments through which an individual can assess a situation on the grounds of his desires, values, and experiences. Images showing the defendant's actions, or representations of his or her deeds are perfectly reasonable when presented to fully depict the nature and the quality of a crime of which the defendant has already been judged as guilty. Punishment should be ideally proportional to the gravity of a crime and the circumstances it happened. Appeals to emotions fulfil the goal of drawing a vivid representation of the whole situation; emotions cannot influence the assessment of the culpability, but are valuable instruments to evaluate how serious the offence was[5]. However, the purpose of assessing the seriousness of a crime is clearly different from persuading an audience of the responsibility of a crime. In this latter case, the appeal to emotions seems to distort the purpose determining the dialog the interlocutors take part to. The purpose of assessing the evidence in order to determine the culpability of the defendant is shifted to the goal of evaluating the possible remedies for the defendant's actions. The emotions risk leading the jury to qualify the very facts (that is, who committed an action) which are to be determined at that stage of the discussion (see also Uviller 1996: 218). This risk is clearly expressed by the federal rules of evidence, used to establish which kind of evidence should be admitted at different stages of trial (Walton 2006: 5):

---

5   In civil law the position of the judges can be expressed by the following statement, setting out that appeals to pity shall not be deemed to be irrelevant when the equity principles, used to determine what remedy is fair, are to be applied (Graf v. Hope Building Corp., 254 NY 1 (1930)): "There is no undeviating principle that equity shall be unmoved by an appeal ad misericordiam, however urgent or affecting. The development of the jurisdiction of the chancery is lined with historic monuments that point another course. Equity follows the law, but not slavishly nor always. If it did, there could never be occasion for the enforcement of equitable doctrine. Let the hardship be strong enough, and equity will find a way, though many a formula of inaction may seem to bar the path"

Case 11: Emotions as Dialogical Shifts

One question that had to be resolved by Judge Ito concerned the evidence of Simpson's abuse of his wife. There were photographs as well as other evidence of Simpson's having stalked and beaten Nicole Brown Simpson. The teams of attorneys on both sides put forward arguments on the relevance of this character evidence and whether it should be admitted in the trial (Park, 1996, p. 748). The defence cited the rule against character evidence, a California rule that is similar to Rule 404 of the Federal Rules of Evidence as the basis of their argument that character was not a relevant issue to be raised. The prosecution cited a California law ruling that domestic violence evidence is in general relevant, even when it is character evidence. They also argued it was relevant because it showed that Simpson had a motive of controlling and dominating Nicole Brown Simpson (Park, 1996, p. 749). Judge Ito admitted some but not all of the spousal abuse evidence on the ground that it showed motive.

Appeal to emotions can therefore be qmanipulations of the presuppositions the dialog between interlocutors is grounded on. The determination of the facts can be shifted to the determination of the quality of the facts, and lead the interlocutors to qualify an action as good or bad without carefully assessing whether this action was committed and by whom. Emotions, on this view, seem to shift a dialog, whose basic presupposition is a conflict of opinion on an issue, to decision making based on different propositions.

Dialog shifts can also occur when a dialog on the definition of an action is shifted to a discussion on the fairness of a classification. The following case can provide an explanation for this move. The defendant challenges the decision of the court of first instance and appeals the judgment. In the Court of Appeals, however, no new evidence is provided, only an argument questioning the fairness of determining the failure of a man in financial difficulties to pay the taxes a tort (*People v. Sonleitner*, 185 Cal. App. 2d 350 (1960)):

Case 12. Emotions as Fallacious Shifts of Issue

Throughout defendant's briefs runs the recurring contention that because the court found that he was financially unable on a given date to deposit the security fixed by the board as a condition to a hearing for redetermination, he should be excused from exhausting his administrative remedies and be permitted to contest the tax in the action brought by [***40] the state on the jeopardy determination. Defendant phrases this contention in his statement of "Issues" as follows: "Can the Legislature and the Board of Equalization compel courts to restrict due process in tax cases to the wealthy?" This, logicians refer to as "argumentum ad misericordium," an appeal to pity. This is of [**541] course a contention which could be made against any tax and can have no relevancy [*371] here. A similar contention was advanced in Modern Barber Colleges v. California Emp. Stab. Com., supra, 31 Cal.2d 720, and thus answered at page 732: "It would be strange indeed if this court were to sanction a practice whereby a taxpayer could regularly refrain from paying taxes, the obligation of which he disputes, and then urge that, by reason of his large delinquency, the ordinary remedies provided for reviewing his liability are inadequate in his particular case."

The defendant, instead of disputing the facts or the relation between facts and classification, disputes the fairness of a law, which cannot be an issue in a Court of Appeals. The attack is on the presuppositions the dialog is based on, namely that the two parties adopt a system of law, which is not at stake at that level of the dialog. The problem of relevance can be easily shown as a manipulation of basic dialogical presuppositions.

All the cases above mentioned are taken from legal contexts, in which the purpose of the discussion and the dialogical rules the participants abide by are clearly defined. However, what in law is established, in ordinary conversation is simply matter of mutual understanding of the communicative purposes. For this reason, while in law the purpose of the dialog is clear and the shifts evident, in situations in which the interlocutors' goals are not evident shifts, or claims against alleged shifts, may work as instruments to manipulate the interlocutor's dialogical intentions. Clear examples of manipulations of dialogical intentions emerge when purported shifts are condemned by the interlocutors, who points out that the purpose of dialog has been not respected by the other party. The speaker claims that the interlocutor pretends to be involved in the type of dialog the interlocutors were committed to, but in fact pursues completely different goals. For instance, we can consider the following argument, advanced by Grinols and Mustard (2001: 9) to support the thesis that casinos had impact on crime. After presenting some arguments against some studies which concluded that gambling was unrelated to crime, the authors advanced the following reasoning:

Case 13: Manipulating the Interlocutor's Commitments

Last, many studies were agenda-driven, conducted or funded by either pro-gambling or law enforcement organizations. Nelson, Erickson and Langan (1996), Margolis (1997) and Albanese (1999) were funded by explicitly pro-gambling groups. Not unexpectedly, they concluded that gambling had no impact on crime.

The personal attack against studies challenging the conclusion that gambling has no impact on crime is grounded on an accusation condemning a dialog shift. The speaker claims that the speaker's intentions could not fit the type of dialog he was actually committed to. Instead of achieving the goal of presenting and assessing evidence in order to reach a fair conclusion, the interlocutor is depicted as trying to persuade the audience by all means. This type of reasoning is represented in figure 2.

This type of argument highlights how crucial the determination of dialogical intentions is for the reasonableness of the dialog. A whole discussion could be focussed on the problem of purportedly biased research, and on the real dialogical intentions of the researchers funded by one of the two sides of a discussion. The crucial problem remains that if the goals of the speakers are actually found to be different, the credibility of the accused interlocutor's arguments drops, and either he is excluded from the discussion or the weight of his arguments is poorly considered.

LEVELS OF A PERSUASION DIALOG

Dialog shifts, as analyzed in the section above, show some crucial aspects of persuasion dialog. First of all, dialogs are characterized by some basic presuppositions, namely the conflict of opinions and the intention to solve it.

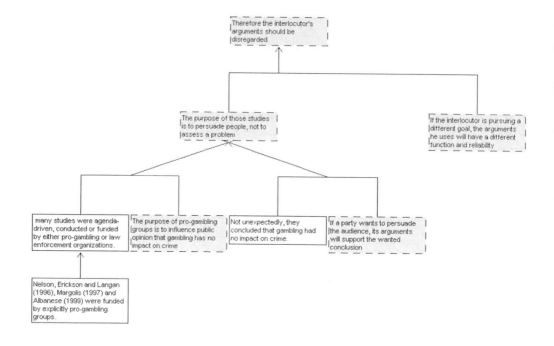

Figure 2. Conflicting dialogical intentions.

Dialogs are distinguished on the grounds of those pre-requisites: the different types of dialog have different goals, emerging from the interlocutors' intentions. However, sometimes those basic commitments to the type of interaction the two parties are engaged in are not clear, or simply change in the course of the dialog. Those basic requirements, which following Vanderveken's terminology we called "presuppositions", but we can also conceive as basic dialogical commitments, are preconditions for a dialog, meta-dialectical requirements (see Krabbe 2003) that have to be respected in order for a dialog to proceed.

The interlocutors, as shown in the cases above, are already committed to those basic propositions when they begin a dialog. The crucial question is who or what establishes those commitments, and what kind of commitments are those.

An answer to this question comes from the Pragma-Dialectical school. On Van Eemeren and Grootendorst's view (see van Eemeren and Grootendorst, 1984, 1992, 2004), a dialog aimed at resolving a difference of opinion, called "critical discussion", is characterized by four stages: the confrontation stage, the opening stage, the argumentation stage, and the concluding stage. The confrontation stage represents the starting point of the dialog, namely the point in which a point of view is expressed by one party and is not accepted by the other party, who challenges it or cast doubts on it. The second stage is a level in which the parties "try to find out how much relevant common ground they share" (Van Eemeren and Grootendorst 2004: 60). At this level the format of the dialog, background knowledge, the values, and the roles are compared and discussed. At the argumentation stage the participants advance their arguments to support their viewpoint, whereas at the concluding stage the parties establish "what the result is of an attempt to resolve a difference of opinion" (Van Eemeren and Grootendorst 2004: 60). On their view, the opening stage corresponds to the negotiation of the participants' commitments; however, the status of this stage as a dialogical level may cause some problems (Krabbe 2007: 238). The first problem regards the completion: as the opening stage proceeds the argumentation stage it is a precondition of, the interlocutors must agree on all possible procedural methods, argument schemes, and shared propositions that might be used at the subsequent dialogical stage. For this reason there might be an indefinite number of propositions to be agreed on. The second problem regards the infinite regress: in order to overcome the difference of opinion regarding a procedural proposition a new critical discussion begins, involving a new opening stage, and so forth. At last, if all propositions object of disagreement are to be solved at the opening stage, it seems that little would be left to the argumentation stage.

On Krabbe's view, one solution to these problems arising from a dialectical level aimed at solving procedural or commitment problems can be found in assigning a separate status to this type of discussion (Krabbe 2007: 240-241). On this perspective, some crucial questions that are tackled in the opening stage can be shifted to a metadialogical level, namely a dialog on the conditions of the dialog (Krabbe 2003: 641; Finocchiaro 2007). Metadialogs are situated at a different level from the dialog (the ground dialog), and their object is the dialog itself.

The pragma-dialectical analysis of critical discussion and Krabbe's theory of metadialogs can provide the grounds to develop an account of the levels and the stages of a persuasion dialog. As seen above, dialogs are characterized by the interlocutors' intentions, but also by a set of shared propositions, which establish what has to be proven and what cannot be disputed. In addition to those two requisites, the dialog is based on some basic principles of communication including for instance the knowledge of argument schemes and the dialogical and argumentative principles of reasonableness allowing one to allocate the burden of proof or to assess an argument. These propositions represent the hidden side of the dialog, which in (Walton and Krabbe 1995) has been described under the label of dark side commitments. However, those commitments are not placed on the same level and do not share the same nature. We represent the different levels of commitments in figure 3.

In this diagram we can notice two levels, the cultural and the contextual dark side commitments. The institutional setting, such as a court of justice, determines the roles of the interlocutors and their relative positions (for the notion of institution and context, see Rigotti 2006: 522); the roles, jointly with the institution, restricts the possible communicative intentions (see Goodnight 2008: 360-364). For instance in courts the counsels' intentions is already determined by the type of hearing and the type of court. The communicative context in its turn determines which propositions belonging to the cultural commitments are relevant in these situations (see Rigotti 2006: 524).

For instance in a persuasion dialog before a judge some types of commonly shared propositions, for example proverbs, are excluded from the types of propositions supporting reasonable presumptions; likewise, some types of argument, like for instance arguments grounded on the defendant's origins supporting a particular value judgment (character evidence), are not considered to be among the relevant types of inference in certain types of discussions. Finally, the institutional setting and parties' intentions also affects the assessment of certain types of reasoning based on inductive or abductive axioms. While in ordinary conversation such arguments could affect the interlocutors' judgment, in courts their probative force is carefully examined, and certain types of proofs commonly considered to be extremely

Levels and nature of dark side commitments				
Communicative context	Institutional setting		P and O are pleading a case in court	
	Interlocutors' roles		P is the counsel for the prosecution	
	Interlocutors' intentions		P wants to persuade the jury that Bob's action was larceny	
Cultural Commitments	Shared propositions (Bob committed the action; Bob is XYZ; ....)			
	Dialogical commitments		Inferential commitments	
	Dialogical reasonableness	P cannot personally attack the counsel for the defense	Commonly accepted propositions	Blood is shed when the being is wounded
	Procedural reasonableness	The burden of proof rests on who asserts, not on who denies	Basic rules of inference	If there is the efficient cause there is also the effect
	Communicative reasonableness	The speaker is committed to what he says	Basic logical axioms	If p then q; p; then q. If p then q; q; then plausibly q.

Figure 3. Architecture of Levels of Commitments in Dialog.

strong, like DNA tests, are evaluated through the analysis of the patterns of reasoning they are grounded on[6]. Parties' intentions also determine the dialogical commitments of the interlocutors. If the participants intend to persuade a third party about the truth of a proposition, they will regard threats, appeals to pity, or personal attacks against the interlocutor as inappropriate. If the intention and the context were different, such moves could be considered to be appropriate. The intentions and the context affect the determination of the procedures: for instance, the burden of proof can be globally determined on the basis of the stage of dialog (pre-hearing; jury trial), the type of trial (criminal, civil), and the type of

---

[6] Goodnight (2008: 365) highlights how the conversational context influences the threshold of assessment for argument: "the threshold for critical testing may be lower for the provider who has seen situations like this before; it may be higher for the client whose resources are limited and risks high, but who does not have the time, knowledge, or standing to put expert advice to the test".

discussion (examine the witness, persuade the jury) (see Keane 2008: 103-115; Allen 2004: 111). Finally, the intentions of the parties and the institutional setting also influence the type of standards of communicative reasonableness. The retraction of a proposition or the commitment to a position depends on whether the parties are engaged in a negotiation, a quarrel, or a persuasion dialog (see Walton and Krabbe 1995). Between the contextual and the cultural commitments there are the shared propositions, namely the commitments the interlocutors can consider to be shared on the basis of their intentions to discuss a specific issue.

As dark-side commitments represent a hidden dialogical level, discussion concerning this type of propositions belongs to metadialogs. Metadialogs intervene to avoid communicative breakdowns, caused by disagreements about propositions that are the precondition of the dialog. Some type of information is rooted deeper than other, and is more crucial as constituting the grounds of interpersonal communication. For instance, a disagreement about the strength of some types of reasoning or the basic principles of communicative reasonableness can easily lead to an interruption of a persuasion dialog and can be resolved only after deep discussions about the standards of dialogical acceptability. On the contrary, disagreements about some commonly accepted propositions, like meaning of words or habits, usually lead to metadialog.

The model of persuasion dialog can be represented as a succession of three stages. The first stage is an opening phase in which the interlocutors express their viewpoints, setting the issue to be resolved by the dialog as a whole. In this stage, the type of dialog and the interlocutors' goals are drawn from the type of institutional setting and the parties' conversational roles. The second stage is an argumentation phase in which the participants have to fulfil a burden of persuasion by inferring new commitments from the old parties' commitments. The third is a concluding stage in which it it determined which side fulfilled its individual goal. These three stages presuppose a set of dark side commitments that are the conditions of the dialog itself; should these commitments be infringed, the dialog may proceed or reach a breakdown. In such a case, the parties need to solve their conflict of dark-side commitments starting a metadialog about the conditions of the dialog.

The starting point for establishing the dialog conditions and characteristics is the opening stage, in which the issue and the conflicting points of view are set forth. The issue determines the nature of the standpoints and what kind of propositions can be considered to be shared by the interlocutors. For instance, if the issue regards the qualification of an action, the interlocutors can consider as dark side commitments the fact that the action has happened, that it has happened in a certain place and time, that it can be defined in a certain fashion, and so on. The nature of the shared knowledge depends on the type of issue. At the argumentation stage, the parties have to support the challenged positions by means of arguments. The conversational context establishes the type of dark side commitments we called above "commonly accepted propositions" which the parties can use as premises for their inferences. Once a challenged proposition has been supported by arguments and accepted by the other party it becomes a commitment. However, the crucial problem at this level is to establish who has the duty to support his own position. Depending on the context, on the type of issue and on the nature of the disputed proposition this type of procedural dark side commitment is determined. At last, at the closing stage, the dialog ideally can be concluded by determining who has to change his commitments on the basis of the propositions he has previously committed himself to. This level is characterized by the standard of argument assessments established by the dialogical context, the interlocutors' intentions, and the type of issue, and the retraction rules (in case of a two-party discussion). The structure of a persuasion dialog is represented in figure 4.

	TYPE OF COMMITMENTS	LEVELS	GOAL OF THE LEVELS
Metadialogs	Shared knowledge; setting burden of persuasion	Opening stage	Determining the claim to be proved or subjected to reasonable doubt
	Managing burdens of producing evidence	*Argumentation stage*	Proving the claim or showing that burden of persuasion is not met
	Standards of argument assessment applied	*Closing stage*	Resolving the conflict of opinions by weighing the arguments on both sides

Figure 4. The three levels of persuasion dialog.

In figure 4 only the dark side commitments have been represented. The interlocutors also have a set of light side commitments, namely propositions which they have committed themselves to during the dialog. This set of commitments increases as the dialog proceeds, and becomes the ground for inferences to other propositions. The dynamic advancement of a persuasion dialog can be represented as shown in figure 5.

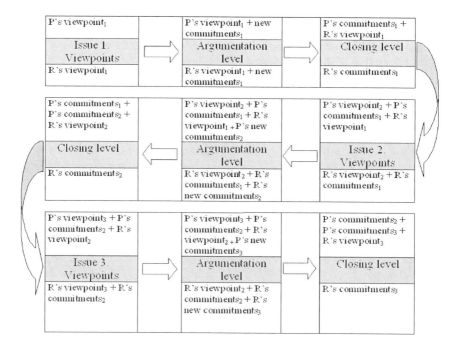

Figure 5. Dynamic advancement of a persuasion dialog.

In figure 5 the two parties are represented as P and R; the starting point is issue 1, on which the two parties commit themselves to their own viewpoint. At the argumentation level, they increase their commitment store with new commitments, and at the closing level the losing party (P, in our case), has to accept the winning party's viewpoint (R's viewpoint, in our example). Once issue 1 has been resolved, the dialog can proceed to issue 2, and the parties commence a new dialog related to the first one. They maintain the commitments of the previous one (commitments$_1$), and in addition they commit themselves to the new viewpoints (viewpoint$_2$). The discussion proceeds through the second and the third dialog, until all 3 issues are resolved.

STRUCTURE OF THE DIALOGICAL LEVELS

Dialogical levels, as mentioned above, are characterized by specific features. The opening stage, for instance, is determined by the type of issue the interlocutors want to discuss about. The type of issue and the contextual presuppositions stemming from the type of institutional setting determines the dark side commitments of the second level, the argumentation stage. These implicit commitments are both procedural, namely the rules for allocating the burden of proof, and "inferential", providing the standards for evaluating the arguments. Those standards constitute also the dark side commitments of the third level, the closing stage.

1. The Opening Level: The Issues

The concept of "issues" can be related to the ancient doctrine of stasis (for an overview of this model, see Calboli Montefusco 1986). Stasis was the basic classification of issues in a case (Braet 1999: 408) which was developed by Hermagoras, who in his turn elaborated a model drawn from Aristotle's Rhetoric (Braet 1999), and Cicero. In the ancient tradition, the model of stasis described what in our model called the opening level. According to Cicero (*De Inventione* 1.10; for the analysis see Heath 1994: 116), "the stasis is the first conflict of pleas which arises from the defence or answer to our accusation, in this way: "You did it "— "I did not do it," or "I was justified in doing it." On this view, the stasis is the conflict of opinions in which the prosecution and the defence disagree on an issue. The questions, namely the controversies, may be about "a fact, or about a definition, or about the nature of an act, or about procedures." (*De Inventione* 1, 10). As Carter puts it (1988: 98), "Stasis was the method by which rhetors in the classical tradition identified the area of disagreement, the point that was to be argued, the issue on which a case hinged. Its most recognizable feature was a set of questions, asked in a particular order, that established the nature of the issue as fact, definition, quality, or sometimes procedure". In order to show the four levels of the issues, we provide the following examples in table 3 (see also Crowley and Hawhee 1999).

In those cases, we can notice how the interlocutors' commitment store is determined by the kind of issue. In non-affirmative defences, the defendant disputes the facts or the elements of the crime charged.

For instance, the defendant charged with the murder of the victim may provide evidence that he or she was somewhere else when the crime was committed; a defendant charged with possession of marijuana may present evidence that the substance was in fact oregano (Brody et al. 2001: 241). An issue about the definition of an offence presupposes that the action has occurred and has been committed by the defendant; however, the classification of the offence may be challenged by showing that the facts can lead to a different classification. For instance, a charge of murder can be challenged by showing that when the homicide was committed under the influence of emotions or rage the malice was not present. In an affirmative defence, aimed at offering excuses or justifications for an action, the defendant admits having committed the crime charged (Brody et al. 2001: 241), but tries to qualify it as a minor offence. At last, the procedural defence does not affect the interlocutors' commitments, but represents a move in which the procedural commitments represent the issue. It is a kind of metadialectical move.

Table 3. The four levels of issues

Stasis	Questions	Examples
Conjecture	Did the accused commit the crime?	O.J. Simpson's ex-wife, Nicole Brown Simpson, and her friend Ronald Goldman were found dead. Who killed them?
Definition	How can the act be defined?	Rourke had teased a younger boy, Harris, about losing a game and pushed him. Harris hit Rourke in the knee with an aluminum bat, then seconds later hit him on the neck, severing an artery. Harris died. Was it murder or manslaughter?
Quality	How serious is the act?	In Beckford v R the defendant police officer was told that a suspect was armed and dangerous. When that man ran out of a house towards him, the defendant shot him because he feared for his own life. The prosecution case was that the victim had been unarmed and thus presented no threat to the defendant. Was the murder justified?
Procedure	Should the act be submitted to some formal procedure?	On the morning of October 2, 1987, David Kifer was driving a green Chevrolet on Christ Road in Evansville when he struck and killed jogger Barbara Mazick. Kifer left the scene of the accident and did not report the incident to police. After 12 years, the State charged Kifer with failure to stop at the scene of an accident resulting in death, a Class D felony. Was the action barred by the five-year statute of limitations for a Class D felony?

The four issues can be thought as a hierarchy of commitments (see Kauffeld 2002; Conley 1990). For instance, if a person is accused of murder, the first potential issue is the conjectural, in which the parties dispute whether the alleged deed was committed or not by the defendant. Once the accused was proved or conceded to have committed the deed, the second issue would be the definition of his action. At last, when the action has been defined, the possible mitigating circumstances of that specific crime can be shown. In addition to these three issues related to the ontology of the matter at stake, the parties can also dispute on the procedural facts, for instance the presence of structural or trial errors. This level refers to the moves made by the other pary, for instance whether the indictment or the complaint was correctly filed; whether the court has jurisdiction over the case; whether the jury was correctly instructed; whether any errors were committed during the trial.

Stasis was conceived in the traditional rhetoric (see Crowley and Hawhee 1999; Heath 1994) as a classification for the invention. The issues help the rhetor to develop an appropriate argumentative strategy: for instance, certain patterns of argument like the argument from the more or the less are inappropriate when the issue regards whether the fact has happened or not, whereas it could be highly effective in issues of quality (was the action right or wrong? Was the action bad or good?). Cicero noticed how the issues influenced the reasonableness of certain types of arguments, determining the strength of some arguments relative to others. For instance, Cicero noticed that in the issue of conjecture arguments from causes, from effects (or rather from signs), from depending circumstances (Cicero *Topica* 87), from the nature of the person (*De Inventione* II, 16) or from witness testimony (Cicero *De Inventione* I 46). For instance to prove that the accused did not commit the crime it can be shown that the evidence found on the scene of the crime did not fit the defendant, or that the accused was elsewhere when the deed happened. The prosecution can provide evidence supporting a causal link between the accused and the crime, or showing that he was on the scene of the crime, or collect testimonies against the accused. The relevance of the issue establishes what arguments can be considered reasonable and what reasoning is extremely weak or inappropriate. For instance, in the conjectural issue deductions are inappropriate, as the facts deductions can be grounded on have not been proved (Cicero *De Inventione* I, 19). At the definitional issue arguments may proceed from definition, classification, consequences, cause and effects; the reasoning is aimed at proving whether or not a definition fits a description of the facts, or whether or not the definition provided is good, or whether a definition reflects the intention of the law. At the last ontological issue, qualification, arguments can proceed from arguments from values, from comparisons, or from emotional appeals (Cicero *Topica* 87).

The ontology of the interlocutors' positions therefore affects the type of dark side commitments at the opening level, and the relevance of the type of arguments and types of reasoning at the argumentation level. The dark side commitments at the second dialogical level, the argumentation level, include also another type of commitment, the presumption, which determines the allocation of the burden of proof.

2. The Argumentation Level: The Burden of Proof

If we consider the legal dialog, which is a particular type of persuasion dialog in which the rules are clearly stated, we can notice how the whole sequence of arguments put forth by the parties is determined by a particular kind of dark side commitment, that is, the burden of proof. In law, like in everyday conversation, it is possible to distinguish between two types of burden of proof: a global burden of proof, which refers to the obligation of one party to defend his or her position, and a local burden of proof, which denotes the specific interlocutors' obligation to prove or disprove some evidential facts or issues which are crucial to the final judgement. In law, what we called 'global' and 'local' burden are called 'burden of persuasion' and ' evidential burden of proof'. The difference can be explained as follows (Murphy 2007: 71):

> The term 'burden of proof', standing alone, is ambiguous. It may refer to the obligation to prove a fact in issue to the required standard of proof, or to the obligation to adduce enough evidence to support a favourable finding on that issue.

Burden of persuasion is set at the opening stage. It establishes which side has to prove what, and what standard of proof is required to prove it, depending on the type of trial. Burden of persuasion does not change during the argumentation stage of the trial, and the jury during closing stage determines whether the burden of persuasion has been met by the one side or the other. The allocation of the burden of persuasion follows general rules relative to the type of issue. For instance, in criminal cases burden is on the prosecution to prove the facts essential to their case (see *Woolmington v DPP* AC 462 (1935)), whereas in civil cases "he who asserts must prove", i.e., the burden rests with the plaintiff (the party bringing the action) (Keane 2008: 98). However, the allocation of the burden of persuasion depends on the issue. In criminal cases, if an accused raises insanity as a defence, or in some cases in which the latter relies on some exceptions for his defence, he bears the legal burden of proving it (Keane 2008: 83). In those cases, we can notice, the issue is not more conjecture, but qualification; the defendant does not dispute the facts, but their qualification. Similarly, in civil cases the burden of persuasion "usually lies on the party asserting the affirmative of such an issue. For example, in an action for negligence, the claimant bears the burden of proving duty of care, breach of such duty and loss suffered in consequence" (Keane 2008: 98). However, the defendant bears the burden of proving any defences different from a simple denial of the claimant's assertion (such as contributory negligence), or, in case of qualification, he has to prove the factors leading to an exception or mitigation (Keane 2008: 100).

Another type of burden of proof is the evidential burden of proof, which corresponds to the burden of proving all elements essential to the claim. As Murphy puts it (Murphy 2007: 71):

> Every claim, charge or defence has certain essential elements, the proof of which is necessary to the success of the party asserting it. For example, a claimant who asserts a claim for negligence asserts: 1) that the defendant owed the claimant a duty of care; 2) that the defendant, by some act or omission, was in breach of that duty of care; and 3) that as a result of that breach, the claimant suffered injury or damage for which the law permits recovery. These elements derive, not from the law of evidence, but from the substantive law applicable to the claim, in the case the law of negligence. They are known as 'facts in issue' or 'ultimate facts'. The proof of these facts in issue depends, however, on the detailed facts of the individual case, which are referred to as 'evidential facts'. Thus, for example, in order to prove the fact in issue, negligence, the claimant might set out to prove the evidential facts that the

defendant drove while drunk, too fast, on the wrong side of the road, and knocked the claimant down, breaking his leg.

In criminal cases, the prosecution has the burden of proving all the essential elements; should the prosecution fail to prove them, the defendant is acquitted. However, if the elements have been supported by evidence, the prosecution establishes a *prima facie* case, namely that should the defendant not disprove any element, the case stands or falls only by this evidence. The defendant bears an evidential burden of proof, namely the burden of adducing some evidence to contradict the claim. The relation between burden of persuasion and the evidential burden of proof is represented in figure 6 (Murphy 2007: 73):

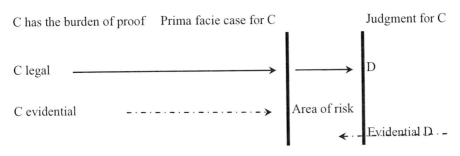

Figure 6. Burden of persuasion and evidential burden.

The burden of proof is established on the basis of a particular type of dark side commitments, that is, presumptions. A presumption is "an inference made about one fact from which the court is entitled to presume certain other facts without having those facts directly proven by evidence" (Hannibal, Mountford 2002: 464). They are commonly known propositions, some of which are taken to be true unless contrary is proven (see Walton 1995: 213). Presumptions are divided in three categories: irrebuttable, rebuttable, and presumptions of fact. Irrebuttable presumptions can be considered as irrefutable dark side commitments; if some facts are proven, other facts must be inferred and no evidence can disprove this conclusion (Hannibal, Mountford 2002: 465). For instance, no children under the age of 10 can be guilty of an offence. Therefore, if a child is proven to be under the age of 10, he is presumed to be innocent and no evidence can rebut this conclusion. Rebuttable presumptions are rebuttable propositions leading from some proved facts to a conclusion. The conclusion of such inferences is valid unless the other party rebuts the presumption. For instance, if the parties wished to marry and a marriage ceremony had been performed, the marriage is presumed to be valid. In this case, the other party has the burden to disprove the conclusion by showing how the proposition taken for granted (usually people who wish to marry and perform a ceremony are validly married) is wrong in the given case. The third type of presumption can be considered a rule of inference from a previous experience of the connection between the premises and the conclusion. For instance, if a man was alive on a certain date, it can be presumed that he was alive on a subsequent date. Whereas the presumptions of law are implicit propositions provided for by law, presumptions of fact can be considered to be logical inferences (9, *Ency. of Evidence*, 882), that is, grounded on commonly known propositions.

In civil cases, the presumption is rebutted either when the other party produces evidence to rebut the conclusion, or when it proves that the presumed facts do not exist by preponderance of evidence (Buckles 2003: 44). According to the theory of presumption, the evidence and or the arguments provided shift burden of proof.

In this account of burden of proof, we can notice how presumption is strictly determined by the issue. The facts to be proven carry dark side commitments on the parties, which affect the allocation of the burden of proof, and therefore the arguments to be produced in the argumentation stage. Moreover, the issues also establish the standard of evidence to be provided in the closing stage.

2. The Closing Level: The Standard of Proof

The closing level of a persuasion dialog highly depends on the type of issue and the type of conversational setting. We consider the legal context, in order to show how issues can affect the type of argument evaluation.

In law, there are different types of standards for evaluating whether the burden of proof has been met or not, and whether the case can be decided for the plaintiff or the defendant (Gordon and Walton, 2009). The most famous standard is "beyond a reasonable doubt", as it is used in criminal cases. The prosecution has to prove the case overcoming any possible doubt based upon reason and common sense (Sand *et al.* 2006: Criminal P4-01 at 4.2). However, in fraud cases, the standard of evidence is lower. The trier of fact must prove the facts by clear and convincing evidence; he has to prove that it is highly probable that the facts are true or exist (*Collins Securities Corp v. SEC*, 562 F.2d 820 (D.C. Cir. 1977)). In civil cases, the standard is by preponderance of evidence (or of probabilities); namely, the trier of fact must believe that it is more probable that the fact is true or exists than it is that it does not exist. In most administrative cases it is required that the party bearing the burden of proof produces relevant evidence as a reasonable mind might accept as adequate to support a conclusion (*Richardson v. Perales*, 402 U.S. 389 (1971)). The issue and the type of legal context can also affect the type of evidence needed to prove a conclusion. For instance, a criminal defendant bears the burden of proving incompetency to stand trial by a preponderance of the evidence (*Meraz v. State*, 714 S.W.2d 108 (Tex.App.-El Paso 1986)). Moreover, in criminal appeals, the "clear and convincing evidence" test must be utilized on appeal to determine whether a criminal defendant's consent to search was voluntary (State v. Ibarra, 953 S.W.2d 242 (Tex.Crim.App. 1997)). Similarly in civil cases, depending on the issue, the standard of evidence can be higher than the preponderance of probabilities. For instance, contempt of court or allegations of criminal conduct must be proved beyond a reasonable doubt (Hannibal, Mountford 2002: 458)

The different types of standard of proof, and the relation between the standards and the judgment, can be represented in the figure below (Murphy 2002: 102). In a civil case, any tipping of the scales, however slight, in favor of the claimant (or party bearing the burden of proof) is sufficient to win. If the scales are tipped the other way, then it is clear that D wins. If the scales remain evenly balanced (i.e. the tribunal of fact is unable to decide) D must also win because the burden of proof has not been discharged on the balance of probabilities. If the scales go no further down than the preponderance of probabilities, or remain balanced, D must win (Murphy 2002: 101).

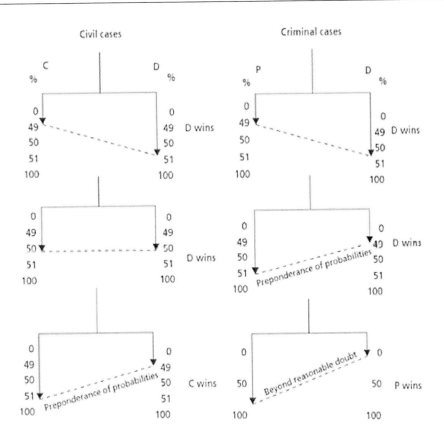

Figure 7B. alancing of the scales of burden of proof.

Dark side commitments are therefore propositions and rules which determine the dialogical procedure and the argument construction and evaluation. These commitments arise from the type of context and the type of issue, and affect the three levels of a persuasion dialog in different fashions.

CONCLUSION

This paper showed how thirteen examples of legal argumentation can be used to identify and analyze significant features of arguments used in persuasion dialog by applying a simple formal model of persuasion dialog to them. The following features were identified and analyzed in the examples: shifts from one type of dialog to another; information-seeking used to open a persuasion dialog, information-seeking as backing in persuasion dialog, different goals displayed in dialog shifts, persuasion in cross-examination, use of *ad hominem* arguments in persuasion dialog, use of *ad hominem* arguments in information-seeking dialog, acceptable uses of arguments from consequences, threats as improper consequences in persuasion dialog, appeals to emotions as reasonable arguments in persuasion dialog, emotions as fallacious shifts of issue, and manipulating the interlocutor's commitments.

The analysis of these examples provided a basis for discussing some of the general characteristics of persuasion dialog, and showing how some of the theoretical problems in modeling persuasion dialog are being solved in current work. One of the most interesting developments we discussed is the distinction between different levels of dialog, and in particular the use of metadialogs to model procedural disagreements kind that would be ruled on by a judge in a legal setting. One special feature we concentrated on was the use of dark side commitments in CBV, where we drew important distinctions between the levels and nature of dark side commitments, including the distinction between dialogical commitments and inferential commitments. We showed how shared knowledge is operative at the opening stage of a persuasion dialogue in determining commitments, how the type of burden of proof commonly called the burden of producing evidence in law is operative at the argumentation stage, and how standards of argument assessment are applied at the closing stage for resolving the conflict of opinions. In law, a determination of which side is held to prevail in a trial is determined by the judge, who applies the standard of proof required by the burden of persuasion set at the opening stage to the argumentation that took place during the argumentation stage. We showed how the traditional stasis theory can be applied to model the notion of burden of persuasion in law, where the whole sequence of argumentation during the argumentation stage it is directed towards the resolution of the conflict of opinions posed at the opening stage.

REFERENCES

Allen, C. (2004). *Practical guide to evidence*. London: Cavendish.

Atkinson, K, T. Bench-Capon, and P. McBurney (2005). A dialogue game protocol for multi-agent argument over proposals for action. *Journal of Autonomous Agents and Multi-Agent Systems* 11:153 - 171.

Barth, E. M. and E. C. W. Krabbe (1982). *From* Axiom *to Dialogue : A Philosophical Study of Logics and Argumentation*. Berlin : de Gruyter.

Bench-Capon, T. (1998). Specification and implementation of Toulmin dialogue game. In Legal Knowledge-Based Systems. JURIX: The Eleventh Conference (5-19). Nijmegen. Gerard Noodt Instituut.

Bentahar, J.. B. Moulin and B. Chaib-draa (2004). A Persuasion Dialogue Game based on Commitments and Arguments. In Rahwan et al. In Proceedings of AAMAS-04 1st International Workshop on Argumentation in Multi-Agent Systems (148-164). New York, NY, July 19.

Braet, A. (1987). The Classical Doctrine of Status and the Rhetorical Theory of Argumentation. *Philosophy and Rhetoric* 20: 79-93.

Braet, A. (1996). On the Origin of Normative Argumentation Theory: The Paradoxical Case of the Rhetoric to Alexander. *Argumentation* 10: 347-359.

Braet, A. (1999). Aristotle's almost unnoticed contribution to the doctrine of stasis. *Mnemosyne* 52(4): 408-433.

Brewka, G. (2001). Dynamic argument systems: a formal model of argumentation processes based on situation calculus. *Journal of Logic and Computation* 11: 257-282.

Brody, D. *et al.* (2001). *Criminal law*. Jones and Bartlett Publishers.

Buckles, T. (2003). *Laws of Evidence*. New York: Thomson.

Calboli Montefusco L. (1986). *La dottrina degli status nella retorica greca e romana.* Hildesheim

Carter, M.(1988). Stasis and Kairos: Principles of Social Construction in Classical Rhetoric. *Rhetoric Review* 7 (1): 97-1 12.

Conley, T. M. (1990). *Rhetoric in the European tradition*. New York: Longman.

Damasio, A. (2000). *The feeling of what happens*. London: Vintage.

Friedman F. (2000). *Cross-Examination Skills*. Albuquerque: New Mexico Public Defender and University of New Mexico Trial School.

Goodnight, T. (2008) Strategic Maneuvering in Direct to Consumer Drug Advertising: A Study in Argumentation Theory and New Institutional Theory. *Argumentation* 22 (3): 359-371

Gordon, T. (1994). The Pleadings Game: an exercise in computational dialectics. *Artificial Intelligence and Law* 2: 239-292.

Hahn, U., and Oaksford, M. (2007). The rationality of informal argumentation: A Bayesian approach to reasoning fallacies. *Psychological Review, 114,* 704-732.

Hamblin, C. (1970). *Fallacies*. Methuen, London.

Hannibal, M. and L. Mountford (2002). *The Law of Criminal and Civil Evidence. Principles and Practice*. New York : Longman

Heath M.(1994). Substructure of Stasis-Theory from Hermagoras to Hermogenes. *The Classical Quarterly, New Series*. 44 (1): 114-129.

Hintikka, J. (1979). Information-seeking dialogues : a model. *Erkenntnis* 38 : 335-368

Jørgensen C. (1998). Public Debate – An Act of Hostility?. *Argumentation* 12 (4) : 431-443

Kauffeld, F. J. (2002). Pivotal issues and norms in rhetorical theories of argumentation. In F. H. v. Eemeren and P. Houtlosser (Eds.), Dialectic and rhetoric: The warp and woof of argumentation analysis (pp. 97-118). Dordrecht: Kluwer Academic Publishers

Keane A. (2008) *The modern law of evidence*. Oxford : Oxford University Press

Krabbe, E. (2007). On How to Get Beyond the Opening Stage. *Argumentation* 21: 233–242

Leenes, R.E. Burden of proof in dialogue games and Dutch civil procedure. In *Proceedings of the Eighth International Conference on Artificial Intelligence and Law,* pages 109-118, ACM Press, New York, 2001.

Lodder, A.R. *DiaLaw. On Legal Justification and Dialogical Models of Argumentation.* Law and Philosophy Library. Kluwer Academic Publishers, Dordrecht/Boston/London, 1999.

Loui, L. (1998). Process and policy: resource-bounded non-demonstrative reasoning. *Computational Intelligence* 14: 1-38.

MacKenzie, J. (1979). Question-begging in non-cumulative systems. *Journal of philosophical logic*, 8:117-133.

Murphy, P. (2007). *Murphy on Evidence*. Oxford: Oxford University Press

Prakken, H. (2001). Modelling reasoning about evidence in legal procedure. In Proceedings of the Eighth International Conference on Artificial Intelligence and Law (119-128). New York: ACM Press.

Prakken, H. (2006). Formal systems for persuasion dialogue. *The Knowledge Engineering Review*: 1-26.

Ravenscroft, A. Wells, S., Sagar, M. and Reed, C. (2009). Mapping persuasive dialogue games into argumentation structures, Symposium in Persuasive Technology and Digital

Behaviours Intervention, Artificial Intelligence and Simulation of Behaviour (AISB) Convention 2009, Edinburgh, April 6-7, Scotland, UK.

Rigotti E. (2006) Relevance of Context-bound loci to Topical Potential in the Argumentation Stage *Argumentation* 20 (4): 519-540.

Rigotti, E. and S. Cigada (2004). *La Comunicazione Verbale*. Milano: Apogeo.

Rigotti, E. (1995). Verità e Persuasione. *Il nuovo areopago* 14(1): 3-14.

Saltzburg S. (2007). *Trial Tactics*. Washington, DC : Criminal Justice. Section, American Bar Association.

Sand et al. (2006). *Modern Federal Jury Instructions*. New York: Matthew Bender.

Solan, L. (2006). *Definition/Rules in Legal Language*. In Keith Brown, (ed.), *Elsevier Encyclopedia of Language and Linguistics*, Amsterdam: Elsevier.

Solomon, R. (2003). Not Passion's Slave. New York: Oxford University Press

Vanderveken, D. (2001). Illocutionary logic and discourse typology. *Revue Internationale de Philosophie* 216: 243-255.

Walton (1984). *Logical dialogue-games and fallacies*. University Press of America, Inc., Lanham, MD.

Walton, D. (2000). Case Study of the Use of a Circumstantial Ad Hominem in Political Argumentation. *Philosophy and Rhetoric* 33 (2): 101-115.

Walton, D. and D. Godden (2005). Persuasion dialogue in online dispute resolution. *Artificial Intelligence and Law* 13:273–295.

Walton, D. and E. Krabbe (1995). *Commitment in dialogue: basic concepts of interpersonal reasoning*. Albany: State Univ. of New York Press.

Walton, D. (1995). *Arguments from Ignorance*. University Park: The Pennsylvania State University Press.

Walton, D. (1997). *Appeal to Pity*. Albany, N.Y.: State University of New York Press.

Walton, D. (2009). Dialectical Shifts Underlying Arguments from Consequences. *Informal Logic* 29 (1): 54-83.

Walton, D.(1989). *Informal Logic*. New York: Cambridge University Press.

Woods and D. Walton (1978). Arresting circles in formal dialogues. *Journal of Philosophical Logic* 7: 73-90.

In: Psychology of Persuasion
Editors: J. Csapó and A. Magyar, pp.35-70

ISBN: 978-1-60876-590-4
© 2010 Nova Science Publishers, Inc.

Chapter 2

PERSUASION ON-LINE AND COMMUNICABILITY: THE DESTRUCTION OF CREDIBILITY IN THE VIRTUAL COMMUNITY AND COGNITIVE MODELS

Francisco V. Cipolla-Ficarra[1]

HCI Lab – FandF Multimedia
ALAIPO – Asociación Latina de Interacción Persona Ordenador, Italy
AINCI – Asociación Internacional de la Comunicación Interactiva, Italy

ABSTRACT

In the era of quality in interactive communications, persuasion is an implicit attribute in the human-computer interaction process and the human-computer interface design. Persuasion avails itself of the new technologies to modify the behaviour of the potential users of the on-line and off-line interactive systems. In our case, we will focus on its presence in the on-line systems aimed at university education. We think of education as being one of the cornerstones of any society, just the same as health care therefore, it is important to discover how persuasion underlies in some environments which can seriously damage the potential users, multimedia content generators, interactive systems designers, etc. Consequently, we present a series of techniques and heuristic methods to unveil the persuasion practiced on-line for the last eight years in a European university context. Through it, it will be possible to analyze and understand each one of the variable components that foster or destroy the validity of on-line information through persuasion. Through the obtained results a heuristic guide is presented in order to detect the presence of persuasion with advice as to how to avoid it in the case that there is no intention to have an influence on behaviour. Simultaneously the power of persuasion in the virtual community of students and teachers will be analyzed, with examples where credibility fades into disappearance in some cases. A linguistic and semiotic analysis will make it possible to establish a series of isotopies along time to discover in our case of study those links in which persuasion can be linked with manipulation and even with destructive

---

1 Communic@tions Corp, (www.alaipo.com), (www.ainci.com), Via Pascoli, S. 15 – CP 7, 24121 Bergamo, Italy – Email: ficarra@ainci.com.

behaviours such as bullying, mobbing, bossing about, stalking, etc. all of them very well disguised in the construction of e-mail messages, for instance.

1. INTRODUCTION

Persuasion is the activity of demonstrating and trying to modify the behaviour of at least one person through symbolic interaction [1], [2], [3]. It is a conscious activity, and it takes place when a threat is perceived against a person's goals and when the source of the information and the degree of this threat are important enough to justify the cost of the effort that persuasion entails. Obviously, here are excluded those situations in which the person –or user, in our case–, convinces himself/herself that someone's behaviour has changed in the wanted direction without the mediation of a symbolic interaction [4], [5]. Convincing oneself that a person or a situation has changed is self-persuasion, which is not considered in the current chapter. Now, it is important to point out that persuasion and communication are activities that involve at least two people, whose combined actions determine the outcome. Persuasion is not something that one person does to other, but something that that person does with another [1]. Even if the persuader feels that the goal of modifying the other person's behaviour has not been achieved, the persuasion activity has taken place. The use of the words 'dynamic persuader' and 'interactive persuaded person' does not mean that persuasion is a unidirectional activity, but rather bidirectional. On few occasions a person does change the other's point of view or behaviour without altering in the process some of his/her own rules. The concepts of persuasion and communication are in direct relationship to the context from which the dynamic persuader and the interactive persuaded person interact [6], [7], [8], [9]. This context is very important, because it can depend from it the degree of persuasion and destruction of truthfulness of the contents in the on-line hypermedia systems, for instance. It is even possible to establish a geographic map of those areas where the destruction of credibility in the virtual community is bigger [10]. Coherence, pertinence and efficacy cannot be defined without taking into account when? how? and for whom? It is also important to include the following rhetorical question: To what purpose or end?

However, we see how some individuals perceive other people's behaviour as a threat to their own goals. For instance, in the educational context between two professors of the same subject the publication on-line of the bibliography or of a more detailed or complete subject programme is enough so that the dynamic persuader activates all the persuasion mechanisms in regard to his/her students or potential interactive persuaded individuals. In this case two conditions may take place: that these people do not share the same rules, and/or that even if they share these rules, they disagree in their logic to apply them. When these two conditions are present, persuasion becomes a double process. The rules repertoire of the person to be persuaded must be modified, and it is necessary to provide a logic that makes the application of the preferred rules sensible. A given behaviour is reasonable for the individuals if they perceive a high degree of correspondence between their context perceptions and the previous conditions specified in the rules that guide behaviour selection. That is to say, in the regulation rules we have some previous conditions and some wanted effects; between them lie the behaviour options (mandatory, prohibited, preferred, allowed, irrelevant, etc.)

Now the fact that people make an interpretation of events means that they can never live reality from first hand. They must create their own reality through the application of cognitive schemes. These schemes make up the basis and the results of communication and persuasion, that is to say, they are binary schemes. These associations or cognitive binary schemes acquire the shape of construals and behaviour rules. In this sense an authority in the theory of the personal construal such as that of George Kelly [1], maintains that people make an effort to make their worlds predictable. They develop construals with the goal of interpreting phenomena. These construals are useful to measure the meaning of an object, of an action or a context. For instance, the users of interactive systems develop a construal to help themselves in the interpretation of a simulated world or emulated on a computer screen. These construals differ from one user to another, because they have different experiences and consequently they generate different construals. Since the context constantly generates many new experiences, the user spends part of his time at the moment of the interaction with the multimedia systems, for instance, in the search and maintenance of prediction and self-evidence at the moment of navigation. Through the daily communication with other people, our dynamic persuader has accumulated a set of rules of conducts that adjust to a certain number of construals. The interpretations are insufficient on their own to lead to action. The wanted effects in a specific context, in our case, in the face of certain metaphors that make up the interfaces and/or other design components in the interactive systems (in our case divided into the following design categories: content, presentation, structure, dynamics, connectability and panchronism –from Greek *pan* and *chronos*, time) and the constructions of previous conditions of the persuaded user, are linked to conducts under the shape of cognitive schemes that are known as rules. The vision of the communication theorists influenced by Kelly's conception about the human cognitive process was developed in a coherent theoretical structure named constructivism [1], [11].

In the current chapter we intend to use the resources of semiotics, linguistics, human-computer interaction, usability engineering, software engineering and primitives used in the design models for the multimedia systems and cognitive models to detect those situations in which the dynamic persuader destroys the information that the persuaded user perceives (it is an intersection of the formal sciences and the factual sciences –to quote Mario Bunge's division of the sciences) [12-19]. The main techniques and methods that the expert in communicability must possess in order to detect such situations are also presented, so that it is possible, for instance, to make the rest of the users of a virtual community aware of them.

2. TECHNIQUES AND METHODS

The methods and techniques used refer to the social sciences (direct observation and analysis of contents). The first of them is also used in usability engineering, especially in the methods of heuristic evaluation. The observation in context of usability engineering has led to creating special laboratories with equipment and staff, with which the studies made have a higher cost to those made for communicability, since they do without the use of laboratories, for instance. In our case, we apply direct observation which is a technique that stems from the social sciences and we eradicate the subjective factors via the elaboration of binary tables, reaching excellent objectivity levels in the results [20]. The compilation of the data is fast and it allows one to make comparative graphics of the obtained results for a better understanding of those environments where the destruction of the credibility in the on-line contents underlies in a blatant or latent way. To this effect we resort to the use of the analysis of the contents that has been used for decades in the traditional communication media: press, radio, television, cinema, etc. These analyses are made according to concepts hailing from linguistics and semiotics. Now in our case we follow the notions of their founders and we do not make up any business-like slang, such as the idea of turning semiotics into engineering when in fact it belongs to the field of the social sciences. For instance, a notion that has been very useful in the field of interactive design and especially in the design of heuristic evaluations is isotopy. The notion of isotopy in semiotics has also been applied, aside from the study of the contents plans and expression stemming from linguistics. Greimas borrowed the term isotopy from nuclear physics [21]. In structural semantics, isotopy describes the coherence and homogeneity of texts. He defines isotopy as "the principle that allows the semantic concatenation of utterances" [21]. Greimas develops the theory of textual coherence on the basis of this concept of contextual semes. In its syntagmatic extension, an isotopy is constituted by all those textual segments which are connected by one contextual seme. Since texts are usually neither unilinear nor univocal, Greimas describes the overlapping of isotopies at various isotopic strata. When a discorse has only one interpretation, its semantic structure is a simple isotopy. The simultaneity of two readings, such as in ambiguities or metaphors, is called bi-isotopy. Te superimposition of several semantic levels in a text is called pluri- or poly-isotopy. The 'enunciator star' works with poly-isotopy in virtual community.

The isotopies are sense lines that act upon the structures. That is to say, from a semantic point of view lines are drawn which unite several components of the multimedia in order to help comprehension of the rest of the multimedia system. The sense lines are independent of our location inside a multimedia, since they draw a unity in relation to the four basic categories used in the heuristic analysis of the system. For instance, if we are inside a guided tour or on the first frame of a certain entity type, we can detect that there is a set of elements belonging to the presentation of the content which do not change (typography, the background to the frames, the positioning of the navigation keys, the icons that represent the navigation keys, the kind of transitions between different frames, the music, the speaker's voice, etc.).

The lines link those elements which remain identical among themselves and which belong to the different categories of design [9]: presentation, content, dynamism, panchronism, structure and connectability (in the current chapter we have focused on the following two categories: presentation or layout and content). For instance, the equality existing in the guided tours and in collections; the colour and the typography in presentation, the organisation of the textual content as is the inverted pyramid, the activation and deactivation of the dynamic media, and the way to reach the hyperbase [22] and structure of the whole of the nodes.

The analysis of the structure of an interactive system, from a semiotics point of view, for instance, allows us to use software engineering notions, hypermedia systems models, human-computer interaction and the cognitive models. The goal is to put apart each one of the design components, studying the links down to the tiniest detail and from several approaches in those websites where the destruction of on-line credibility is detected. Therefore, the examples that will accompany the next pages are real, and of free access in the Internet, especially in the university context of Southern Europe. This task of inter-disciplinary analysis also allows one to elaborate a non-ambiguous language for the future designers, programmers of interactive systems in the Internet and especially the evaluators of on-line and off-line communicability. The goal is to work out models and guidelines for interactive design with the highest transparency, credibility and veracity of digital information.

3. MODELS AND GUIDELINES FOR INTERACTIVE DESIGN

Traditionally, a model is a theoretical scheme, generally belonging to the formal sciences, as it is the case of mathematics, of a system or a complex reality, which is elaborated to facilitate its comprehension and the study of its behaviour. Also from the point of view of art it is something —an object— which can be in its natural state from the point of view of dimension and scale, for instance —which comprises a series of qualities to be imitated and/or produced. That is to say, an object or a set of them made in relation to a same design. Most of the designers of interactive systems with commercial purposes need a series of design rules for the production of systems in the least possible time and with the lowest costs. In regard to this we find in the literature of interactive design interesting research works related in some cases to the software and/or hardware in computers, for instance in the case of the Macintosh and Windows [23], [24]. Today our attention is strongly drawn to the fact that these models and guidelines which have served for years in the design of the systems are criticized in order to destroy their validity since the passing of time is not taken into account. That is, it is illogical to compare operating systems and/or software from the beginnings of the commercial multimedia era to the computers at their peak in the mid-nineties in many European countries with the current ones avaible. This destructive criticism is a ploy used by our manipulator/persuader also called the 'star enunciator' (see your profile in annex #1).

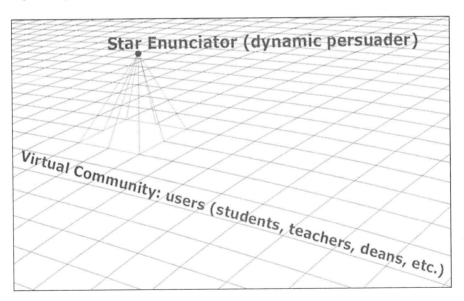

Figure 1. Star enunciator –Superiority and manipulation.

In the current work the term 'star enunciator' refers to the author or website designer in a virtual community, such as a university professor, for instance, who has as his goal to gain visibility on-line by resorting to a series of stratagems and techniques which destroy the credibility of on-line. This notion stems from social semiotics and sociology [11], [13], [21], since he will take the central place in the interrelations with the persuaded and/or users, but not at the same level but at a higher position. That is to say, graphically in the Internet, it is as if somebody pulled from a node until turning it into a cobweb with the shape of a pyramid. At this summit node is our star enunciator to be found. Besides, we understand as a 'virtual community' the number of users who continuously participate in chats, videoconferences, etc. in Internet or intranet, whether it is in long distance courses, semipresential courses, etc. or other users with the purpose of establishing bidirectional interactive communication links among them. In the case of Internet, these users establish additional links thanks to the Web 2.0 phenomena with applications such as Linkdln, Facebook, Twitter, Naymz, etc. [25].

Evidently, the diachronic factor is not considered by the on-line credibility destroyer at the moment of making his comments [26]. Sometimes, these comments are disguised as false studies of usability engineering or lack of orientation of the users in the multimedia systems because of designers' mistakes. What actually happens is that the person who makes such criticism does not have an adequate training and/or experience in the social sciences environment since he has some rudimentary university studies belonging to the formal sciences such as are mathematics and/or computer science, added to some short-lasting master in marketing and/or public relations. For example, these days, we can find professors from some Lombardian universities with direct criticism, in Internet, and to be listened in the iPods, to a book which has served for years as a guide for millions of multimedia and hypermedia interfaces designers: Apple Guidelines [23]. One of the main problems in the Italian universities is that a bachelor with a master of 6 months more or less, which may even have been obtained through the Internet, has more power than a PhD in multimedia, for instance. It is necessary to count in communicability with a new professional profile which is the intersection between formal sciences and factual sciences [27].

3.1. Professionals for Cognitive Models and Design

Now at the moment of design it is when these intersection knowledges are applied. In regard to this we find in the late 80s and early 90s a rich and varied literature about cognitive models and design guidelines [28], [29], [30]. For the cognitive approach to human-computer interaction and human-computer communication theories in cognitive science and cognitive psychology are applied to the human computer interface to make the processing of information by the human easier and more efficient [28]. However, here it is necessary to make an anchoring operation of the notions or concepts as they are made inside the semiotics context [5], especially among the studies of social sciences and the training of professionals in the context of the new technologies, between the English-speaking and the Latin peoples, for instance. In the English speaking environment it is easy to find interdisciplinary work teams in the framework of the new technologies, that is to say, the collaboration of sociologists, social communicators, designers, computer experts, experts in usability, communicability, etc. In contrast in the Latin environment of Southern Europe the eternal discrepancies between training and profession can be seen. For instance, a young philologist in English, who is familiar with commercial programmes aimed at design and who has passed an eight months long master in introduction to the cognitive models in Spain claims to be an expert in cognitive models. Obviously, when it is not possible to have an interdisciplinary team for economic reasons as it happens in many places in the European Mediterranean zone, it is better to foster training the Latin countries. In short, lacking previous studies in psychology or social communication, for instance, this alleged expert in cognitive models will only resort to the destruction of credibility on-line through the virtual communities which are close to him in order to spread those lies.

In the cognitive models and similar to other human-based tasks, the computer user perceives, stores and retrieves information from short- and long-term memory, manipulates that information to make decisions and solve problems, and then carries out responses [29]. That is to say, a set of typical activities akin to those performed by a specialist in the social sciences, who resorts to certain sociology and statistics techniques to present the obtained results. Now, in these tasks for the design process in the interfaces, for example, it is necessary to remember that there is a classic triad among the conceptual model, the mental model and the interface design. Besides, there is a triadic relation with the communicability. Graphically:

Between each one of these elements there is a bidirectional relationship. Following Norman's concepts, the conceptual model is a design model maintained by the designer of the interactive system, in engineering or programming terms, so that it is accurate, consistent, and complete. In this design, if it is done carefully, the designer should consider the user's task and capabilities [29]. A way to know these user's tasks is through an assessment of the usability of a multimedia system, for instance.

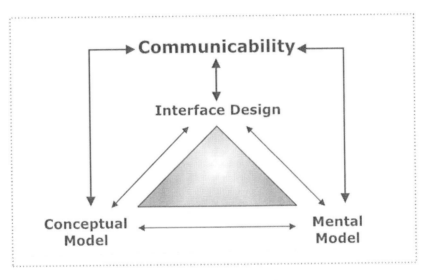

Figure 2. Communicability for Cognitive Model and Interface Design.

The mental model is the model that the user forms of how the interactive system, this mental model guides how the user structures the interaction tasks [29].

3.2. Models and Metaphors: Empathy and Inference for Interfaces

Now from the prospect of communicability the conceptual model and the mental model may be boosted through empathy [31]. Empathy is a quality attribute that facilitates the design of the interactive systems. The goal for an interface designer is to try to choose the information to represent on the display so that the mental model can, like the conceptual model, be accurate, consistent and complete. In this representation of contents on the computer screen it is always necessary to make a difference between emulation and simulation of the reality [32] on the one hand and always consider the potential international users, even in the case of the hypermedia systems developed in an off-line support. In the case of emulation and simulation of reality, the metaphors still play a very active role even in the new distance games systems which allow the real movement of the user in front of the television or computer screen, such as Wi-Fi or the current Microsoft Project Natal (the system works through the recognition of the body movements, voice and face of the users).

Those metaphors will be developed in the design process of the interface in relation to the software and the hardware available, following certain models or principles of the periphericals for the coming-in and going-out of data and/or information. Some of them hail from outside the computer context, such as was the keyboard of the typewriters 'qwerty' and which with the passing of time has become a model to be followed in computer hardware. In this case, the movement of the arms of these new interactive systems should foresee the situations of those people who have some kind of disability, such as is the amputation of a hand or an arm. Perhaps a new age is being opened for those people through a cyberarm, that's to say, a computerized arm to interact with the multimedia systems aimed at leisure, training, etc.

The correct use of metaphors, for instance, can provide us another kind of communication which is that known as direct manipulation, such as the icons of the operating systems in the computer screen, videogames, CAD/CAM applications, etc., based on the principle "What You See Is What You Get" [23]. In these cases, it is necessary that the users have a previous acquaintance with these icons, since many vary with regard to the different cultures. For instance, the classic wastepaper basket of Windows or Mac, towards which we move the documents, programs, etc. for their elimination, had to be modified in Thailand and some small crosses be inserted that depicted flies, because in that country, from a cultural and conceptual point of view, garbage is related to flies.

The remaining techniques and models in this chapter all claim to have some representation of users as they interact with an interface, that is, they model some aspect of the user's understanding, knowledge, intentions or processing. The level of representation differs from technique to technique –from models of high-level goals and the results of problem-solving activities, to descriptions of motor-level activity. The formalisms have largely been developed by psychologists, or computer scientist whose interest is in understanding user behavior [28].

Classically, in the computer interface, the set of mental models is the key to understand the methods and the techniques which can be used in an efficient interfaces design. However, the communicability issue has always been left behind. This indicates the lack of expert professionals in interactive systems who are the result of the interaction of the social and fact sciences. Starting from these cognitive models and the models used for the design of hypermedia systems, on the basis of aspects which range from the interface to the structuring of the information, a series of quality attributes have been created which are aimed at the user's skill in the moment of interacting, such as is the prediction or the anticipation of behaviour in some actions. When it comes to multimedia or hipermedia systems, the model that a user has of the system or the user model governs her interactions with it. Predictions or inferences will be based upon the model: thus, in designing an interactive system, a lot of care and work should go into making the user model as clear and obvious as possible to the user. If the system's behavior can be describe by different user models then the question of choosing a good user model or even designing a new one to describe the behaviour is also of importance. Evidently all of this was developed with the momentum of usability engineering so that the users could interact quickly with the interactive systems. Now many persuasion aspects belonging to the user-computer communication were included in these models, but no detailed studies were made to determine the main variables, especially with the aegis of Internet in the mid-nineties in Southern Europe, for instance. Today it is necessary to go deeper into these variables, because the star enunciators who exert their influence in the virtual communities are destroying in many cases the veracity of on-line information.

3.3. Models For Interactive Users: Diachronic Evolution

Setting the user as the central axis in the cognitive models we have two main aspects from the first studies made in the human-computer interaction context: competence and performance. Competence models tend to be ones that can predict legal behaviour sequences but generally do this without reference to whether they could actually be executed by users. In contrast, performance models not only describe what the necessary behaviour sequences are but usually describe both what the user needs to know and how this is employed in actual task execution. Traditionally, the study of competence models, therefore, represents the kinds of behaviour expected of a user, but they give little help in analyzing that behaviour to determine its demands on the user. Performance models provide analytical power mainly by focusing on routine behaviour in very limited applications [32]. In some cases, these two terms have been used as quality attributes in the design of the hypermedia systems, inside a non-orthogonal relationship with the five usability principles [33].

With the spread of personal computers, the premise of the easy use of usability engineering has been pivotal in the studies of the different kinds of users. On the basis of these studies the first models centred on the users started to be made in the 90s. Now in these models we find different main components of the sciences and its disciplines, such as psychology, sociology, communication and computer sciences. In the specific case of the interfaces, we have users with or without previous experiences in the use of computers, the observation of that interaction by the different groups of users: children, teenagers, adults, elderly people, etc., the interaction between the user and the computer, the abstraction of the information by the designer at the moment of generating that interface. Obviously, in this process we can see the difference between the physical aspects and the conceptual aspects of the user model, and how information is an essential part of the user model. It is in this stage where the primary data, through the process of the designer becomes an information which is aimed at the potential users. An information that later on has to be communicated through the dynamic and static means that make up the content of the on-line and off-line interactive systems. In the information and the communication we have two environments where persuasion is always present to a greater or lesser extent. We can also talk about information manipulation, however, in the current work we will only refer to this destructive factor of credibility on-line.

The use of cognitive psychology in the new technologies and especially in the context of the communications has its origins at the end of the XIX century with the studies made by the psychologists Bryan and Harten for the telegraph [2]. These general studies hold for and applied cognitive psychology, and on the same general ground that they hold for all sciences. However, it is worth detailing the three main yields for cognitive psychology that can flow from a robust applied cognitive psychology. The information processing revolution in cognitive psychology is beginning. An example in the past decade was usability engineering. Another of the still existing environments is the human-computer interaction, and a novel field to be explored in the coming years is communicability. The second contribution is to the style of cognitive psychology rather than to its substance. For example, the human-computer interaction area with its emphasis on task analysis, measurement and approximation, is also appropriate for basic cognitive psychology. The existing emphasis in psychology on discriminating between theories is certainly understandable as a historical development. The third contribution is simply that of being a successful application, though it sounds a bit odd to say it that way. Modern cognitive psychology has been developing now for 50 years, more or less. If information-processing psychology represents a successful advance of some magnitude, then ultimately it must both affect the areas in which psychology is now applied and generate new areas of application. Finally, the yield for computer science that can flow from an applied psychology of human-computer interaction is engineering methods for taking the properties of users into account during interactive system design [2].

These studies have made apparent a kind of fashion in the university departments of the United States of America and Canada, related to software engineering, languages and computer systems, etc. such as the involvement of anthropologists, psychologists, sociologists in their projects. The purpose of the inclusion of these professionals was to reach a maximum quality in software, in the 90s [34], [35]. Obviously, the academic reality of the computer science in the study plans of these two countries differs from the rest of countries in Europe and Asia. For instance, in some Latin American countries in the 80s the programmers, analysts, systems engineers, etc., had mandatory subjects of the social sciences (social psychology, sociology, public relations, marketing, etc.) to reach a higher level of professionalism at work. The current study plans in the universities of many European countries and even the new Bologna model of the alleged convergence of the university degrees do not foresee this wealth of vision for the professional studies. Consequently, we will find bachelors in arts or engineers in computer science, telecommunications, electronics, etc., who once they have finished their studies will take some short-duration master without high academic requirements but aimed at the social sciences. The goal of these professionals is not quality, but rather how to increase the technical knowledge of persuasion and manipulation for groups leadership, direction of projects, human and public relationships, etc.

4. FROM HUMAN-COMPUTER COMMUNICATION TO HUMAN-COMPUTER INTERACTION

In the framework of the communication between human beings and computers it is possible to establish the following listing of relationships:

- Computer-computer communication.
- Computer-human communication.
- Human-computer communication.
- Human-human computer (using a computer desktop).

In all these relationships the process of bidirectional interaction between the user and the computer is implicit, excepting the first case. In the remaining cases, it is interesting to search the existing possibilities to establish an excellent communication between the aspects of hardware/software of the new technologies and the human factors that intervene in the process of interaction between the user and the computer.

When we talk about interaction and communication we obviously need a natural language, a direct manipulation of the peripheral input/output, data/information to the processor, whether it is through the keyboard, sight, voice, movement, etc., and formal languages. Here is one of the main central issues of the research in human-computer interaction. One of the main goals of human-computer interaction is the combination of the modes of interaction to obtain multimodal communication. Now the most prominent medium in human-human communication is natural language. The high degree to which natural language is mastered by humans, as well as a series of different possible applications: Here is a brief listing of the traditional fields of study of natural language [28]:

- Combined language and graphic systems.
- Linguistic, word processing: automatic spelling correction, automatic retrieval of strings, etc.
- Automatic translation.
- Dialogue systems.
- Creation, editing and query of databases in natural language, etc.

Evidently here is an interesting link to artificial intelligence. The application of natural language in the user interface not only considerably increases the number of potential users, but is also of great value for the professional user, since the conceptualization of the user's intentions is no longer inhibited by an artificial language. Well, from the point of view of language and in the framework of the formal sciences also some distortion has been made, such as can be considering semiotics as an engineering [36]. Here is another example of how in some specific university or institutions of private teaching which are akin to parochialism, such as Saussure defines it [37]. This parochialism is usually a very important source in the destruction of on-line credibility. Oddly enough, the business-like purpose of these private institutions is one of the features of this star enunciator who promotes himself in the virtual community like a commercial product (see annex #2). In annex section we can see some examples (some aspects have been left out because of privacy reasons). The right to the privacy of on-line information in some countries sometimes prevents the denunciation of star enunciator and their persuasive behaviours, which in some extreme cases may even turn out to be regrettable and belonging to the kind of actions prosecuted by the law, such as intimidation, coercion and academic bossing or bullying. These are illegal actions, manipulative of the real interest of the star enunciators, and they enjoy the unanimity that the Internet gives, when it comes to international law of digital information on-line [38], [39].

The formal languages interaction style denotes essentially formal languages in the mathematical sense, programming and command languages and other classical user-initiated interaction styles with restricted conceptual and semantic models. In this kind of interaction it is necessary that the user be an expert, since the learnability and the acceptance with unskilled users is low in the normal users. Formal languages are best suited to environments where highly trained users need great flexibility of commands and parameters.

The evolution process of these three interaction models leads us to the issue of gesture interaction. Perhaps one of the fastest ways of communicating among people depending on the cultures, where words may be constantly accompanied by the movement of arms, hands, etc. as it happens in many peoples of the Mediterranean. However, here it is also necessary to take into account the contextual and/or cultural factor where the interactive system will be used since some gestural meanings vary from one people to another [5]. One of the environments where it was intended to boost this intersection of communication modalities is that of virtual reality, in the mid-70s in Europe, as a natural evolution of the interactive multimedia systems. However, there were two main factors that have not allowed the relationship between the users and the virtual community, the cost factor of the hardware/software (gloves, helmets, etc.), and the feeling of balance that the usually normally loses at the moment of the interaction in the tridimensional environments. Other experiments were made with some systems that combined the voice with a word processor, that is to say, instead of writing, the user could dictate the text inside Microsoft Word, as was the case with the IBM Via Voice.

On the other hand, these combinations of modes of interaction require great financial resources (laboratories, special equipments, staff, etc.), in order to obtain reliable results. Perhaps an environment where some mistakes in the combination on these modalities go unnoticed is the artistic one, since in many cases the level of abstraction is high and no accuracy is required in the triadic relationship, as stated by Pierce [13], [42]. Evidently, for those who do not have a solid foundation in the social sciences many of the aspects belonging to the social communication, this will sound like a real novelty, but in fact these are issues that since the appearance of the social or massive means of communication such as can be radio, television, etc., are being studied in a systematic way, especially the effects that the emitter has on the message receptors.

4.1. Competence of the Interactive System and the User's Change of Behaviour

Competence is a quality attribute which indicates the ability of the interactive system to adapt itself to the different kinds of users in the navigation. It is a design quality attribute and which can be measured through a series of techniques and heuristic methodologies without great costs and in an efficient way. This attribute at the moment of design makes up the designer's cognitive model in regard to the potential users. Implicitly the designer must take into account behaviour changes of the user for which he will resort to persuasion.

Now inside the framework of the star enunciator/persuader's changing behaviour pattern towards the potential users, it can be seen that the persuader know why a person takes up a certain attitude in given situations, and so he is then in a better position to encourage this change. Change may be achieved by convincing the user (a) that his current attitude does not lead any longer to the satisfaction he is yearning after (b) that another attitude will satisfy more easily the user's needs, or (c) that the user should reconsider the value of his attitude in the light of the new information [1]. In short, there is a kind of bidirectional triad concerning the rules on which the persuasion incentives are founded: coherence, pertinence and efficacy. Graphically:

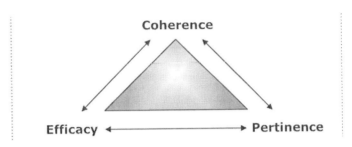

Figure 3. Star enunciator and changing behavoir towards the users.

The two first incentives belong to communicability, whereas efficacy is one of those attributes cited by Nielsen in usability engineering [15]. Obviously, although the rules applied in a given situation may be coherent, pertinent and effective from the perception that the subject to be persuaded has about the previous conditions and the desired effects, these perceptions may be inaccurate. The source of the inaccuracy may stem from the lack of consideration of the contextual aspects in which our international user is immersed. In these cases, the persuader must help the subject to persuade in the reconstruction of the previous conditions of the context, such as can be the motivation in the fruition, before making any appeal to coherence, pertinence or the efficacy enclosed in the message or credibility of the source. In the case of a star enunciator who devotes himself to put the same contents in the same personal sites of the university server, writing each statement in English and Italian for instance, this connotes an approach to the context of the potential user to motivate navigation in these contents, however, it denotes a high power of persuasion as source of information.

The credibility of the source has been treated as a factor that facilitates the effect of the message rather than as a more pivotal or significant aspect of the persuasive process. It is a questionable statement in relation to a series of studies made in the context of the social sciences in the last fifty years. For instance, in the studies carried out by Rosenthal [1], according to which focusing on the effect of the message, the theory and research on communication blinds us in regard to the complexity of the communication among people and currently in the virtual community, thanks to the new technologies, with important implications in the future of the study of persuasion and the interactive means based on computers. An example where on-line persuasion destroys the credibility of the source is that in which the university professor (start enunciator) inserts a daily counter in his pages to make the rest of the community believe (students and colleagues) that his websites are visited on-line by a great number of users (an average of 500 visits per day, which the home page of some Lombardian universities do not have). In reality it is the day after the exams of his subjects, where there is no advertisement board with the listing of the grades in paper support, and all the students have to visit his personal website to find out the grades (see annex #3).

Bitzer [1], on his side, describes the context of communication as an invitation to create an adequate answer (obviously, it is not the case of the former example). This entails the existence of normative forces dependent on the context and which are imposed on the options of the communicators. In our example, the rules are set by the star enunciator, since the rest of the professors use the digital systems (on-line) and the analogical (the classic list of paper grades in the advertisements board). Simons claims that the meaning is always contextual, and the achievement of communication depends on the ability that the communicator has to anticipate the sense of logic of the situation that the receptor has [1]. In the case of our student and receptor (interactive persuaded person), he/she wants to know his/her grades, and besides he/she must navigate through the personal website of the professor. Quite absurdly, the reading the professor makes of this situation is the exponential increase of the visitors since that favours his personal mania with statistical data, even if they are false. Besides, the star enunciator's behaviour does not open other communicative alternatives for the student community.

Now, in each behaviour underlies a logic that consists in constructs and rules. This construct is based on reasons that may take one of these two shapes: prospectives and retrospectives. The prospectives reasons make up the argumentations that people use to select and order their rules before proceeding (the student who wants to see his grades must access the professor's website and unwillingly increase the counter of these sites). The retrospective reasons are the arguments that people use for the behaviour after their decision (the persuader enunciator may prove statistically in the meetings with his colleagues that his contents on-line on a text format, audiovisual, etc., are visited by a great part of the student virtual community). As long as the persuaders may recognize the argumentation of which the potential navigator to be persuaded avails himself to use constructs and apply rules according to his own observations and demands of retrospective reasons, his chances of achieving acquiescence, accommodation, commitment or cooperation increase.

However, these chances are not exclusively determined by the ability that the persuader has to take up a social perspective, (a way to conceal this lack of social perspective is through the insertion of promotional banners related to national and/or international volunteering activities). Some contexts do not lead to coercive ways of persuasion. For instance, in formal organizations of a vertical structure, such as the organization of a school or a university with the principal, the dean or the 'star professors', at the summit of the power structure, they create conditions (status, visibility, disciplinary punishments, etc.) which make acquiescence and accommodation more frequent than commitment and cooperation. For instance, in the case of figure 4 it can be seen how the star enunciator complains in an authoritarian way about the students' lack of orientation to reach his office or tutoring activities:

Figure 4. Star enunciator and authoritarianism (scream style and red colour for the messages).

That is to say, in the same website of a professor or star enunciator we find the nonexistence of the competence quality attribute, for instance, the visual accessibility in the text, the persuasion at the service of the promotion of authoritarianism and the destruction of credibility through the inadequate use of statistics (see annex #3).

5. PERSUASION: MAIN VARIABLES OF COMMUNICATION IN THE VIRTUAL COMMUNITY

As a rule, in those situations in which the existence of the destruction of credibility manifests itself in a latent way, an analysis of the main variables of persuasion used in the designer's cognitive model may be very positive to aid understanding of the main variables in the communication and in communicability. That is to say, there is a kind of manifest pretension in each act of the persuader, in shifting his ego/I to the user or receiver, regardless of the personality of the persuaded person and the context where he/she is immersed. The bigger or lesser ease to achieve that goal will jeopardize the credibility of the source in relation to the persuaded user. These elements persist in a direct and indirect way at the moment of interacting with the systems developed by the star enunciator under a cognitive model. In other words, the persuasion variables may be used to shift the focus from the "I" towards the context of the user to be persuaded. The result is a reorganization of the rules whose knowledge makes easier for the persuader his choice of appeals to belonging, coherence or efficacy. For instance, getting the curriculum vitae of a colleague may mean automatically not only the loss of the workplace, but also the birth of a professional copycat. In the context of persuasion, the expression "professional copycat" refers to the fact that in the scientific environment a star enunciator may take the place of another person through the continuous plagiarism of all his former works, present and future, without the persuaded people knowing it.

Essentially, as far as the persuader can carry out that shift from the focus of the "I" to the context of the individual, the appeals to belonging become more adequate. To the extent in which the "I" becomes prevailing, the appeals to coherence are those that have bigger chances of bringing about behaviour changes. For instance, in the websites of the star enunciator it can be seen these prevailing through continuous sentences to draw attention, for instance the hard work he does in the correction of his exams or in the tutor ships —thus underplaying his assistants' work—, inserting the total of corrected exams (the everlasting number mania), etc. In the cases in which the consequences are more important than belonging and coherence, the most useful will be the appeals to efficacy. The star enunciator will resort to a myriad persuading variables to increase his status as a reliable source.

The credibility of the source is a multidimensional construct. The components of credibility may not be the same through all the situations, but they depend on the function that a communicant is expected to fulfill in a given context. For instance, the degree of persuasion and/or manipulation is easier to achieve in environments where the real or virtual students community is small, especially in cities or towns with few inhabitants, and with a low educational-university level, statistically speaking. The credibility studies also differ in the degree of attention that they lend to the characteristics of the emitter and the audience. On the other hand, the research in the context of the social sciences tends to ignore the interaction between the characteristics of the emitter –in our case, star enunciator– and of the individual (narcissistic personality, destructive and Machiavellian). The studies made during the past decades about the influence of the designer of the cognitive model and the potential users have indicated a bidirectional influence [4].

To the extent in which the contexts in which we will find ourselves will require information about the source, it is likely that we see ourselves forced to remember them. In other cases, the subjects (individuals) seem very capable of accepting and even respecting the emitter, although at the same time they reject his message. In some cases, there is an unexpected positive impression in the face of the source as a result of a rule pattern which inclines the members of the virtual community to respond positively when they lack a previous experience concerning the star enunciator (for instance, how a personal website is structured: biography, publications, on-line notes, programme of the subjects, etc.). It is obvious that the members of the virtual communities usually grant the benefit of doubt to the enunciators who are not familiar to them [43]. The quality of the message in the Internet seems to be usually enough to induce the individuals to create a rather favourable perception of the source. One would say that the members of the virtual community thought that such a good message could only come from a very good source. There are of course some traces that indicate falseness, urge for power, or authoritarianism of the source (the eyes that see everything, the use of the red colour in advertisements, the childlike sentences to reward or punish university students, the use and abuse of statistical data, etc., such as can be seen in the annexes #2 and #3, for instance). It is important to take into account that the personality inside a given context entails several variables to be always considered in the case of persuasion [1], [44]:

- A personality is not manipulated in the same way as the emitter's credibility.
- The persuasive messages may adapt to the individual characteristics.
- People usually experience a sense of detachment when a deed they perform is inconsistent with a stable feature or their personality.

However, Rosenthal admits that a persuasive message can't provide an abundant information, but it does give some information, and the individuals use it to create their own impressions [1]. It is the case of the on-line publicity to foster E-commerce. As a rule, advertisers normally use well-known sources to increase the credibility of their message and to set the ground for implicit or explicit appeals to the belonging (cinema or television actors, cinema melodies, etc.). The credibility of the source is important whether it is in the classical studies of the traditional means of social communication as in a virtual community, because the use of highly reliable sources may (a) stimulate identification, making useful the appeals to incoherence, (b) give additional value to the belonging claims or (c) inform the individual about the efficient resources to achieve the wanted effects [1], [45].

6. PERSUASION COMPLEXITY: DYNAMIC PERSUADER AND INTERACTIVE PERSUADED PERSON

Intelligence has been the focus of a lot of attention in terms of its relationship to persuasion. Mc Guire has suggested that intelligence may make a person more susceptible to persuasion thanks to the growing attention and comprehension it entails, but that this susceptibility decreases by increasing the resistance against complacency [1], [46]. As a rule, people of average intelligence are usually easier to persuade than people with a high or low intelligence. Here lies one of the main problems in the metrics aimed at assessing the destruction of credibility and communicability. The star enouncers belonging to the education sector and with knowledge in marketing become real specialists in persuasion and manipulators of information, but not in a positive way, rather in a negative way. Besides, by aiming all their actions at the students, not only the interactive context of a virtual community is affected, it reaches also the real environment, damaging the current and future generations of users and the veracity of the interactive contents.

In many cases, communicability becomes a mere transmission of persuasive contents, whose purpose is to foster the authoritarianism masked in a democratic context which should be the virtual communities. Obviously, to achieve such a goal a star enunciator needs to absorb the greatest amount of information sources within his reach and carry out a continuous plagiarism of contents. In some cases he may even undergo a metamorphosis in his personality plagiarizing not only the colleagues' scientific aspects, but also the fashion and the way to behave. Consequently, we may expect that some individuals surpass others in this, simply because they lay a bigger stress in interactive communication. Besides, users integrate their previous experiences in remembrable messages that they can evoke to explain certain specific problems in certain contexts and aim their action at this context. In the annex # 1 there is a listing about how to detect the star enunciators from the prospect of design, especially in the categories of presentation and content.

A very important variable which is always to be considered in persuasion is the textual content of the message. The star enunciator must gain visibility on-line and therefore will focus there all his persuasion resources (it is necessary to resort to all the basic notions of the hypertext and the access to the hyperbase [22], that is to say, kinds of links, nodes, indexes, etc.). The metaphorical expressions which are opposed to literal ones may strengthen the persuasive effect. The studies made by Kaisa Väänänen-Vainio Mattila in this visual context are of great interest, and also the distribution of the information on the computer screen [47]. Another variable that is usually associated to the reactions of the receiver to the source is the intensity of the language, such as the range of the lexical skills in the emitter (wealth of vocabulary) and verbal immediacy (when an emitter is related to the subjects of the message). Obviously, it is always necessary to consider the context of the messages. The strategy of the message, that is, how the arguments are presented in a sequential way, juxtaposed, implicit conclusions, repetition of contents, etc. For instance, Zimbardo and Ebbesen [1], [44] suggest that it is important to present an aspect of the argument when the virtual community is mostly friendly, or the position of that who introduces the issue is the only one that will be presented, or when the speaker wants a temporary change of view, even if temporary.

Now, when one, after another points of view are presented, the last one to be exposed will probably be the most effective. The repetition of a message adds something to the persuasive effect of a message, such as it happens in a radio or television broadcast (even though the supports are currently digital, for instance podcasting, digital tv, many of the persuasive techniques carried out by the analogical media can be applied to the new information supports. Lastly there is the pre-eminence of the subject chosen by the emitter. This variable stands in a direct relationship to the usefulness of the information. There are members in the virtual community who are seeking to establish contact links with the communicator, and that the accepted information to be judged on the basis of whether its acceptance favors the achievement of that goal.

Each one of these analyzed variables may be regarded as a contribution to the predominion of the context as opposed to the predominion of the "I" (enunciator). The credibility of the source may be used to strengthen an appeal to belonging, assuming that other significant for the individual perceive the source as an opinion leader. Here is another of the goals of the star enunciator, to be a leader in certain fields, within record time, even he does not have the knowledge or the ability or the experience in the subjects, but thanks to persuasion he/she can present himself as a valid leader, although he has filched those subjects from other colleagues in the virtual or real community. To the extent in which a source is used with identification purposes, an appeal to coherence may turn out to be more effective.

The variables of the message can also be manipulated to influence on the perception that the receptor has of the source, or to surpass expectations, and therefore influence the resistance that the receptor opposes to persuasion. The information about personality provides a certain orientation to determine the persuasion strategy, since it can indirectly indicate the autonomy level of the possible "I" in a given context. To the extent in which behaviours that indicate a personality type are absent, we may assume that the context prevails. For instance, here the fact of inserting the most outstanding data of the biography of the star enunciator as something indispensable or a requisite to be fulfilled inside the usability as defined by Nielsen [48]. Of course Nielsen does not speak about the paranoid deformations of personality when persuasion becomes something obsessive that only destroys the credibility of the on-line information through the constant manipulation of the statistical data, the plagiarizing of the contents of the colleagues, the obligation of the attendants to set up links to the star enunciators, the activation of websites which do not have contents except by being redirected to personal university websites, inscription to all the Web 2.0 sites (Facebook, Geocities, Naymz, LinkedIn, etc.), all of this with the purpose of gaining visibility in search engines. Obviously a modus operandi of the persuader inside the context that he can manipulate and persuade, such as students and collaborators, he will use some of the techniques to obtain conformity to focus on his goals in a speedy way and without leaving written traces.

The persuaders always operate on the basis of incomplete information. The worst mistake that can be made in the case of a destructive persuader is to give him the most possible information, for instance, in the case of working colleagues, a detailed curriculum vitae. Starting from it, he/she has the necessary elements to empower himself of the other's personality (in this case the colleague to be destroyed) or foster small clone-like individual among his assistants. A typical case is that his collaborators follow studies in the same teaching centres where the colleague to be destroyed has either studied or worked. Now, in the case of having incomplete information, his perceptions of a given relation or interaction are never exactly the same as those of the subjects to be persuaded. However, in an effort to simplify the task of predicting what strategies the individuals may use to persuade others, a series of taxonomies have been created. Obviously, in the framework of the social sciences they were accepted by some and turned down by others as time elapsed. The strategies followed in annex #4 can be divided into three basic types: punishment, instruction and altruistic.

The punishment strategies are aimed at increasing the possibility of the wanted answer through the offering of punishments and rewards by the emitter. The instruction strategies provide the emitter with reasons or justifications to prefer a way to answer. The altruistic strategies focus on the relationships between subject and emitter as the basis of the appeals. Regardless of the criticism or praise received by the taxonomy, many experts in the social sciences started to make experiments with them as in the case of Miller et al. [1] [11], who reached the conclusion that two strategies are exceptionally used in interpersonal relationships: negative esteem and adverse stimulation. The situations with long-term consequences seem to be marked by a high degree of possibility of the use of promises, positive alternative models, and altruism, whereas in situations like this the resort to adverse stimulation is unlikely.

7. PERSUASION, EDUCATION AND NEW TECHNOLOGIES

Persuasion has always been present in the communicative process. One of the rhetorical questions of human communication, is: For what purpose is a communication process established? For instance, in the case of audiovisual communication, interactive and informative of the digital mass-media and according to the legislation in communication, it may be information as well as formation, as it is in Spain or simply for information as it is in Italy. Obviously, the designer of an interactive system applies a cognitive model for the potential user and should take into account the legislative context in which the user is immersed. Besides, this cognitive model must be built on the basis of the long experience of a designer in the graphic arts and the context where the user is immersed. This experience allows to a neat difference to be established when the interface of a hypermedia design is being designed to be used, whether it is in the traditional personal computers or in what is currently known as mobile computers. That is to say, all those devices that include a central data processing unit (CPU) of small dimension, such as a PDA, multimedia telephone, electronic book, iPod, Tablet PC, etc. Mistakenly, these days, designers of content and hypermedia interfaces think that their knowledge in psychology or training are enough to address the difficulties of the cognitive models in an efficient way. However, it is necessary to start from the perspective of communication, bearing in mind the empathy in the design, for instance, until reaching communicability, that is: qualitative communication in the current interactive systems [27], [31], [49].

Now in the cognitive process the first traces of persuasion by the designer in the interactive communicative process can be detected, since in many cases it can generate the destruction of the credibility of on-line content. The latter frequently happens in the on-line multimedia information, favoured by two factors: the low cost to change hypertextual information and the ease in the on-line data edition. These continuous changes under the shape of updating of the websites make detection easier. However, it is necessary to establish a series of techniques and "ad hoc" methods to locate them and expose them.

A study in the persuasion and destruction of on-line credibility in the university educative websites must start with the professors' environment. Many of these websites are made following cognitive models of richness in design from the graphical point of view and others are more austere. The latter theoretically tend to connote a high credibility. However, in many cases it is not so, since they depict examples where the destruction of the credibility in the virtual on-line community is very high. Using one of the heuristic techniques that stem from the social sciences such as direct observation, it is possible to elaborate a table of assessment of persuasion aimed at the destruction of credibility in the virtual community and cognitive models (see annex 2). As a rule, in those websites which have been created, for example, in accordance to Nielsen's usability principles, there is an implicit enunciation: it is necessary that they be "subjectively pleasing" [15]. Here is the first clue to detect a persuasive-destructive website, the appearance in the speech of the star enunciator as if he were some kind of showman (see annex #5).

7.1. Educational Websites and Credibility Factors

The theoretic and technical notions of the cognitive models in the environment of multimedia communication are not to the service of the potential users, but rather in the sale of the star enunciator as if it was a commercial product or a marketing campaign. These are websites with practically no educative content, since there are no links to the on-line and free access lessons. In the case where they do exist, the links take to a university intranet system, where the user needs key words to have access to the information. We see a kind of personality cult, from the semiotic perspective of language, because the first area of the website is dedicated to the curriculum vitae of the star enunciator. Obviously it is not easy to detect the truthfulness or falsehood of the information in this area because all the study certifications or work experiences are not available. In some countries, it is customary to insert the numbers of the certifications of the diplomas, or make known the contests where access to the university places was gained. In other countries, this information is hidden because there is no transparency in the selection process, and access to the working posts in the public institutions are more related to friendship or family relationship factors, than to the previous knowledge and/or experience of the candidates. For instance, in the case of the countries of the European Mediterranean, many university posts are generated in relation to the candidates previously chosen by the departments. The implicit goal is that there can be no competition for that post from other candidates from other universities. This is a contextual factor whose diachronic analysis denotes an increase in the destruction of the credibility inside the virtual academic community.

With regard to the levels of academic achievement of the star enunciator, usually he/she mixes up the several titles and degrees in order to increase the power of persuasion and decrease the communicability of the website where he has stored that distorted information. A classic example is the use of the abbreviation "dr" in Italian. Many think that it is a PhD, that is, a person who has continued his college studies, but in reality it denotes just a simple bachelor degree. This has to do with the linguistic picaresque of Italian in relation to English, where "dottore" is said of any person who has reached a bachelor degree in law, geography, social sciences, languages, etc, and whose real abbreviation is "dott.-dottore" in men and "dott.ssa-dottoressa" in women.

However, many use in the north of Italy the abbreviation in English "dr" as if it were a researcher, scientist or physician in the case of Spanish. We find the destructive factor of credibility on-line we find it in those Lombardian bachelors in computer science who present themselves PhD in the Latin America websites when in fact they are not. In the Lombardian websites, others, however, use incorrectly the "dr" abbreviation instead of the Italian "dott." or "dott.ssa". Simultaneously, to conceal that destruction of credibility, these "dottori" or Italian BA take part the administration board of the Italian faculties. That is to say, that if some doctor with a degree or an engineer wants his university diplomas to be recognized, they will be assessed by these pseudo PhDs.

Consequently, lack of credibility may have serious consequences outside the context of the virtual community, since a BA is evaluating not only the titles or study plans which are similar to his own, even superior in the case of those who present the titles or posts of study similar to their own in the case of those who have a masters degree or a PhD. Therefore, the credibility of the on-line information is essential to carry out a previous selection where to hand in the paperwork to submit to the titles homologation process in some European countries. Currently it is not the Ministry of Education who carries out these activities, but each one of the colleges according to the degree of autonomy they enjoy. Now, the credibility information is very poor, especially in academic education from Web 2.0. For instance, LinkedIn website:

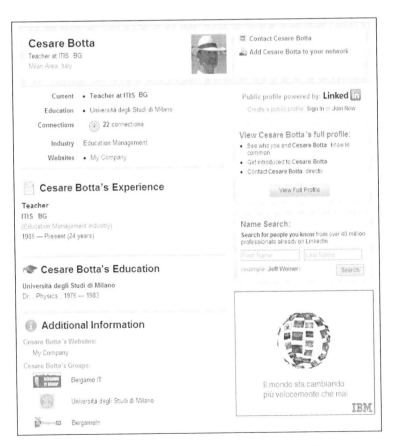

Figure 5. Dynamic persuador has a B.A. in Physics but we can see 'Dr' in education area (this is an example of false PhD).

Another of the elements to be analyzed is the presence of personal aspects such as hobbies related to leisure time; walking, trips, etc. Here there also is in reality a concealment of the tourism promotion or associations to make trips to specific places, damaging the correct circulation of the information in the cultural heritage environment, through the on-line multimedia systems (see annex #2).

The goal is that the students register for these associations.

 Cristina Bus's Education

Universitat Ramon Llull
PhD , Telecommunications Engineering , 2003 — 2007

Universitat Pompeu Fabra
Master , Journalism and Audiovisual Communication , 1993 — 1995

Universitat de Barcelona
Degree in Geography & History , 1st & 2nd cycle in Anthropology & Art History , 1987 — 1992

Universitat de Barcelona
Degree in Psychology , 1st & 2nd cycle , 1986 — 1991

 Giancarlo Zicchi's Experience

Me Srl
(Information Technology and Services industry)
May 2003 — Present (6 years 3 months)
    System engineer, System analyst

Figure 6. Meteoric and motley formation Figure 7: Engineer and analyst from "experience".

Inside the conceit of on-line communication, the star enunciator will try to conceal the goals he is pursuing at the moment of listing his publications. At first he will hide all those that do not have a straight relationship to the post he is holding at the university, for instance. Later on, he will start to publish articles –resorting to style plagiarism, if necessary– akin to the post he is holding. What matters is to justify his current position in the university and in the virtual community in a fast way. That is the way in which a simple bachelor in arts turns himself into a researcher, the typical activity of a PhD, thanks to the associations of international standing: ACM (*Association for Computing Machinery*), IEEE (*Institute of Electrical and Electronics Engineers*), etc.

Obviously 80% of these publications do not hold him as author, but rather as co-author, since he doesn't know the issues that are treated in these publications. The prevailing of deceit in interactive communication, such as is the example of the publications in the website of the star enunciator, indicates to what extent the persuader in the virtual community keeps his image of himself and his relationships. Most of the members of the virtual community do not seem especially apt at detecting the deceit. This is because the ability to generate deceit conditions does not seem to be equaled by our aptitude to recognize it. Besides, the star enunciator knows that the truth is relative. Everything which can be true can also be false, according to the receptors of the contents and the circumstances. The definitions of truth and deceit depend, therefore, on the user of the interactive system and the context where he is immersed. As if it were a commercial product, the star enunciator tries little by little to become an international prestige brand, bolstered by associate publications and associations, even if he doesn't have the necessary knowledge to hold the position he is taking at the university.

Another stratagem the persuader will use for the destruction of credibility in the university virtual community are the referential links to a set of alleged friendly websites (it is another ploy to deceive the potential users). In fact, these are direct relatives, such as a brother-in-law, those ex-students from whom he has exploited to the utmost their final project works to take hold of them in a disguised way and to start the publication in international associations such as ACM, IEEE, etc. He/she will overlap the order of the authors in those publications of scarce scientific value, giving priority to the ex-students and even in some cases he/she will wipe out the students altogether, and he will appear as the only author. In both situations the content of the presented work is always the same. That is to say, this is another factor that alters the persuader's behaviour and that of the interactive persuaded person. Persuasion brings about changes in people's attitude. Attitudes exert a coercion on behaviour, they condition the answers. Persuasion triggers changes in what people will and will not do, because it affects attitudes which in turn affect behaviour. Knowing that the users prefer to keep a coherence in the patterns of behaviour to be followed, and that the user wants to appear doing what is regarded as appropriate and efficient.

The persuaders may create the conditions for change by questioning the coherence, the pertinence or the efficacy of the behaviour of the individuals to be persuaded. Sometimes, the persuaded user sacrifices coherence at the expense of pertinence/efficacy, or vice versa, thus easing changes in behaviour. When it comes to choice of incentives, the persuader must decide, according to the specific conditions in the context, whether it is coherence, pertinence, or efficacy which has the highest priority in the spirit of the individual to be persuaded. Obviously, in the university context the persuader may achieve the pre-set goals in an easy way, for instance by offering a paid post to his students in return for their giving away the intellectual property of the works that have been done, or that they cooperate in the promotion of his personality in the Internet global village as if he were a Hollywood cinema star. An easy way to detect this situation is to watch whether the former students –the same university– of the persuader/manipulator have become teachers or participants of the courses of the star enunciator. Simultaneously, to find out whether they have referential links from their websites, to the star enunciator. This is another ploy that the persuader uses to destroy credibility in the university virtual community, since it consists of increasing the number of links to hold the first positions in the search engines, such as: Google, Yahoo, MSN, etc.

7.2. A Set of Main Components that Foster the Validity of on-Line Educational Information through Persuasion

Now the persuasion process often entails the act of exerting influences on a person so that he/she responds to an object or word in the same positive or negative way in which the individual responds to another object or word. However, sometimes there is the need to change previous associations. This is done through counter-conditioning. Counter-conditioning may entail associating a stimulus that triggers a negative answer with another that triggers a positive answer. It is possible to the extent in which the positive stimulus-response link is stronger than the negative stimulus-response link. For instance, the word "informatics" may cause a slightly negative response for an inexpert user of computers, the association of that stimulus with more working opportunities, higher salary, entertainment, technological advance, etc., increases the possibility that in the future the word "informatics" (computer science) arises a positive answer.

The new stimulus must be strong enough as to discredit the negative connotation that had for the user previously the original stimulus. One of the most common techniques in persuasion is the association with the object of change of some other negative or positive stimulus. The credibility of the source operates essentially on this association principle. A high credibility source associated with a message increases the possibility of acceptance of that message. The subliminal messages of the areas of interest kind may influence in an imperceptible and surreptitious way the cognitive associations. Evidently, the main goal is that the students participe in these areas of the interest to switch from a virtual community – some kind of coterie or clique which obeys the star enunciator at 100%.

In the case of the key words or interest areas it has to be pointed out that they are used to gain visibility in Internet search engines. As a rule, the star enunciator will constantly change them, and they don't even interest them if they are redundant. The goal is no other than appearing in the first positions within a subject range, city, region or country. He will analyze the rest of those pages that appear in the search engines and will extract the key words to be found in the Html language. Starting from there, he will insert them randomly in his pages. Here is another of the techniques used for the destruction of the credibility in the virtual community.

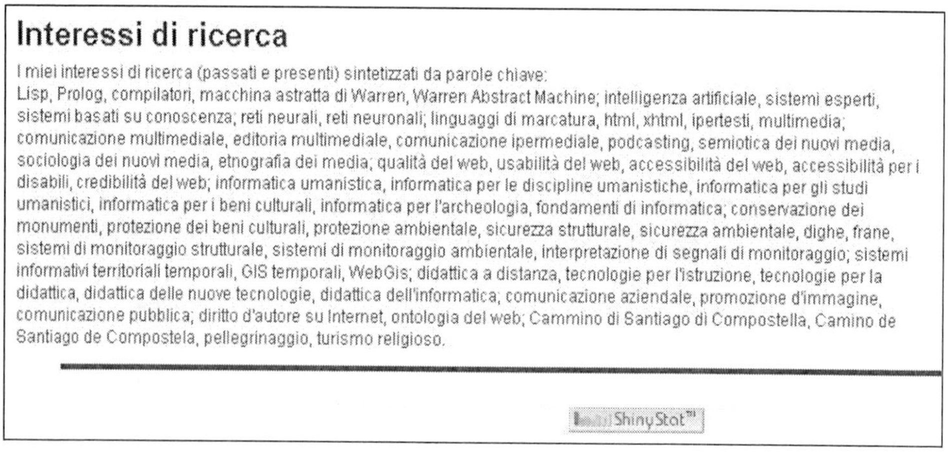

Figure 8. Star enunciator has 63 areas of the interest –keywords for Google, Yahoo, etc. (2008).

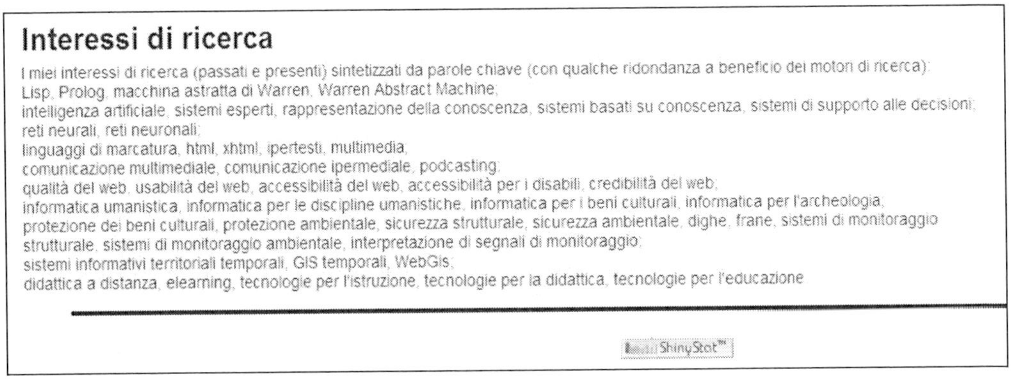

Figure 9. Now, star enunicator shows 41 areas of the interest (2009).

Obviously it is almost impossible to deny the efficacy of the formation of associations as a means of persuasion, but the different kinds of learning seem to imply much more than a simple association. Even in the case that the disguised associations make up the basis of all learning and therefore of persuasion, human beings are capable of identifying and deciding acceptance or rejection of those inappropriate or incoherent associations when they regard them as contrary to other social and personal rules. Some examples of disguised associations by a star enouncer are: the austerity of the personal website (the real aim is to gain visibility on-line; that is why numerous dynamic and static means are not included, excepting the links to television interviews to increase his stardom), the manner of dress (ties, for instance), the nepotistic links (buddies, relatives, former work mates, etc.), didactic laziness (links to other on-line courses so as not to have to develop the themes accessible to all), the corrupt attendants who easily forget the other professors and show a total lack of respect towards older people, with a wider knowledge and previous experience, etc. In short, human beings may change their own associations through a higher reflexion level, but in the case of the persuaders who are aware of their position and the control they exert on the virtual or real clique, thanks to favours stemming from economical factors (working posts, grants, stays abroad, etc.) this premise is usually not kept.

8. LESSON LEARNED AND CONCLUSION

Something happens to the on-line credibility of the obtained results through certain search engines. The passing of time allows us to see how these search engines become something like a personal obsession for some enunciators or pupils of star enunciators, to reach the highest possible number of Internet links, as if it were some kind of spam through the search engines. This can be achieved, in a simple way, by generating a small open source programme and distributing it for free, with a link inside it to the author. Evidently the free distribution is due to the fact that if it has been made through programmers of a virtual community and many of them will stay forever anonymous, the promoters of spam and viruses in Internet get subsidies from the regional authorities for these projects. That is to say, that the lack of credibility on-line may be bankrolled in Europe with public funds. Of course this belongs to parochialism as stated by Ferdinand de Saussure makes these star enunciators preach with a bad example. These 'modus operandis' to ruins not only the credibility but also communicability on-line.

In the work made it has been seen how the purpose of persuasion in the free access virtual communities in Internet is the boundless promotion of the star enunciator. This notion that we have introduced in the current work has already shown from the start that we are in the face of an authoritarian and vertical attitude in the context of virtual communication. It is not easy to detect his presence since this entails knowing some real data about the star enunciator. However, we find in the first analysis table of on-line credibility the metrics of binary presence in the components (presence or absence). This table allows to establish a first approach to detect the situations which destroy the veracity in on-line information and very especially in the university education context. At the same time it is important to stress two main aspects in the on-line contents. In the first place, the volatility of the information, that is to say, once a star enunciator is detected this or his team can eliminate in a total or partial way those elements which easily give away the presence of a star enunciator-persuader. The legal immunity enjoyed by the individuals who devote themselves to destroying the credibility and veracity of on-line information. In this regard, it is necessary to establish a legal framework in the international computer context, or else the veracity of the information in digital and free access support will be slowly destroyed, regardless of its goal, whether it is educative, commercial, entertainment, etc. The main problem is how to stop this phenomenon in one of the cornerstones of any culturally developed community, that is, education, and very especially the university context, which is the highest pillar for the progress of the information society in a free and democratic way.

The democratization of the Internet has allowed the free access to knowledge and training to millions of users in the whole planet. It is necessary to eliminate the star enunciators or dynamic persuaders for its expansion to continue. The main problem currently is not only he/she, but his/her disciples, who will damage in an exponential way the credibility of on-line information, the clearness of the sources, the veracity and transparency of the contents. This may mean the end of the virtual communities in the next years. Maybe it will be necessary to implement a system of quality rules like those that exist in the software, that is to say, a ISO normative, in each one of the members who promote themselves through the free instruments of the Web 2.0. Also some international icon can be incorporated to refer to the fact that such a community does not have star enunciators who devote themselves to constantly sabotage the authenticity and/or veracity of on-line information. It has been made apparent in the current study the presence of members of the virtual community who, prompted by a boundless eagerness for protagonism destroy the quality criteria known as credibility. An expert in communicability can detect these situations, starting in some cases with real information to carry out the parallelism between the truth and falsehood. The problem is that once these falsehood situations are detected, the volatility of digital information on-line allows one to erase the traces of those star enunciators and their collaborators. It is necessary to resort to ethical and legal international codes. Otherwise, we will be witnessing the beginning of the end of on-line credibility.

ACKNOWLEDGMENTS

The author would like to thank Emma Nicol (University of Strathclyde), Maria Ficarra (ALAIPO and AINCI), Lucindo Bolatti (UNC), Jorge Vivas (UNVM), Teresina Gamba (Bergamo, Italy), Miguel (Canada, Spain and Italy) and Carlos (Barcelona, Spain), for their helps and contributions.

ANNEX SECTION

Annex #1. First Profile of the Star Enunciator and Heuristic Table of the Persuasion Evaluation

The profile of the star enunciator is the result of the heuristic evaluation of university websites from 1995 up to our days.

- There are three types of those: the cinema star, the pixel psychedelic and the anonymous. Among the first group, they choose to hire the photographic services of real professionals in the sector because they define themselves as artist, creative, communicator, idea makers, "human", etc. In the second group, we have those who use the passport format. Some of them manipulate the images with special effects, for instance; the blurry look. However, in all of them they appear smiling in the best style of "the hyenas or the mocking" modalities existing in the multimedia system for the learning of languages. If there are no photographs of the star enunciator himself, they usually insert graphics which denote gaiety, that is, a happy person (obviously, their whole work consists in manipulating and persuading the virtual community).
- The fashion aspect in the pictures of the star enunciators mustn't be ruled out, especially since in semiotics there are studies which speak about the tyranny of fashion, i.e., Roland Barthes. It is common that those characters defined as disciples of the star enunciator use without need spectacles with thick glasses or frames in black, like those models of the 50s or 60s, with the purpose of drawing the attention or selling the image of young researchers or scientists.
- They need to constantly promote their activities as if they were a news agency. We usually find their daily notebooks on-line, the pictures when they come back from their trips abroad (flickr, for instance), etc.
- There is a mania towards statistic and gaining visibility on-line. Their names must appear in the first slots in the main search engines such as Google, Yahoo, MSN, Ask, etc.
- Existence of endogamy-style links towards their personal websites posted by their collaborators or virtual community.
- A thorough analysis of the curriculum vitae or resume makes it apparent that in their origins they do not have any training in interactive systems, but they have been able to fill that void by working as a team, that is to say, co-authorship. Once their issues are defined they start their publication in an individual manner. In the first of them, there is an endless roster of names of people in the gratitude section (over 20),

because in fact the work or the knowledge stems from those people (let us not forget that he/she has no previous knowledge and/or experience of the issue he/she is introducing).

- They resort systematically to the art of disguised plagiarism. This art consists in copying and gluing the bibliographical sources from other authors. He or she will even become a kind of copycat of those he/she will constantly plagiarize. For instance, a bachelor in computer science, instead of busying himself with those aspects related to information structure, such as may be the data search algorithms, the different kinds of databases, the natural languages, artificial intelligence, etc. prefers to tackle issues which are totally alien to him/her from both the training and the experience standpoint: semiotics, quality, design, history of interactive systems, colours, digital newspapers, podcasting, etc.

- Their areas of interest are multifarious and may surpass the 12-15 subjects, simultaneously.

- In the first years of the stardom he/she will constantly change the name of the subjects. It is the period of major plagiarizing until getting settled in a theoretical and practical context. To this effect he will count with the help of assistants who daily control his/her competence –colleagues or workmates-, in and outside university.

- The study diplomas do not match the areas of interest and activities.

- University titles and working experience obtained in a record time. For instance, one or two BAs, a master and a PhD, simultaneously; department management, direction of interdisciplinary teams, holding of university posts, etc., in less than 15 years.

- Total or partial elimination of the possession of university jobs. For instance, professor in a university but in reality is a school industrial for professional formation.

- Fake assumption of titles by the investigator or systems engineer, for instance in the Facebook, Naymz, LinkedIn, etc. but they lack university studies.

Component and Credibility Attributes for Star Enunciator or Dynamic Persuader	Design Categories: Presentation = P and Content = C	Yes	No
- Photographies: Individual and group. Style: Hollywood, special effects (Fx), anonymous. Gesture: Smiling, serious, makes to faces.	P		
- Fashion: oppressive and tyrannical.	P		
- Journalism activities (emission news and product/service information sites, i.e., digital radio, TV, press, etc.).	C		
- Statistical information and manipulation of the contents.	P, C		
- Spam effects of the contents (high level of diffusion on-line and reusability of the information).	P		
- Promotion of endogamy-style (links towards their personal websites).	P, C		
- He/she has the website with links to distant relative or relation in-law in the same university, for example.	C		
- He/she uses more than one language for on-line promotion.	C		
- Curriculum vitae or resume with false contents in Web 2.0 portals, i.e., Facebook, Naymz, LinkedIn, Geocities, Flickr, Twitter, etc.	C		

Component and Credibility Attributes for Star Enunciator or Dynamic Persuader	Design Categories: Presentation = P and Content = C	Yes	No
- He/she changes constantly the contents in personal website.	C		
- twelve or more areas of interest.	C		
- The keywords in personal pages on-line change are homogeneous.	C		
- The content are originals (plagiarism tasks, i.e. copycut).	C		
- The use of phrases that ridicule the acting of the members of a real or virtual community.	C		
- The use of capital letters in the text (i.e. email), red colour (personal communications) or traffic lights for evaluation of the students.	P, C		
- He/she provocates a confusion constantly between academic contents and personal marketing or business.	P, C		
- He/she introduces icons or symbols on-line for the omnipresence of an information manipulator.	P		
- The dynamic persuader and/or your collaborators attack others websites in virtual community.	C		

Annex #2. Examples of the Destruction of Credibility in the Virtual Community

Figure 10. The star enunciator –universitary teacher, provocates a confusion constantly between academic contents (teacher, writer, press, resume, etc.) and personal marketing or business ('tienda' – shop).

Figure 11. Those eyes give away the omnipresence of an information manipulator. The thick eyebrows reveal authoritarianism and control towards all those who access the content.

Figure 12. The dynamic persuaders to promove false tours into virtual community for your potential copycut activities.

Annex #3. Dynamic Persuader and Stadistical Information for Users Manipulation

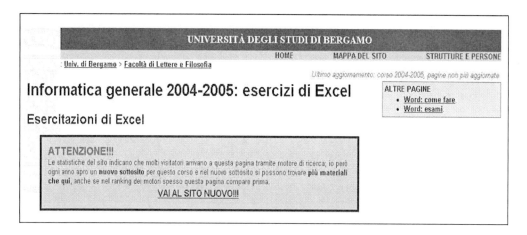

Figure 13. Star persuader or dynamic persuader likes very much the false statistical information .

In the figures 12 and 13 we see how two counters reach the same number on two different days (05/27/2009 = 501 visitors and 05/29/2009 = 492) and 23:30 hours, more or less, the counter is to start from scratch.

The digital newspapers are also evidence of this context: persuasion on-line and destruction of credibility. Sometimes, the news which is closest to the interests of these power groups surpasses in reader numbers the news from the front page of the papers. For instance, information technological news in the digital version of "El País" (www.elpais.es) as compared to the news on the coverpage of the paper version. This alleged reading record was reached in only 4 hours (248 punctuation –very interesting).

Figure 14. Total visitors = 501.

Figure 15. Total visitors = 492.

Figure 16. ShinyStat system shows only 7 visitors 5/29/2009 –not 500, more or less. Evidently, there is a direct manipulation of the counters (star enunciator and/or collaborators) at the access to the on-line pages.

Annex #4. Conformity Obtainment Techniques in Daily Life Situations

1. Promise: if you obey, I will reward you.
2. Threat: If you don't obey, I will punish you.
3. Experience (positive): If you obey, you will naturally have a reward.
4. Experience (negative): If you don't obey, you will be naturally punished.
5. Sympathy: The persuader shows himself friendly and cooperating with the individual to gain his good disposition in such a way that he fulfills what he requires.
6. Anticipation: The persuader rewards the individual before asking his conformity.
7. Adverse stimulus: The persuader continuously punishes the individual, making depend the suspension of the punishment on his obedience.
8. Debt: You owe me obedience because of the favors I did you in the past.
9. Moral appeal: If you don't obey, you are immoral.
10. Yes feeling (positive): You will feel better with yourself if you obey.
11. No feeling (negative). You will feel bad with yourself if you disobey.
12. Alternative model (positive): A well-natured person would obey.
13. Alternative model (negative). Only a bad-natured person would disobey.
14. Altruism: I very much need you to obey, do it for me.
15. Esteem: (positive). The people you love will be happy if you obey.
16. Esteem (negative). The people you love will think badly of you if you don't obey.

ELPAIS.com > Tecnología

Dos jóvenes españoles sacan partido de Google Earth

Panoramio.com permite compatir fotografías e incorporarlas en el sistema de imágenes vía satélite

EFE - Madrid - 11/12/2006

248 votos | Vota

El portal de internet Google Earth, que ofrece vistas del mundo tomadas desde satélites, ha incluido en su servicio las imágenes de Panoramio.com, un proyecto creado por dos jóvenes españoles que permite compartir fotografías y situarlas en el mapa.

La noticia en otros webs
- webs en español
- en otros idiomas

Panoramio.com es una comunidad virtual, creada hace algo más de un año por Joaquín Cuenca y Eduardo Manchón, en la que los cibernautas pueden compartir gratis sus fotografías y situarlas cartográficamente en el lugar donde fueron captadas, gracias, precisamente, a imágenes de satélites proporcionadas por Google Maps.

La integración de Panoramio en el portal de Google Earth hace posible visualizar de manera combinada las imágenes de satélite en tres dimensiones de ese portal y las fotos tomadas de cualquier lugar del mundo. Las fotos se representan sobre el mapa con pequeños iconos azules y para visualizarlas basta abrir Google Earth.

publicidad

Suscríbete ahora a las alertas de EL PAIS.com en Vodafone live!

Lo más leído | ...enviado

1. Dos jóvenes españoles sacan partido de Google Earth
2. "Como mucho iría a 140"
3. Gritos y abucheos contra la única representante ejecutivo chileno en el funeral de Pinochet

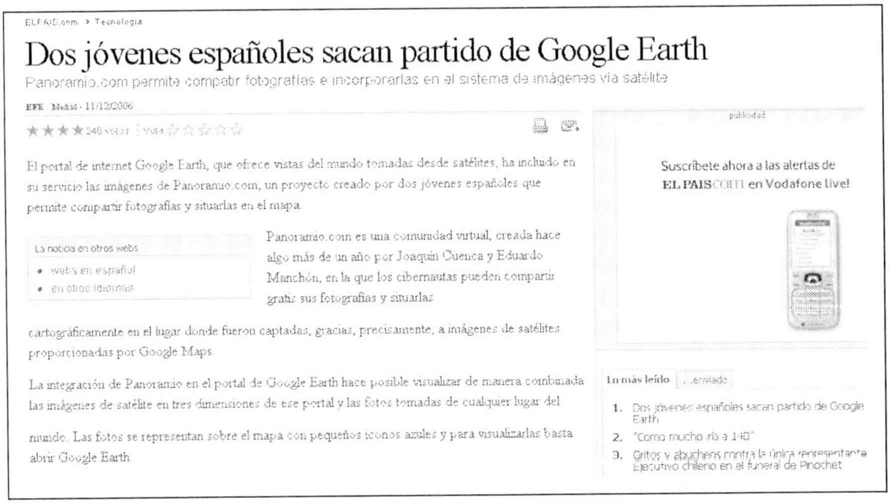

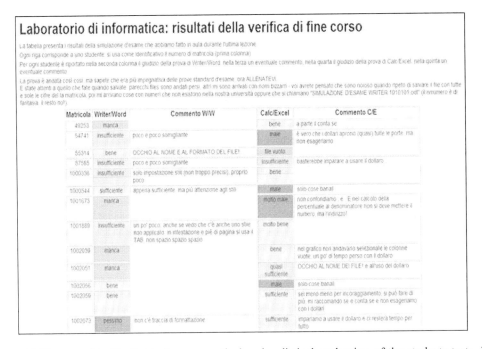

Figure 17. Community virtual and manipulation of the information in digital newspapers .

Among the 16 conformity obtainment techniques, the techniques from 9 to 13 appeal to the coherence with the image itself, whereas the remaining ones appeal to the personal need of approval by the persuader (1,2, 5, 7, 8 and 9) or by others (3, 4, 15 and 16). Authors: Maxwell and Smith [1], [44], [45].

Annex #5. Dynamic Persuader and Statistical Information for Interactive Persuaded Person

Laboratorio di informatica: risultati della verifica di fine corso

La tabella presenta i risultati della simulazione d'esame che abbiamo fatto in aula durante l'ultima lezione.

Ogni riga corrisponde a uno studente: si usa come identificativo il numero di matricola (prima colonna).

Per ogni studente è riportato nella seconda colonna il giudizio della prova di Writer/Word, nella terza un eventuale commento, nella quarta il giudizio della prova di Calc/Excel, nella quinta un eventuale commento.

La prova è andata così così, ma sapete che era più impegnativa delle prove standard d'esame, ora ALLENATEVI.

E state attenti a quello che fate quando salvate: parecchi files sono andati persi, altri mi sono arrivati con nomi bizzarri - voi avrete pensato che sono noioso quando ripeto di salvare il file con tutte e sole le cifre della matricola, poi mi arrivano cose con numeri che non esistono nella nostra università oppure che si chiamano "SIMULAZIONE D'ESAME WRITER 1010101.odt" (il nnumero è di fantasia, il resto no!)

Matricola	Writer/Word	Commento W/W	Calc/Excel	Commento C/E
49253	manca		bene	a parte il conta.se
54741	insufficiente	poco e poco somigliante	male	è vero che i dollari aprono (quasi) tutte le porte, ma non esageriamo
55314	bene	OCCHIO AL NOME E AL FORMATO DEL FILE!	file vuoto	
57585	insufficiente	poco e poco somigliante	insufficiente	basterebbe imparare a usare il dollaro
1000336	insufficiente	solo impostazione stili (non troppo precisi): proprio poco	bene	
1000544	sufficiente	appena sufficiente, ma più attenzione agli stili	male	solo cose banali
1001673	manca		molto male	non confondiamo ; e . E nel calcolo della percentuale al denominatore non si deve mettere il numero, ma l'indirizzo!
1001889	insufficiente	un po' poco: anche se vedo che c'è anche uno stile non applicato; in intestazione e piè di pagina si usa il TAB, non spazio spazio spazio	molto bene	
1002039	manca		bene	nel grafico non andavano selezionate le colonne vuote; un po' di tempo perso con il dollaro
1002051	manca		quasi sufficiente	OCCHIO AL NOME DEI FILE! e all'uso del dollaro
1002056	bene		male	solo cose banali
1002059	bene		sufficiente	sei meno meno per incoraggiamento, si può fare di più, mi raccomando se e conta.se e non esageriamo con i dollari
1002073	pessimo	non c'è traccia di formattazione	sufficiente	impariamo a usare il dollaro e ci resterà tempo per tutto

Figure 18.The use of traffic lights for a sarcastical and sadistical evaluation of the students tests, i.e., poor, banal, unsatifactory, illeterate, bad, insufficient, etc.

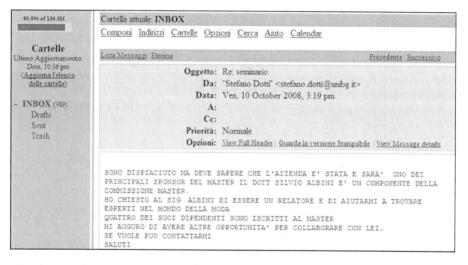

Tesi in tecnologie per l'istruzione

Con gli studenti della specialistica in consulenza pedagogica sono disponibile per tesi relative al mio insegnamento di Tecnologie per l'istruzione.
Ci sono due requisiti: competenze informatiche e buon inglese. Non dico altro.

Regole d'oro per chi vuol fare la tesi / prova finale con me

1. Prima di venire a parlarmi, leggetevi "Come si fa una tesi di laurea"
2. Prima di venire a parlarmi, leggetevi la lista dei temi di ricerca che mi interessano e quella delle tesi che ho già seguito.
3. Se mi chiedete la tesi / prova finale e poi la fate con un altro docente, usatemi la cortesia di segnalarmelo, così vi tolgo dalla lista e libero un posto per qualcun altro (non ve ne dimenticate, potrei capitarvi in commissione di laurea...).
4. Se scopro che avete copiato / parafrasato da libri o siti Internet, vi faccio saltare la sessione. Inutile dirmi che tutti copiano, LO SO.
5. Se state facendo la tesi / prova finale con me e decidete di **posticipare la laurea**, fatemelo sapere.

Figure 19. The use of phrases that ridicule the acting of the members of a real or virtual community (topic: Internet, books, final project and plagiarism).

Figure 20. The use of capital letters in the text gives away authoritarianism in the electronic messages (scream/shouting). In the example, it is a cover-up behaviour to defend the extra-academic coterie to which belongs the writer of the message

REFERENCES

[1]   Reardon, K. (1981). Persuasion. Theory and Context. Sage Publications: London.

[2]   Card, S., Moran, T., Newell, A. (1983). The Psychology of Human-Computer Interaction. LEA: New Jersey.

[3]   Sharp, H. et al. (2007). Interaction Desing: Beyond Human-Computer Interaction. John Wiley: West Sussex.

[4]   Sears, A. (2007). The Human-Computer Interaction Handbook: Fundamentals, Envolving Technologies and Emerging Applications. LEA: New York.

[5]   Cipolla-Ficarra, F. (2005). An Evaluation of Meaning and Content Quality in Hypermedia. In CD-ROM Proc. Las Vegas: HCI International.

[6]   O'Neill, S. (2008). Interactive Media: The Semiotics of Embobied Interaction. Springer-Verlag: London.

[7]   Dubberly, H., Pangaro, P., Haque, U. (2009). What is Interaction? Are There Different Types? Interactions of ACM, pp. 69-75.

[8]   Reeves, B., Nass, C. (1998). The Media Equation –How People Treat Computers, Television, and New Media Like Real People and Places. Cambrigde University Press: Cambrigde.

[9]   Cipolla-Ficarra, F., Cipolla-Ficarra, M. (2009). Computer Animation and Communicability in Multimedia System: A Trichotomy Evaluation. New Directions in Intelligent Interactive Multimedia. Heildeberg: Springer-Verlag, pp. 103-115.

[10] Preece, J. (1998). Empathic Communities. Interactions of ACM, vol. 5, pp. 32-43.

[11] Ander-egg, E. (1986). Techniques of Social Investigation. Hvmanitas: Buenos Aires.

[12] Bunge, M. (2008). Semántica I: Sentido y referencia. Gedisa: Barcelona.

[13] Eco, U. (1979). A Theory of Semiotics. Indiana University Press. Indiana.

[14] Holdcroft, D. (1991). Saussure –Signs, System and Arbitrariness. Cambridge University Press. Cambridge.

[15] Nielsen, J. (1993). Usability Engineering. Academic Press: London.

[16] Pressman, R. (2005). Software Engineering –A Practitioner's Approach. McGraw-Hill: New York.

[17] Cipolla-Ficarra, F. (1997). Evaluation of Multimedia Components. In Proc. IEEE Multimedia Conference on Multimedia Computing Systems. IEEE Press: Ottawa, pp. 557-564.

[18] Kirlik, A (2006). Adaptive Perspectives on Human-Technology Interaction: Methods and Models for Cognitive Engineering and Human-Computer Interaction. Oxford University Press: Oxford.

[19] Ishii, H. (2008). The Tangible User Interface and Its Evolution. Communications of the ACM, vol. 51, pp. 32-36.

[20] Cipolla-Ficarra, F. (1996). The Resolution of the Problem of Objectivity in a Method of Evaluation for Interactive Applications. ACM SIGWEB. ACM Press: New York.

[21] Nöth, W. (1995). Handbook of Semiotics. Indiana University Press: Indianapolis.

[22] Tompa, F. (1989). A Data Model for Flexible Hypertext Database System. ACM Transactions on Information Systems, vol. 1, pp. 85-100.

[23] Apple (1992). Macintosh Human Interface Guidelines. Addison-Wesley: Massachusetts.

[24] Schneiderman, B., Plaisant, C. (2009). Designing the User Interface: Strategies for Effective Human-Computer Interaction. Addison-Wesley: Cambridge.

[25] Murugesan, S. (2007). Understanding Web 2.0. IT Professional Vol. 9 (4), pp. 34-41.

[26] Cipolla-Ficarra, F., Cipolla-Ficarra, M. (2008). Interactive Systems, Design and Heuristic Evaluation: The Importance of the Diachronic Vision. New Directions in Intelligent Interactive Multimedia. Springer-Verlag: Heildeberg, pp. 625-634

[27] Cipolla-Ficarra, F. (2008). Communicability design and evaluation in cultural and ecological multimedia systems. In Proc. MSCommunicability '08. ACM Press: New York, pp. 1-8.

[28] Blattner, M., Dannenberg, R. (1992). Multimedia Interface Design. ACM Press: New York.

[29] Eberts, R. (1992). User Interface Design. Pretince-Hall: London.

[30] Card, S., Moran, T., Newell, A. (1983). The Psychology of Human-Computer Interaction. LEA: New Jersey.

[31] Cipolla-Ficarra, F. (2005). HEDCDEH: A Heuristic Evaluation Disk for Communication and Design in Hypermedia. In CD-ROM Proc. HCI International: Las Vegas.

[32] Dix, A. *et al.* (2004). Human-Computer Interaction. Pretince-Hall: London.

[33] Garzotto, F., Mainetti, L., Paolini, P. (1995). Communication of ACM, 38 (8), pp. 74-86.

[34] Basili, V., Musa, J. (1991). The Future Engineering of Software: A Management Perspective. IEEE Computer 24 (9), pp. 90-96.

[35] Basili, V. *et al.* (2004). New Year's Resolutions for Software Quality. IEEE Software 21(1), pp. 12-13.

[36] De Souza, C. (2005). Semiotic engineering: bringing designers and users together at interaction time. Interacting with Computers. Vol. 17 (3), pp. 317-341.

[37] Saussure, F. (1990). Course in General Linguistics. McGraw-Hill: New York.

[38] Boyle, J. (1997): Shamans, Software, and Spleens –Law and the Construction of the Information Society. Harvard University Press: Cambridge.

[39] Darrell, K. (2009). Issues In Internet Law: Society, Technology, and the Law. Amber Book Company: London.

[40] Aykin, N. (2007). Usability and Internationalization: Hci and Culture. Springer-Verlag: Berlin.

[41] Yunker, J. (2002). Beyond Borders: Web Globalization Strategies. New Riders Publishing: Indianapolis.

[42] Fabbrichesi, R. (2008). Semiotics and Philosophy in Charles Sanders Peirce. Cambridge Scholars Publishing: Cambridge.

[43] [43] Boyd, D., Ellison, N. (2007), Social Network Sites: Definition, History, and Scholarship. *Journal of Computer-Mediated Communication,* Vol. 13 (1).

[44] Mulholland, J. (1994). Handbook of Persuasive Tactics: A Handbook of Strategies for Influencing Others Through Communication. Routledge: London.

[45] Cialdini, R. (1998). Influence the Psychology of Persuasion. Collins: New York.

[46] Dillard, J., Pfau, M. (2002). Persuasion Handbook. Sage Publications, Thousand Oaks.

[47] Koskela, T., Väänänen, K. (2004): Evolution towards smart home environments: empirical evaluation of three user interfaces. Personal and Ubiquitous Computing, Vol. 8 (3-4) pp. 234-240.

[48] Nielsen, J. (1999). The Top Ten Web Design Mistakes of 1999. Available at: http://www.useit.com/alertbox/990530.html

[49] Goodwin, K. (2009). Designing for the Digital Age: How to Create Human-Centered Products and Services. John Wiley: Indianapolis.

[50] Cipolla-Ficarra, F. (2009). Virtual Learning Environment: Quality Design for Foreign Languages in Multimedia Systems. New Directions in Intelligence Interactive Multimedia System. Springer-Verlag: Heildeberg, pp. 117-127.

In: Psychology of Persuasion

Editors: J. Csapó and A. Magyar, pp.71-99

ISBN: 978-1-60876-590-4

© 2010 Nova Science Publishers, Inc.

Chapter 3

REGULATORY FIT AND PERSUASION: ROLES OF ELABORATION AND TRANSPORTATION LIKELIHOOD

Leigh Ann Vaughn[*]

Ithaca College, Ithaca, N.Y., USA

ABSTRACT

This chapter puts current research on regulatory fit and persuasion into the larger contexts of elaboration likelihood and transportation likelihood (the likelihood of becoming experientially engaged with a narrative). I lay groundwork by describing regulatory fit with prevention focus and promotion focus, how regulatory fit is operationally defined, and how it can affect judgments through feelings-as-information, metacognitive, and other processes. Then I review current research on how regulatory fit affects persuasion through advocacy messages and through narratives, noting where interpretational ambiguities exist. Finally I speculate about how effects of regulatory fit on persuasion might differ according to elaboration or transportation likelihood and according to whether the regulatory-fit experience results from an initial event unrelated to the communication or from engagement with the communication itself.

Keywords: regulatory fit, prevention, promotion, persuasion, metacognition

INTRODUCTION

Positive and negative value can be attached to attitude objects, one's thoughts, or styles of processing information. Often, value may come from considerations such as the pleasure or pain of an actual or imagined outcome. In the past decade, however, a new and growing area of research has addressed a different source of value: regulatory fit, which is a good match between one's self-regulatory orientation and the means of engaging with a task (e.g., Higgins, 2000, 2005, 2006). Regulatory fit can affect persuasion through adding value to and

---

[*] Leigh Ann Vaughn, Department of Psychology, Ithaca College, Ithaca, N.Y. Correspondence concerning this work should be addressed to Leigh Ann Vaughn, Department of Psychology, Ithaca College, Ithaca, NY 14850. E-mail: Lvaughn@ithaca.edu

enhancing engagement with advocacy messages (which use logical arguments to present a case for a position) and narratives (which present characters immersed in events that have a beginning, middle, and end). In this chapter, I review how regulatory fit could enhance and at times reduce persuasion relative to regulatory nonfit (which is a mismatch between self-regulatory orientation and means of engaging with a task).

Imagine how regulatory fit could enhance mental engagement with a story, for example, and make the story seem more persuasive. In this example, a person I will call Jill had heard a lot about the book, *The Da Vinci Code* (Brown, 2003) so she decided to buy a copy and read it. Initially she did not find it very involving. Although she considered setting the book aside for good, she decided to stick with it for a while. Then, about one-fifth of the way through, she became much more engaged in the story. It wasn't clear what about the story had changed, but Jill was much more transported than she had been. Now reading the book wasn't so much like reading: when she was really into it, *she* didn't seem to be present at all. In her imagination, she was a character with the events of the story happening to her. When she put down the book after a few chapters, she was a little surprised to find herself - *as* herself - in her home. She even started thinking about how the conspiracy in the book could be real. She understood why many conservative Christians seemed so upset by the book and why so many people had written books debunking the conspiracy it portrayed. Everything in the book just seemed so plausible. She now returned from her experiences in the story world slightly changed – more persuaded, with more story-consistent beliefs.

In fact, however, in this example Jill's enhanced feelings of rightness, her mental engagement, and the apparent change in the story's persuasiveness didn't come from any changes in the book at all. They came from events at Jill's work. Shortly after beginning the book, Jill started a new project at work that was an especially good fit with her usual, cautious style of doing things. This experience of regulatory fit created vague, lingering feelings of rightness that – because she still had them while reading the story but wasn't thinking about where they came from – she unwittingly attributed to the story.

Compared to regulatory nonfit, how could regulatory fit enhance engagement with a narrative? For that matter, how could it enhance engagement with advocacy messages - such as commercials or political speeches - that rely on well-crafted and logical arguments?

In this chapter, I will review current research on regulatory fit and how it influences persuasion through advocacy messages and through narratives. There are many possible mechanisms by which regulatory fit may influence persuasion. Such mechanisms differ in their likelihood of occurring when motivation and ability to engage with the communication is low, unconstrained, or high. Accordingly, they also relate to the depth which people process persuasive appeals, which makes these mechanisms important to understand because deeper processing enhances the strength and behavioral impact of resulting attitudes (e.g., Petty & Cacioppo, 1986; Petty & Wegener, 1999).

When I describe regulatory fit effects throughout this chapter, I will contrast regulatory fit with regulatory nonfit experimental conditions. In part, this is because regulatory fit theory specifies how regulatory matching and mismatching conditions should differ from each other (e.g., Higgins, 2000, 2005), but it is silent about how they should differ from some sort of ultimate control condition. Indeed, given that regulatory fit is a high-match state and regulatory fit is a low-match state, it is difficult to imagine what some sort of ultimate control state would be with regard to regulatory fit/nonfit. Additionally, regulatory-fit experiments usually only compare fit and nonfit conditions (cf. Hong & Lee, 2008, Study 2), so this is the contrast I will implicitly or explicitly draw in the current chapter.

REGULATORY FIT, FEELING RIGHT AND ENGAGEMENT STRENGTH

People experience regulatory fit when their way of engaging with a task sustains their self-regulatory orientation or interests in the task (e.g., Higgins, 2000, 2005). Although most research on regulatory fit has worked with the distinction drawn between promotion focus and prevention focus (e.g., Higgins, 1997), fit effects can occur with other motivational orientations as well. These include locomotion and assessment orientations (Avnet & Higgins, 2003) and tendencies associated with perceiving that a task is meant to be important versus that is meant to be fun (Bianco, Higgins, & Klem, 2003). All currently-published research on regulatory fit and persuasion has addressed differences between promotion and prevention orientations, strategies, and/or outcomes, so it is on this research that I focus my review.

According to regulatory focus theory (e.g., Higgins, 1997), people in a promotion focus strive for growth and accomplishment through pursuing ideals, hopes, and aspirations, whereas people in a prevention focus strive for security and protection through pursuing "oughts," duties, and obligations. Strategies preferred in a promotion focus are eagerness-related (e.g., doing extra reading for a class), which naturally fit a concern with aspirations and accomplishment. In contrast, strategies preferred in a prevention focus are vigilance-related (e.g., avoiding distractions while studying), which naturally fit a concern with security and protection (Crowe & Higgins, 1997; for reviews, see Higgins, 2000, 2005, 2006). Regulatory focus can be situationally activated, and tendencies toward promotion and/or prevention also can be chronic (e.g., Higgins et al., 2000; for research on or using measures of chronic regulatory focus see, e.g., Higgins, Bond, Klein, & Strauman, 1986; Higgins et al., 2001; Lockwood, Jordan & Kunda, 2002; Ouschan, Boldero, Kashima, Wakimoto & Kashima, 2007; Shah, Brazy, & Higgins, 2004; Shah, Higgins, & Friedman, 1998; Summerville & Roese, 2008).

Compared to regulatory nonfit, regulatory fit generates feelings of rightness (e.g., Camacho, Higgins, & Luger, 2003; Cesario, Grant, & Higgins, 2004; Cesario & Higgins, 2008; Freitas & Higgins, 2002; Freitas, Liberman, & Higgins, 2002; Higgins, Idson, Freitas, Spiegel, & Molden, 2003; Vaughn, Harkness & Clark, in press; Vaughn, Hesse, Petkova & Trudeau, 2009; Vaughn, Malik, et al., 2006; Vaughn, O'Rourke, et al., 2006), confidence (Cesario et al., 2004), and enjoyment (Freitas & Higgins, 2002). These feelings may be a manifestation of processing fluency/ease, which researchers have found to be positively related to regulatory fit (Lee & Aaker, 2004; Vaughn, 2007; also see Reber & Schwarz, 1999). For example, Vaughn (2007) found that a commonly-used method of varying regulatory fit significantly impacted subjective processing fluency (the method is from Freitas & Higgins, 2002, Experiment 2, and I describe it in more detail in the section on eliciting experiences of regulatory fit). At the end of this regulatory-fit manipulation, participants reported their processing fluency by responding to the question, "Sometimes coming up with strategies to pursue a goal feels very fluent - it just flows. When you were coming up with strategies to pursue the goals you listed, how fluent did it feel?" using a 1 (*not at all*) to 7 (*extremely*) scale. A Regulatory Fit (fit vs. nonfit) X Regulatory Focus of Goals (promotion vs. prevention) ANOVA revealed only a significant main effect for regulatory fit $F(1, 28) = 4.45$, $p = .04$, $\omega^2 = .53$; other $ps > .82$. Participants in regulatory fit conditions reported more processing fluency ($M = 4.88$, $SD = 1.41$) than those in regulatory nonfit conditions ($M = 3.75$, $SD = 1.48$).

As is the case with other subjective experiences such as mood, familiarity or ease (e.g., Clore, 1992; Schwarz & Clore, 1983; 2007), people can use the subjective experience of regulatory fit as information for judgments as long as they (implicitly) attribute this experience to the focal task (e.g., Camacho et al., 2003; Cesario et al., 2004; Freitas & Higgins, 2002; Higgins et al., 2003; Vaughn, et al., in press; Vaughn et al., 2009; Vaughn, Malik, et al., 2006; Vaughn, O'Rourke, et al., 2006). Importantly, however, although regulatory fit appears to be more enjoyable than regulatory nonfit (like feeling happy relative to feeling sad), positive and negative moods do not account for regulatory-fit effects on judgments (e.g., Camacho et al., 2003; Cesario et al., 2004; Forster, Higgins & Idson, 1998; Higgins et al., 2003; Hong & Lee, 2008; Shah et al., 1998; Vaughn, 2009; Vaughn et al., 2009; Vaughn, Malik, et al., 2006; Vaughn, O'Rourke, et al., 2006). This reflects how regulatory fit can create value apart from hedonic considerations of pleasure and pain (e.g., Higgins, 2000, 2005, 2006).

The impact of feelings of regulatory fit on judgment and task engagement is especially clear in studies that vary regulatory fit in an initial task and then ask some participants how the initial task made them feel (cf., Clore, 1992; Schwarz & Clore, 1983). Feelings resulting from an initial event can be used as information for later judgments if people attribute these feelings to what they are later judging (for a review, see Schwarz & Clore, 2007). If people use feelings from an initial event as information in a later, focal activity (e.g., judgment task) because they are confused about the source of these feelings, then reducing this source confusion should reduce the effect of the feelings on the later judgments. Consistent with this "feelings-as-information" logic, regulatory-fit effects disappear when participants' attention is drawn to an earlier event as a source of their feelings of rightness, apparently because doing so renders these feelings irrelevant for the focal activity (Cesario et al., 2004; Vaughn et al., in press; Vaughn et al., 2009; Vaughn, Malik, et al., 2006; Vaughn, O'Rourke, et al., 2006).

Regulatory fit can enhance engagement strength (Higgins, 2006) when people (implicitly) attribute feelings of regulatory fit to what they are currently doing or thinking. Whether this has a positive or negative impact on judgments and performance depends on what people have in mind. Regulatory fit is more enjoyable than regulatory nonfit (e.g., Freitas & Higgins, 2002), so it can enhance the favorability of judgments about people or things if making such judgments is what people have in mind (e.g., Cesario et al., 2004; Higgins et al., 2004; Vaughn et al., in press). For example, several experiments have shown that an initial experience of regulatory fit enhances the favorability of judgments about the trustworthiness of specific acquaintances (Vaughn et al., in press). Regulatory fit also enhances confidence (Cesario et al., 2004), so it can enhance the extremity of either positive or negative thoughts people have about something, if metacognitions about thought confidence are what people are considering at the time. For example, participants who receive instructions likely to enhance metacognitive monitoring of their thoughts about a persuasive message may report more positive opinions of what the message is proposing when their thoughts about the message are positive, but more negative opinions when their thoughts about the message are negative (Cesario et al., 2004, Study 4). Additionally, the enjoyment and confidence associated with regulatory fit could - if experienced before a focal activity and they are not attributed to something other than the activity - serve as a "go" signal for usual or accessible styles of task engagement (e.g., Vaughn, 2009). For example, when an accessible goal is to continue a task as long as it is enjoyable, desirable feelings of regulatory fit enhance perseverance, but when the accessible goal is to continue a task until one has done enough, regulatory fit diminishes perseverance (Vaughn, Malik, et al., 2006).

Finally, there is evidence suggesting that regulatory fit can enhance ability and motivation to process information, at least when the fit is integral to focal tasks (e.g., Aaker & Lee, 2001; Evans & Petty, 2003). Because different ways of eliciting the experience of regulatory fit may have different effects on persuasion, I turn next to how regulatory fit can be varied.

ELICITING EXPERIENCES OF REGULATORY FIT

Regulatory fit can result from events incidental or integral to a focal task (cf. incidental versus integral mood effects; Bodenhausen, Mussweiler, Gabriel & Moreno, 2001). To create incidental experiences of regulatory fit/nonfit that can carry over to influence later judgments and activities, researchers often prime these experiences by asking participants to list two promotion-related goals (e.g., hopes and aspirations, or things participants ideally would like to gain or improve on) or prevention-related goals (e.g., duties and obligations, or things participants believe they should not lose or let deteriorate) and to provide either five eager strategies or five vigilant strategies for each (Cesario et al., 2004; Hong & Lee, 2008; Koenig, Cesario, Molden, Kosloff & Higgins, in press; Vaughn, 2009; Vaughn et al., in press; Vaughn et al., 2009; Vaughn, Malik, et al., 2006; Vaughn, O'Rourke, et al., 2006; also see Freitas & Higgins, 2002, who used this procedure as a manipulation of integral fit). Regulatory fit conditions pair promotion goals with eager strategies (or prevention goals with vigilant strategies), and regulatory nonfit conditions pair prevention goals with eager strategies (or promotion goals with vigilant strategies). This brief, approximately 3-minute-long procedure does not create a strong enough state of promotion or prevention focus to be noticeable in subsequent tasks (e.g., Hong & Lee, 2008; Vaughn, 2009; Vaughn, Harkness, & Clark, in press; Vaughn et al., 2009; Vaughn, Malik, et al., 2006; Vaughn, O'Rourke, et al., 2006). Nonetheless, it creates a strong enough experience of regulatory fit to affect subsequent judgments and activities. Consistent with the idea that regulatory fit can influence later task engagement through a feelings-as-information process, drawing attention to the initial regulatory-fit task as a source of feelings of rightness eliminates these effects (Cesario et al., 2004; Vaughn et al., in press; Vaughn et al., 2009; Vaughn, Malik, et al., 2006; Vaughn, O'Rourke, et al., 2006).

Ways in which researchers have elicited integral experiences of regulatory fit are considerably more varied. Most commonly, researchers have set up interactions between temporary or chronic regulatory focus and characteristics of focal tasks. These focal-task characteristics include eager or vigilant message framing (e.g., Cesario et al., 2004), nonverbal cues suggesting eagerness or vigilance (Cesario & Higgins, 2008), thinking about gains or losses (thinking about gains is a better fit for promotion focus; Higgins et al., 2003; Idson, Liberman & Higgins, 2000; Lee & Aaker, 2004), abstract or concrete language (abstract, broad language fits promotion better; Semin, Higgins, de Montes, Estourget & Valencia, 2005), instructions to use emotion or cognition to choose a product (use of emotion fits promotion better; Avnet & Higgins, 2006; Pham & Avnet, 2003), presenting promotion or prevention-framed goals (e.g., Evans & Petty, 2003), and presenting independence- or interdependence-framed goals (Aaker & Lee, 2001; Vaughn, 2006; independence fits promotion better; also see Lee, Aaker & Gardner, 2000). Additionally, promotion- and prevention-focused goals have been paired with individual differences related to promotion or prevention strategic orientations, such as Openness or Closedness to Experience (Vaughn, Baumann & Klemann, 2008) and individual or culture-related differences in independence and interdependence (Aaker & Lee, 2001; Lee et al., 2000). Finally, if regulatory fit is construed broadly as what people experience when they engage in activities consistent with their self-regulatory orientation, promotion and prevention fit could happen in other ways as well (see Aaker & Lee, 2006).

REGULATORY FIT WITH MEANS OF ENGAGEMENT AND WITH OUTCOMES

There has been some controversy about how best to operationally define regulatory fit (e.g., Aaker & Lee, 2006; Cesario, Higgins & Scholer, 2008). Some researchers have argued that regulatory fit can be operationalized as a fit between a self-regulatory orientation (e.g., promotion) and ways of engaging with a task (e.g., enacting eager strategies) as well as a fit between a self-regulatory orientation and outcomes to which people with that orientation are sensitive (e.g., thinking about gains; Aaker & Lee, 2006). Others have argued that only a match with ways of engaging with a task is regulatory fit; a match with outcomes is regulatory relevance or message matching (Avnet & Higgins, 2006; Cesario et al., 2004; Cesario et al., 2008). From existing research, it is not clear that regulatory relevance and regulatory fit are empirically distinguishable concepts (Aaker & Lee, 2006). In the following section I review a wide variety of published research on regulatory focus and persuasion, including some research on message matching. With that said, I also indicate whether experiments examined fit with means of engagement (i.e., regulatory fit) or fit with outcomes (i.e., regulatory relevance; message matching).

PERSUASION THROUGH ADVOCACY MESSAGES

Advocacy messages present logical arguments, evidence, and claims supporting a position. They include messages in media such as editorials, political speeches, and public education campaigns (e.g., Green & Brock, 2002). A great deal of research has addressed persuasion through advocacy messages (e.g., see Chaiken, Liberman, & Eagly, 1989; Chen & Chaiken, 1999; Eagly & Chaiken, 1993; Petty & Cacioppo, 1986; Petty & Wegener, 1999, for reviews). In this section of the chapter, I will describe two leading models of persuasion through advocacy messages. Then I will describe how researchers often assess the amount of careful thought about a message and provide an overview of recent research on the role of metacognition in persuasion. Finally, I will discuss research on how regulatory fit affects persuasion through advocacy messages.

The two dominant models of persuasion through advocacy messages are the elaboration likelihood model (ELM; Petty & Cacioppo, 1986) and the heuristic-systematic model (HSM, Chaiken et al., 1989). Although the two models differ in their specifics, they both propose that there are two routes to persuasion at either end of a continuum that ranges from low to high elaboration. Elaboration is the logical consideration/evaluation of arguments presented in persuasive appeals (e.g., Petty & Cacioppo, 1986). This appears to be a divergent process (Green & Brock, 2000) in which individuals use their own schemas and experiences to assess the strengths/weaknesses of the arguments. High elaboration, which is called the "central route" in the ELM and "systematic processing" in the HSM, takes effort and requires both motivation and ability to engage in critical thinking about the message. Factors that enhance motivation or ability to think carefully enhance elaboration likelihood. For example, motivation to think carefully about a message increases with high personal relevance (e.g., Petty & Cacioppo, 1986) or need for cognition (the tendency to engage in and enjoy effortful thought; Cacioppo & Petty, 1982), and ability to think carefully increases with factors such as higher intelligence and lack of distraction or time pressure (Petty & Cacioppo, 1986). Message quality matters a great deal when elaboration likelihood is high: under these conditions, people generally have more positive thoughts about – and are more persuaded by – messages with strong arguments than by messages with weak ones (e.g., Petty & Cacioppo, 1986). Low-elaboration processing, which is called the "peripheral route" in the ELM and "heuristic processing" in the HSM, involves relying on cues peripheral to the merits of message arguments - such source expertise and the length or number of arguments - in order to arrive at judgments. This occurs without much thought about the content of the message itself (see Eagly & Chaiken, 1993, for a review), and as a result, argument quality matters less when elaboration likelihood is low. Under these conditions, people generally are no more persuaded by messages containing strong arguments than by messages containing weak ones.

The extent of elaboration can be assessed in various ways. One is by examining the number of thoughts generated in response to a message; the more carefully people consider a persuasive appeal, the more thoughts they should generate about it (e.g., Petty & Cacioppo, 1986). Another way is by examining the content of thoughts people generate, particularly the valence of these thoughts (e.g., Cacioppo, Harkins & Petty, 1981). Generally speaking, the more people engage in elaboration about a message, the more positive their thoughts about the message should be in response to strong arguments, and the more negative their thoughts about the message should be in response to weak arguments (e.g., Petty & Cacioppo, 1986).

The number and valence of thoughts about a message alone do not predict persuasion. Recent research shows that metacognition – awareness of, or thoughts about, one's thoughts – is an important predictor as well (e.g., Brinol & Petty, 2003; Brinol, Petty & Barden, 2007; Brinol, Petty, Valle, Rucker & Becerra, 2007; Petty, Brinol & Tormala, 2002). People need to generate thoughts about a message in order to engage in metacognition about these thoughts. Such thought generation is likely to occur when people think carefully about a persuasive appeal (e.g., Brinol, Petty, Valle, et al., 2007) and/or when they learn they will be asked questions about thoughts they have about the message content (e.g., Cesario et al., 2004). Metacognition about how valid one's thoughts are should also involve extra effort beyond just thinking about a message. Thus, metacognitive consideration of thought confidence may have the biggest impacts on persuasion when elaboration likelihood is high (e.g., Brinol, Petty, Valle, et al., 2007) or when people receive metacognition-activating instructions (e.g., Cesario et al., 2004). When people think carefully about a message and perceive their thoughts about the message to be valid, they should give their thoughts more weight when forming or revising an attitude in light of the persuasive appeal. Factors that self-validate – i.e., enhance one's confidence about - one's thoughts should increase persuasion when thoughts about the message are positive and decrease persuasion when thoughts about the message are negative.

RESEARCH ON REGULATORY FIT AND PERSUASION THROUGH ADVOCACY MESSAGES

Many experiments have addressed how integral fit between regulatory focus and the content of advocacy messages affects persuasion (e.g., Aaker & Lee, 2001; Cesario et al., 2004; Cesario & Higgins, 2008; Lee & Aaker, 2004; Semin et al. 2005) and others have addressed how incidental regulatory fit affects persuasion (Cesario et al., 2004; Koenig et al., in press). In describing these bodies of research, I first will discuss work on persuasion and regulatory fit with means of engagement and then will discuss work on persuasion and regulatory fit with outcomes.

Fit with Means of Engagement

Integral fit with means of engagement. Clearly, the most fundamental question about regulatory fit and persuasion is whether regulatory fit affects persuasion. The answer is that it does. Especially when it comes to experiments that have varied integral fit with means of engagement, the very clear, consistent finding is that this form of regulatory fit enhances persuasion (Cesario et al., 2004, Experiments 1 & 2; Cesario & Higgins, 2008; Semin et al., 2005, Experiment 3).

An additional question is whether such effects are really due to regulatory fit. Could they be due to mood instead? After all, both positive mood and regulatory fit are desirable experiential states relative to negative mood and regulatory nonfit. The answer appears to be no: mood has not accounted for the persuasive effects of integral fit with means of engagement (Cesario et al., 2004, Experiment 2; Cesario & Higgins, 2008).

When it comes to the question of how these effects occurred, conclusions are more varied. Feeling right about what a persuasive appeal is advocating can mediate the regulatory-fit effect on post-message attitudes (Cesario & Higgins, 2008). It is possible, then, that these feelings could be involved in many, if not all, such effects. If so, perhaps integral regulatory fit with outcomes enhances positive responses to persuasive appeals through people using feelings associated with regulatory fit – such as rightness and enjoyment – in a "feelings-as-information" manner; i.e., as a heuristic cue (e.g., "If it feels right, it must be right"). It is important to note, however, that all currently-published experiments on this form of regulatory fit and persuasion appear to have used messages containing only strong arguments. If people think carefully enough about such messages to generate thoughts about the arguments in them, the content of these thoughts should be positive. Given that regulatory fit is enjoyable (Freitas & Higgins, 2002), and enjoyment can be motivating (e.g., Vaughn, Malik, et al., 2006), the positive effect of integral fit with means of engagement could reflect more motivation to think carefully about these strong messages. Additionally, regulatory fit can enhance feelings of confidence (Cesario et al., 2004), and as a result it could enhance people's confidence in their own thoughts about a message. This also would tend to enhance persuasion if the message content is strong. Furthermore, some studies on integral regulatory fit with outcomes have paired messages with participants' chronic prevention and promotion orientations (Cesario et al., 2004; Experiment 2). In these cases, fitting messages could seem more personally relevant, which itself could enhance motivation to think carefully about them (see Evans & Petty, 2003). This motivation could affect persuasion in an objective manner that is sensitive to argument strength (a process that may not be obvious when argument strength is uniformly high), or in a biased manner that results in more positive evaluations of fitting than of nonfitting messages ("If it fits the way I prefer to do things, it must be right"), regardless of argument strength (see Cacioppo, Petty, & Sidera, 1982; Lavine & Snyder, 1996).

Considering regulatory-fit effects from a less feelings-oriented perspective, regulatory fit also enhances objective processing fluency (e.g., Lee & Aaker, 2004). This could increase people's ability to think carefully about persuasive appeals. For example, regulatory-fitting mental representations of goals and means of engagement presented in the same message could mutually activate each other, enhancing people's ability to think carefully about the message (as in Cesario et al., 2004, Experiment 1). Regulatory fit also can occur between chronic prevention or promotion orientations of message recipients and the means of engagement implied by a message (Cesario et al., 2004, Experiment 2; Cesario & Higgins, 2008; Semin et al., 2005). When these chronic orientations are strong, they could serve as highly-accessible knowledge structures for organizing information in the appeals, making the appeals easier to understand (see Evans & Petty, 2003). In short, regulatory fit could enhance ability to process messages regardless of whether integral fit is varied entirely within the message or involves the fit between the message and a chronic regulatory focus.

Many hypotheses therefore remain to be tested about how the experience of integral regulatory fit with means of engagement influences persuasion. In testing these hypotheses, varying argument strength would help clarify whether observed effects are better attributed to heuristic processing (in which case argument strength would not have much of an effect) or more systematic processing (in which case regulatory fit could augment message-strength effects on resulting attitudes). Assessing moderation by factors that could affect motivation or ability to think carefully about messages (such as need for cognition and/or perceived time pressure) could shed light on whether the persuasive effects of integral regulatory fit with means of engagement depend on elaboration likelihood being high, unconstrained, or low.

Incidental fit with means of engagement. The findings of experiments on the effect of incidental regulatory fit on persuasion also suggest a variety of ways that regulatory fit can affect persuasion through advocacy messages. At the same time, there are fewer plausible explanations for the findings of any one incidental-fit experiment. All of the experiments in this section employed the usual incidental regulatory-fit manipulation (the strategy and goal listing task by Freitas & Higgins, 2002) that I described earlier.

A question remaining from initial experiments on persuasion and integral regulatory fit with means of engagement (Cesario et al., 2004, Experiments 1 & 2) was whether all regulatory-fit effects on persuasion are limited to integral fit with the content of a message. If so, they could be interpreted as a special case of message matching (e.g., Petty & Wegener, 1998; cf. Cesario & Higgins, 2008). They are not. An initial experience of regulatory fit can carry over to affect persuasion through messages that have nothing to do with the initial experience (Cesario et al. 2004; Experiments 3 & 4). This results from a feelings-as-information process: drawing participants' attention the initial regulatory-fit manipulation as a source of feelings of rightness eliminates these regulatory-fit effects on persuasion, apparently by rendering the initial regulatory-fit experience irrelevant to the subsequent persuasion task (Cesario et al., 2004, Experiment 3; also see Clore, 1992; Schwarz & Clore, 1983).

The effect of incidental regulatory fit on post-message attitudes can be positive (Cesario et al., 2004, Experiments 3 & 4), especially when people's attention most likely is on what a persuasive appeal is advocating (Cesario et al., 2004, Experiment 4). For example, when participants learned before reading a message that they would be asked how they felt about what the message proposed, regulatory fit had a positive effect on post-message attitudes. This effect did not depend on the valence of thoughts about the message, which suggests these participants may have used the subjective experience of regulatory fit as a heuristic cue (e.g., "If it feels right, it must be right"). In other words, the favorability of the regulatory-fit experience may have transferred directly to the favorability of subsequent judgments. In contrast, it is less plausible that regulatory fit in an initial task enhanced participants' ability to think carefully about a subsequent, unrelated message or enhanced their motivation to think carefully about the message by making it seem more personally relevant.

Yet incidental regulatory fit does not always have positive effects on persuasion. Whether it does depends on what is most likely occupying people's attention at the time they are arriving at their attitudes. Although regulatory fit may serve as a heuristic cue when attention is directed to what a persuasive appeal is proposing, it may serve as input for thought confidence when attention is directed toward one's thoughts about the message. In Cesario et al.'s (2004) Experiment 4, some participants learned - before reading a message about an after-school program - that they would be asked how they felt about the message. These instructions should enhance attention to participants' message-related thoughts. When these participants initially experienced regulatory fit rather than nonfit, their attitudes about the program were more positive when they had more positive thoughts about the message and more negative when they had more negative thoughts about the message. Orienting peoples' attention to their thoughts about a message may have allowed the subjective experience of regulatory fit to serve as information for assessments of thought confidence, increasing engagement with whatever the thoughts happened to be (Cesario et al., 2004; cf. other influences on thought confidence in persuasion, e.g., Brinol & Petty, 2003; Brinol, Petty & Barden, 2007; Brinol, Petty, Valle, et al., 2007; Petty et al., 2002).

In addition to possibly serving as a heuristic cue or as input for thought confidence, regulatory fit also can serve as information for how much to rely on heuristics in persuasion. Koenig et al. (in press) found that whereas incidental regulatory fit enhanced the influence of an easily-processed heuristic cue (source expertise), incidental regulatory nonfit enhanced the influence of more difficult-to-process information (message strength) and increased resistance to counterpersuasion (suggesting deeper processing under nonfit). This research shows that incidental regulatory fit can enhance people's engagement with what seems to be the default style of thinking about advocacy messages, which is to use heuristics (e.g., Chaiken et al., 1989; Chen & Chaiken, 1999). Because heuristics can be thought of as the application of general processing schemas to specific information (Nisbett & Ross, 1991; also see Bless & Schwarz, 1999), this research further suggests that regulatory fit can enhance use of general knowledge structures (e.g., heuristics; Nisbett & Ross, 1991; also see Bless & Schwarz,

1999). It also is consistent with the hypothesis that incidental regulatory fit can serve as a "go" signal for engaging with usual or accessible styles of processing (Vaughn, 2009; Vaughn, Malik, et al., 2006; for related work on happy and sad moods, see Bless et al., 1996; Clore et al., 2001; Gasper & Clore, 2002).

Summary and conclusions about fit with means of engagement. In short, research on integral and incidental fit with means of engagement shows that regulatory fit can - but does not always - enhance persuasion. The picture with integral fit with means of engagement is very clear in terms of results but less clear in terms of how these results may have occurred. Integral fit with means of engagement could serve as a heuristic cue (cf. mood effects on persuasion when elaboration likelihood is low; e.g., Brinol, Petty & Barden, 2007; Chaiken, 1987). It also is associated with enjoyment (Freitas & Higins, 2002) and processing fluency (Lee & Aaker, 2004), so it could enhance motivation and/or ability to think carefully about messages relative to regulatory nonfit. Furthermore, integral fit with means of engagement could enhance thought confidence, especially if people are highly motivated and able to think carefully about the messages (cf. mood effects on persuasion when high elaboration likelihood is high; Brinol, Petty & Barden, 2007), a process that could enhance persuasion when message arguments are strong. Future research that adds moderators such as message strength, personal relevance manipulations (other than regulatory fit), and individual differences related to elaboration (such as need for cognition) could clarify underlying processes and boundary conditions of what appears to be the basic, positive effect of message-integral regulatory fit with means on persuasion. Research on integral fit with outcomes has done this to some extent, as I will describe shortly.

The research on incidental fit with means of engagement has more complex results but provides somewhat clearer interpretations. Feelings of rightness from incidental fit with means of engagement can enhance persuasion through a later advocacy message as long as people do not attribute the feelings to the initial, message-irrelevant task (Cesario et al., 2004, Experiment 3) and they are thinking about what the message is proposing (Cesario et al., 2004, Experiment 4). Under these conditions, feelings of rightness from this source of regulatory fit/nonfit may serve as a heuristic cue. When experimental instructions instead direct participants' attention to their own thoughts before reporting their attitudes, feelings of rightness from earlier fit with means of engagement may enhance people's confidence in these thoughts (Cesario et al., 2004, Experiment 4). Furthermore, research varying message strength and easily-processed heuristic cues has shown that incidental regulatory fit can enhance engagement with what appears to be people's usual, heuristic style of processing advocacy messages (Koenig et al., in press).

At present, research suggests that integral and incidental fit with means of engagement should not always affect persuasion in the same ways. Task-incidental methods of varying regulatory fit are constrained to affect subsequent persuasion through feelings-as-information processes that should not impact ability to think carefully about the persuasive appeal. In contrast, message-integral fit could influence both ability and motivation to think carefully about a message. At the same time, message-integral fit seems unlikely to affect elaboration likelihood because it would not register fully on participants until they were well into the persuasive appeal. (A possible exception would be if the fit is between chronic regulatory focus and a blatantly regulatory-fitting title of the appeal. In this case, regulatory fit could register on people before they engage much with the appeal and affect how much they go ahead and think about it in a default, heuristic way.) I will expand on these hypotheses in the upcoming section on the impact of regulatory fit on persuasion at different levels of elaboration likelihood.

Fit with Outcomes

Research on persuasion and regulatory fit with outcomes has been conceptualized in various ways, including regulatory fit and message matching (e.g., Aaker & Lee, 2001; Evans & Petty, 2003; Lee & Aaker, 2004; Petty & Wegener, 1998). This research addresses somewhat different issues from research on fit with means of engagement. Most strikingly, current research on persuasion and regulatory fit with outcomes has only examined message-integral fit. In the future, researchers may wish to experimentally vary regulatory fit with outcomes in an initial task to see whether value from this experience can transfer to subsequent tasks. To keep this section related to prevention focus and promotion focus (the self-regulatory orientations in the research on persuasion and fit with means of engagement), I will only describe persuasion research that explicitly concerns fit with prevention and promotion orientations or outcomes.

Positive effect of outcome fit on persuasion. As with integral fit with means of engagement, the primary question regarding integral fit with outcomes is whether this style of fit can enhance persuasion. The answer is that it can (Aaker & Lee, 2001; Evans & Petty, 2003; Lee & Aaker, 2004). For the most part, the experiments (Aaker & Lee, 2001, Experiments 1 & 4; Lee & Aaker, 2004, Experiments 1 & 2) showing this basic effect have the same alternative explanations as in the research showing the basic, positive effect of integral fit with means of engagement. Importantly, however, one of the experiments on fit with outcomes found evidence of attitude change that lasted for at least two weeks (Aaker & Lee, 2001, Experiment 1). This finding suggests that participants in fitting conditions engaged in more elaboration about the message they received, because the more carefully people think about a persuasive appeal, the stronger and longer-lasting their attitudes about the message topic tend to be (e.g., Petty & Cacioppo, 1986; Petty & Wegener, 1999).

Factors that might account for this effect. Follow-up studies to the first experiment by Aaker and Lee (2001) assessed various factors that could account for the positive fit-with-outcomes effect on persuasion: processing fluency, amount of thoughts listed about the message, judgments of message effectiveness, and recall of information from the message (Aaker & Lee, 2001; Lee & Aaker, 2004). Altogether, this set of studies suggests that integral fit with outcomes could enhance ability and/or motivation to process messages. In support of an ability explanation, regulatory fit enhanced how easily-processed messages appeared to be (Lee & Aaker, 2004, Experiment 4A), how fluently participants identified words from earlier-presented messages (Lee & Aaker, 2004, Experiment 4B), and how well participants remembered information in a message (Aaker & Lee, 2001, Experiment 2). In support of a motivation explanation, processing fluency is enjoyable (e.g., Reber et al., 2004), so it is possible that regulatory fit could enhance motivation to think carefully about a message. Whether regulatory fit had a positive effect on motivation to process messages in these studies is not clear, however, because self-reported involvement in reading a message did not mediate regulatory-fit effects on persuasion via that message (Lee & Aaker, 2004, Experiment 4A). Additionally, the judged effectiveness of a message was a better mediator of regulatory-fit effects on persuasion than was the number of positive thoughts participants generated about what the message proposed (Lee & Aaker, 2004, Experiment 5).

Additional evidence: Moderation by message strength and/or need for cognition. If integral fit with outcomes can enhance motivation and/or ability to think carefully about a persuasive appeal, then this form of regulatory fit should enhance the impact of argument strength on persuasion. This appears to be what happens. Several experiments on fit with outcomes have systematically varied the strength of messages participants received (Aaker & Lee, 2001, Experiment 3; Evans & Petty, 2003). These studies found that post-message attitudes were more favorable in response to stronger arguments when participants received a message that fit their regulatory focus but not when they received a message that did not fit their regulatory focus. Fit with outcomes enhanced the impact of message strength on persuasion.

An additional question is when this effect is most likely to occur. Specifically, does integral fit with outcomes enhance message processing most among people not already inclined to think carefully (e.g., because of low need for cognition), or does it enhance message processing for everyone? Although fit with outcomes enhances the impact of message strength on persuasion, Evans and Petty (2003) found that this effect was particularly strong among people low in need for cognition, who would not ordinarily be motivated to think carefully about the message. They speculated that this could have occurred because message matching enhanced motivation to process through enhancing personal relevance. Additionally, they noted that it could have occurred because message matching increased ability to process, through chronic prevention or promotion focus-related self-guides serving as highly-accessible knowledge structures for organizing information and making it easier to understand (Evans & Petty, 2003). Future research should assess whether these effects replicate with other forms of regulatory fit, including incidental and integral fit with means of engagement.

HYPOTHESES ABOUT THE INTERPLAY OF ELABORATION LIKELIHOOD AND REGULATORY FIT IN PERSUASION THROUGH ADVOCACY MESSAGES

It is clear that regulatory fit affects persuasion, but not always in the same way, and many questions remain. For example, do different operational definitions of integral regulatory fit (as fit with means of engagement and as fit with outcomes) have the same effects on persuasion and its mediators? Do integral and incidental regulatory fit affect persuasion differently, and if so, how? How might elaboration likelihood interact with different operational definitions of regulatory fit to influence persuasion? In this section I will propose how incidental and integral regulatory fit may affect persuasion at different levels of elaboration likelihood. I will not distinguish between integral fit with means of engagement and integral fit with outcomes in these hypotheses, because currently it is not clear that these operational definitions of regulatory fit have distinguishable effects on persuasion. In contrast, I will highlight differences between incidental and integral fit, which evidence already suggests can affect persuasion differently.

When Elaboration Likelihood is Low

When ability factors (such as time pressure) and/or motivational factors (such as a message lacking in personal relevance or participants low need for cognition) constrain people's chances of thinking carefully about a persuasive message, incidental regulatory fit should tend to serve as a heuristic cue in persuasion. Incidental regulatory fit feels right (e.g., see Avnet & Higgins, 2006; Higgins, 2005, for reviews) and fluent (Vaughn, 2007). When people are not thinking carefully about a message, desirable feelings of rightness and fluency from an initial experience of regulatory fit could directly inform attitudes about what a message is proposing. This feelings-as-information process should depend on whether people implicitly attribute the regulatory-fit experience to what the message is proposing. If it is clear that the initial regulatory-fit/nonfit task is a source of feelings of rightness/wrongness, this should reduce or eliminate the regulatory-fit effect on post-message attitudes (e.g., Cesario et al., 2004).

Integral fit may be able to serve as a heuristic cue in a similar way, especially if the fit is with chronic regulatory focus (e.g., "If this message speaks to how I prefer to do things, it must be good"; e.g., Evans & Petty, 2003; also see Snyder & DeBono, 1985). However, if regulatory fit is manipulated entirely within the message and people are not motivated or able to think carefully about the persuasive appeal, integral regulatory fit should have little if any effect on persuasion.

When Elaboration Likelihood is Unconstrained to be Either High or Low

When elaboration likelihood is unconstrained, incidental and integral regulatory fit could have distinct impacts on persuasion. Incidental regulatory fit appears to be able to function as a "go" signal for engaging with usual or accessible processing styles (Vaughn, 2009; also see Vaughn, Malik, et al., 2006; Vaughn, O'Rourke, et al., 2006), much like happy mood relative to sad mood can (e.g., Clore et al., 2001). People's default style of engaging with persuasive appeals is to use heuristics and to be persuaded by message-peripheral factors (e.g., Chaiken et al., 1989; Chen & Chaiken, 1999; Petty & Cacioppo, 1996; Petty & Wegener, 1999). Incidental regulatory fit enhances these default tendencies relative to regulatory nonfit through what appears to be a feelings-as-information process (Koenig et al., in press). If so, it should be possible to eliminate such effects on persuasion by directing attention to the initial regulatory-fit task as a source of feelings of rightness.

In contrast, when elaboration likelihood is unconstrained, message-integral regulatory fit enhances careful thought about persuasive appeals (e.g., Aaker & Lee, 2001; Evans & Petty, 2003). It may do so through enhancing motivation or ability to process, as described earlier. In contrast to incidental regulatory fit, integral regulatory fit should not enhance engagement with heuristic processing of messages, unless regulatory fit can register implicitly or explicitly before people engage much with the persuasive appeal.

When Elaboration Likelihood is High

When people are highly motivated (e.g. by high need for cognition and/or factors enhancing personal relevance) and able to think carefully about a persuasive appeal, incidental regulatory fit should be able to serve as information about confidence in these thoughts. This self-validation process (e.g., Petty et al., 2002) should enhance persuasion when thoughts about the message are favorable and should reduce persuasion when thoughts about the message are unfavorable. A caveat to this prediction is that it may be possible to set this self-validation process in motion without high elaboration likelihood. It may simply take a combination of incidental regulatory fit and instructions that direct people's attention to their message-related thoughts before reporting their attitudes (Cesario et al., 2004, Experiment 4; cf. Brinol, Petty & Barden, 2007; Brinol, Petty, Valle, et al., 2007).

It is unclear whether a similar, self-validation process could occur with integral fit. Certainly, integral fit with outcomes did not impact persuasion among people high in need for cognition in Evans and Petty's (2003) research. Whether integral fit can self-validate message-related thoughts may depend on whether participants know in advance that they will be asked about these thoughts (similar to some conditions in Cesario et al., 2004, Experiment 4). If they do, feelings of fluency and rightness – even those resulting from the process of engaging with the message - should be able to enhance confidence in message-related thoughts. This is because participants would experience these feelings as they are generating their thoughts.

PERSUASION VIA NARRATIVES

Having reviewed existing research on regulatory fit and persuasion through advocacy messages, I will turn now to research on persuasion via narratives. Narratives are stories in which characters are immersed in events with a clear beginning and end, and they include stories in books, TV shows, news reports, documentaries, movies, advertisements, and other media. Although much less research has addressed how narratives persuade than how advocacy messages persuade, narratives are nonetheless a powerful source of social influence (e.g., Green & Brock, 2000, 2002). I will begin this section with a review of research on how persuasion via narratives can happen, how researchers assess experiential engagement with narratives, and aspects of narratives that can impede mental transportation and persuasion. Then I will describe published and new research on how regulatory fit can affect engagement with and persuasion via narratives. In part to facilitate comparisons with the previous section on persuasion through advocacy messages, I will introduce a concept I call transportation likelihood: the likelihood of engaging in transportation. Finally, I will present hypotheses about how regulatory fit should affect engagement with and persuasion via narratives at different levels of transportation likelihood.

TRANSPORTATION AND PERSUASION

People tend to engage with narratives experientially - through becoming mentally immersed or transported into narrative worlds (e.g., Green & Brock, 2000, 2002). Although transportation and elaboration both can lead to belief change, existing theory and research suggest that they are independent processes (Green & Brock, 2000, 2002; also see Escalas, 2007). In terms of depth of engagement, one's optimal experience with a narrative appears to be more like emotional and cognitive absorption in a rich mental simulation than like critical thinking (e.g., Escalas, 2004, 2007; Green & Brock, 2000, 2002).

Transportation via narratives involves vivid imagery, strong attachments to characters, and cognitive and emotional responses that converge on the story while leaving behind facts and events in the "real world" outside the narrative (Green & Brock, 2000, 2002). As in the state of flow (Csikszentmihalyi, 1990), transportation appears to involve devoting complete attention to what one is doing, namely – in the case of narrative transportation - mentally constructing the story's meaning and imagining one's self in the story settings and events through identifying with one or another character in the story (Busselle & Bilandzik, 2008). This experience is measured by Green and Brock's (2000) Transportation Scale, which contains 15 items assessing aspects of the transportation experience: ease of imagining the events in the story, emotional involvement, attention to the story, feelings of suspense, unawareness of surroundings, and vividness of mental imagery.

The more people are transported by a narrative, the more persuaded they should be (i.e., the more they should endorse story-consistent beliefs; e.g., Green & Brock, 2000, 2002). In part, this is because people's default tendency when approaching information in a narrative may be to accept it as true as soon as they comprehend it (Gilbert, 1991). Only with effort would people disbelieve it, and this may be especially true when they are engaging with narratives (e.g., Richter, Schroeder & Wohrmann, 2009). Additionally, immersing one's self in a narrative world requires an intense allocation of cognitive and emotional resources, so it should leave fewer resources than usual for critically evaluating information (e.g., Busselle & Bilandzic, 2008; Green & Brock, 2000, 2002). Furthermore, individuals engaged in transportation may be disconnected to some extent from their prior schemas and experiences (Green & Brock, 2000) in preference for the internal logic of the narrative world, regardless of whether the story is fact or fiction (e.g., Busselle & Bilandzic, 2008; Green & Brock, 2000, 2002). For these reasons, people who are more transported by a narrative should be more persuaded by it. This is a consistent finding in research on narrative transportation (e.g., Escalas, 2004, 2007; Green, 2004; Green & Brock, 2000, 2002; Green, Garst & Brock, 2004, Mazzocco, Green, & Brock, 2007; Wang & Calder, 2006).

In contrast to processing of advocacy messages, in which the default approach appears to be reliance on heuristics (e.g., Chen & Chaiken, 1999; Chaiken et al., 1989), the default approach to processing narratives appears to be mental transportation (e.g., Bilandzic, 2006; Busselle & Bilandzic, 2008; Green & Brock, 2000, 2002). However, narratives do not always support this endeavor; they can have parts that impede transportation, initiate story-divergent thinking, and ultimately reduce transportation-mediated persuasion. Low narrative realism and low external realism are qualities of stories that should impede persuasion (Busselle & Bilandzic, 2008). The former occurs when story elements are internally inconsistent. For example, imagine that a character described in one scene as sweet-tempered and as wearing a blue shirt ends this scene committing murder in a yellow shirt – with no explanation why. Readers' transportation would probably suffer and they probably would not be as persuaded by the story's implicit themes as if it did not have this flaw. Low external realism occurs when story elements are inconsistent with mental models of the real world and/or with mental models of that type of story. For example, imagine that in a straightforward historical romance set in the middle ages, a character pulls out a cell phone. Readers' transportation would probably suffer. Yet if the story bridges historical romance and sci-fi genres and if the character has a time machine, the story genre could mitigate this inconsistency, and the appearance of the cell phone could enhance rather than diminish readers' engagement and the story's persuasiveness. In short, the more strongly a story element violates either type of consistency, the more strongly people should shift their attention away from constructing meaningful images of the story world and instead toward disputing the narrative (Busselle & Bilandzic, 2008). Research shows, for example, that written stories containing explicitly inaccurate historical information can slow down reading speed – which may reflect an effortful change in processing style from transportation to critical thinking (Rapp, 2008).

It is not clear, however, that some elaboration about parts of a narrative would significantly reduce transportation via the narrative as a whole. For example, Wang and Calder (2006) found that people who, overall, were highly transported by a written story were also the most likely to report that what could be considered a flaw in the story presentation was intrusive (namely, an ad inserted into the middle of the narrative). They also were the most likely to report negative attitudes about the intrusive ad. This was especially true when the ad was personally relevant, suggesting that these participants engaged in some elaboration about it. Individuals most likely to engage with a story via transportation may also be most distracted by parts of the story that do not seem to fit – but they also can return to being transported by the story.

Distraction followed by a return to the transportation experience should not be a rare occurrence. There probably is no such thing as a perfect narrative. Nonetheless, people are transported by many stories. At least sometimes, people should find a story as a whole to be transporting enough to return to immersing themselves in it. It may be that people usually – and perhaps implicitly - monitor the balance of story enjoyment and the severity of story flaws. Factors enhancing enjoyment that is attributed to the story could enhance the chances of people re-engaging experientially with the story if they encounter a story flaw. They should stay engaged in the transportation experience as long as immersing themselves in the story is enjoyable enough. When criticism of a narrative occurs, however, factors that enhance confidence in one's own thoughts should enhance the intensity of disputing the story, thereby reducing transportation and transportation-mediated persuasion (cf. Brinol & Petty, 2003; Brinol, Petty & Barden, 2007; Brinol, Petty, Valle, et al., 2007; Petty et al., 2002).

RESEARCH ON REGULATORY FIT AND PERSUASION VIA NARRATIVES

Incidental Regulatory Fit

Incidental regulatory fit can enhance engagement with default or accessible styles of processing (e.g., Koenig et al., in press; Vaughn, 2009; Vaughn, Malik et al., 2006; Vaughn,

O'Rourke, et al., 2006), and transportation appears to be the default mode of engaging with narratives. As a result, incidental regulatory fit could function as a "go" signal for engaging experientially with narratives. Specifically, when people read a story, feelings of rightness from incidental regulatory fit could suggest that the story is "right on" relative to feelings of wrongness from regulatory nonfit. Individuals who are experiencing feelings of rightness could engage more with the narrative and be more persuaded by its implicit messages. Two experiments provide support for these hypotheses (Vaughn et al., 2009).

In the first (Vaughn et al., 2009, Experiment 1), participants did the usual, incidental regulatory-fit manipulation (e.g., Cesario et al., 2004; Vaughn, Malik, et al., 2006). Then they received one of two randomly-assigned short stories to read and completed the Transportation Scale (Green & Brock, 2000) about their assigned story. Regardless of the story, participants were more transported when they had experienced regulatory fit in the initial task. Additionally, the regulatory-fit effect on transportation was not limited to one or the other story, even though the stories were not equally transporting.

A follow-up study (Vaughn et al., 2009, Experiment 2) examined the role of feelings of rightness in the effect of regulatory fit on transportation and whether regulatory fit would, through enhancing transportation, enhance endorsement story-consistent beliefs (i.e., persuasion via narratives). This experiment varied regulatory fit in an initial task, then varied attention to this task as a source of feelings of rightness by asking some participants how "right" the task felt; this question should render these feelings irrelevant for the later narrative (e.g, Cesario et al., 2004; Vaughn, Malik, et al., 2006; Vaughn, O'Rourke, et al., 2006; also see Schwarz & Clore, 1983). When participants' attention was not drawn to the initial task as a source of feelings of rightness, those who initially had experienced regulatory fit were more transported and persuaded via the narrative. Transportation mediated the regulatory-fit effect on persuasion. In contrast, drawing participants' attention to the regulatory-fit task as a source of feelings of rightness eliminated these effects. These findings showed that regulatory fit can enhance transportation and persuasion relative to regulatory nonfit through creating feelings of rightness that individuals attribute to the story.

As in the initial experiments on how regulatory fit can enhance persuasion through advocacy messages, it is not completely clear how incidental regulatory fit enhanced narrative transportation and persuasion in Vaughn et al.'s (2009) research. It is unlikely that incidental regulatory fit enhanced the personal relevance of these stories or people's actual ability to process them (as integral regulatory fit might). It is more likely that regulatory fit served as a "go" signal for engaging experientially with the narrative and/or as a source of enjoyment attributed to the story that could have helped people remain experientially engaged with it.

Integral Regulatory Fit with Experimentally Effective but Not-Transporting Narratives

Although regulatory fit could often enhance transportation via narratives, it should not always do so. Initial research shows that story-integral fit with outcomes can reduce transportation when narratives are not very involving (Vaughn, 2006). In this experiment, I randomly assigned 58 undergraduate students (participating for extra credit in their psychology courses; 45 women) to conditions in the Narrative X Regulatory Focus Prime, between-subjects design. Participants initially completed a regulatory-focusing task (e.g.,

Vaughn, Malik et al., 2006, Experiment 2): the promotion-prime condition asked participants to list five hopes or aspirations and to rate the personal importance of these goals, and the prevention-prime condition asked participants to list five duties and obligations and rate the personal importance of these goals.

After a short filler task, participants read one of two short stories that were based on an independent-interdependent self-construal priming task used in earlier research (Trafimow, Triandis & Goto, 1991; also see Gardner, Gabriel & Hochschild, 2002). Called "Sostoras' Decision," both stories began with these paragraphs:

> Long ago, in the ancient city of Sumer, there lived a king named Sargon. The great city of Sumer was full of palaces and gardens, and the people prospered. For that reason, King Sargon sought to extend his kingdom to the entire land of Mesopotamia. Sostoras was a brilliant and brave warrior in King Sargon's army. Over several years, King Sargon did extend his rule over almost all of Mesopotamia, largely thanks to Sostoras. In return, the king rewarded Sostoras with a small kingdom of his own to rule.
>
> Ten years passed, in which time Sostoras set aside battle himself in order to train young warriors and tend to the other business of his kingdom. One day, a messenger from King Sargon arrived with word that the king was conscripting warriors for a new war. Sostoras understood that he was to send a detachment of soldiers to aid the king. Warriors he had, and they would be ready to go at a week's notice. However, Sostoras also had to decide who to put in command of the detachment. It was a weighty decision.

The independent prime continued with the following paragraph, which highlighted the individual merits of the chosen general:

> Sostoras thought about it for a long time. Eventually, he decided on Tiglath, who was the most talented general in his army. Sostoras knew this appointment had several advantages. One was that in providing General Tiglath with this opportunity, he would ensure that the general would want to do even more for Sostoras than he already had. That would support Sostoras' rule. Another advantage was to Sostoras' own prestige in Mesopotamia – if Tiglath did well, it would reflect very well on Sostoras' judgment. Finally, Sostoras knew that if Tiglath performed well, King Sargon would be enormously grateful, ensuring that the king would do more for Sostoras and his kingdom.

The interdependent prime continued with the following paragraph, which highlighted the chosen general's family relationship:

> Sostoras thought about it for a long time. Eventually, he decided on Tiglath, who was a member of his family. Sostoras knew this appointment had several advantages. One was that in providing Tiglath with this opportunity, Sostoras would be showing his honor and devotion to his family, which would deepen his family's loyalty to him. That would support Sostoras' rule. Another advantage was to the power and prestige of Sostoras' family in Mesopotamia – if Tiglath did well, it would reflect well on Sostoras' entire family. Finally, Sostoras knew that if Tiglath performed well, King Sargon would be indebted to Sostoras' family, which would help Sostoras' kingdom as a whole.

Then both stories ended with the following paragraph:

The day of the troops' departure was at hand. As General Tiglath and his troops passed Sostoras' palace on their way out of the kingdom, the general saluted Sostoras with great appreciation and respect. Sostoras anticipated the news that the coming weeks would bring.

Recall that independence fits a promotion focus and interdependence fits a prevention focus (e.g., Aaker & Lee, 2001; Lee et al., 2000), so pairing regulatory-focus priming and in-story self-construal priming would vary integral regulatory fit. Immediately after reading their assigned story, participants completed the Transportation Scale (Green & Brock, 2000), which contained story-consistent imagery items about Sostoras, King Sargon, General Tiglath, and the troops passing Sostoras' palace (Cronbach's $\alpha = .91$).

Although the independent and interdependent versions of this story were revised from the originals to make them somewhat more story-like, there is little character development or imagery, and the decision Sostoras had to make was unlikely to be personally relevant to participants. As expected, pilot testing ($n = 18$; between-subjects design) showed that Sostoras' Decision was not very transporting: on a 1-7 scale on which higher scores reflect more transportation, $M = 2.79$, $SD = 1.01$. (There was no significant difference between how transporting independent and interdependent versions were.) This finding contrasts with how transporting participants in Vaughn et al.'s (2009) Experiment 1 found their assigned stories, as rated on the same 1-7 scale: "Two Were Left" (H. B. Cave, in Berger, 1956) transportation $M = 4.36$, $SD = 0.66$; "Crossing Spider Creek" (D. O'Brien, in Thomas, Thomas & Hazuka, 1992) transportation $M = 3.99$, $SD = 0.96$.

With these versions of "Sostoras' Decision," which were not very transporting, regulatory fit should enhance engagement in story-divergent thinking. Consistent with this hypothesis, participants who received the promotion prime were less transported by the fitting, independence-framed story ($M = 2.87$, $SD = 0.80$) than by the nonfitting, interdependence-framed story ($M = 3.51$, $SD = 1.32$), while participants who received the prevention prime were less transported by the fitting, interdependence-framed story ($M = 2.99$, $SD = 0.98$) than by the nonfitting, independence-framed story ($M = 3.71$, $SD = 1.03$); Narrative X Regulatory Focus Prime ANOVA on transportation, $F(1, 54) = 5.60$, $p = .02$, $\omega^2 = .64$.

In short, this experiment suggests that regulatory fit (at least integral fit) does not always have positive effects on transportation. Rather, when the narrative is not very transporting, regulatory fit can decrease transportation. This could result from regulatory fit enhancing criticism of the story and/or the confidence with which participants held story-critical thoughts. Future research should examine how regulatory-fit (and other) effects on transportation and persuasion differ according to story quality, and how story-integral regulatory fit may enhance transportation and persuasion with highly-transporting stories.

TRANSPORTATION LIKELIHOOD

In reviewing and suggesting future research on the impact of regulatory fit on persuasion through advocacy messages, it helped to work within the framework of elaboration likelihood and to distinguish between occasions when it is low, not constrained to be high or low, or high. I will do something similar with what I call *transportation likelihood*. Transportation likelihood is a function of situational and personal factors that influence people's motivation and ability to mentally engage with the story. Like elaboration likelihood, transportation likelihood is a continuum. The higher people's transportation likelihood is, the stronger their attempts to engage experientially with a narrative will be.

I have not included story quality in my definition of transportation likelihood, even though narrative transportation cannot take place without a story that can support it. For example, narratives of exceptionally poor quality - with inconsistent, minimal, or no imagery, plot, and/or characters (e.g., the quasi-narrative, "The story begins: I couldn't care less about him. Now I love him. Joy! Well, it's time for ice cream. Want a spoon? End of story.") - should not be able to support the intense, story-convergent processing involved in the state of transportation. In contrast, elaboration – being critical thinking – can occur with anything, including message arguments that are weak. One option, then, would be to include narrative quality in the definition of transportation likelihood. The problem is that motivation and ability to engage in transportation should have very similar - and likely additive - effects on transportation, but story quality should interact with motivation and/or ability to engage in transportation. To facilitate hypothesizing about effects of regulatory fit and story quality on transportation and persuasion, I have given story quality a role in my transportation likelihood model that is roughly analogous to the role of argument strength in the elaboration likelihood model.

Numerous factors could influence transportation likelihood. Situational factors like distraction, time pressure, and fatigue could reduce people's ability to be transported. Dispositional factors such as chronic tendencies to become psychologically absorbed in activities (Tellegen & Atkinson, 1974), transported by narratives (Dal Cin et al., 2004), or generate vivid imagery (Sheehan, 1967) could enhance transportation likelihood. Additionally, people who find a story's themes personally irrelevant should have little motivation to immerse themselves the story (e.g., Bilandzic, 2006), especially compared to people with a moderate amount of experience with these themes. An interesting possibility, however, is that people who have a great deal of experience with a story *setting or character's attributes* may be especially motivated to critically evaluate the realism of the story, enhancing self-focus and reducing their likelihood of being transported (Bilandzic, 2006). For example, an Albuquerque resident watching a TV crime drama set in Albuquerque may devote so much attention to figuring out where each scene was filmed that he or she barely pays attention to the story. Finally, the presence or absence of a strong desire to take a break from the real world could influence transportation likelihood (e.g., Green & Brock, 2005). It may be possible to vary such a desire experimentally by randomly assigning some participants to recall aspects of their daily lives that are tiring, confusing, or stressful – and from which they would like to take a break – and others to recall aspects of their daily lives that are energizing, enjoyable, or relaxing - and that they would like to continue. This is not meant to be an exhaustive list, and future research may add to or subtract from it.

The lower people's transportation likelihood, the more distant they should feel from a story and the less story imagery they should generate (Bilandzic, 2006). Story quality should have less of an impact on engagement and persuasion, to the extent either occurs. People should also be less likely to think critically and/or negatively about aspects of a narrative that do not ring true. They may not even notice them. Instead, they may only follow the general trend of the plot and keep general track of the main characters and setting.

A special case of low transportation likelihood may occur when people approach a narrative intending to be critical of it (e.g., Bilandzic, 2006). In this case, low transportation likelihood could be the same as high elaboration likelihood. Importantly, however, need for cognition is unrelated to transportation (Green & Brock, 2000), suggesting that this relationship would not result from transportation and elaboration normally being opposites. Both elaboration and transportation are high-engagement states. In many cases of low transportation, one's engagement with a communication – via transportation or via elaboration – may simply be low.

The higher people's transportation likelihood, the more willing and able they are to engage experientially with the narrative. This does not mean they always will. Story quality could have increasing effects with increasing transportation likelihood. Enjoyment of the narrative being equal, the more flawed the narrative, the more that highly-engaged people should turn their attention away from experientially engaging with the story and toward disputing the narrative (e.g., Bilandzic, 2006).

EFFECTS OF REGULATORY FIT ON NARRATIVE TRANSPORTATION AND PERSUASION: HYPOTHESES ORGANIZED BY TRANSPORTATION LIKELIHOOD

When Transportation Likelihood is Constrained to be Low

When people lack motivation and/or ability to engage experientially with a narrative, transportation should not occur. People may be too distracted to enter the story world, for example, or may lack the skills to try with much success. Under these conditions, persuasion would not occur, either – at least not through the process of mentally immersing oneself in the narrative. To the extent that any persuasion occurs because the communication is a story, per se, it may be through regulatory fit serving as a heuristic cue about obvious story themes.

When Transportation Likelihood is Unconstrained to be High or Low

When transportation likelihood is unconstrained, story-incidental and story-integral regulatory fit should have different influences on transportation and persuasion via narratives. Feelings of rightness or fluency from incidental regulatory fit could enhance the confidence with which people engage in what appears to be the default, experiential processing style with narratives. A likely moderator of this effect is the relative lengths of the regulatory-fit induction and the narrative. If incidental regulatory fit results from a chronic source (e.g., the fit between a person's dispositional prevention focus and the strategies required by one's job – as in the opening narrative of this chapter), the length of the narrative should not matter in the persistence of regulatory-fit effects. However, if the incidental regulatory-fit manipulation is brief and a narrative is lengthy, the incidental regulatory-fit effect on transportation and persuasion should be particularly strong at the start of the narrative.

In contrast, story-integral regulatory fit (e.g., with chronic regulatory focus) could influence transportation and persuasion in numerous ways, with perhaps not always positive effects. Regulatory fit with story themes could enhance the actual fluency with which people process the narrative. Additionally, the enjoyable experience of processing fluency could enhance motivation to stay engaged with the narrative. However, extremely strong correspondence between story events, settings, and/or characters and the person's own attributes (which could include chronic regulatory focus) may enhance self-focused attention and critical thinking about the realism of story events, reducing transportation and transportation-mediated persuasion (see Bilandzic, 2006).

Additionally, when transportation likelihood is unconstrained, a poor-quality narrative or a blatant flaw in an otherwise good story should route people's psychological engagement away from transportation and toward criticizing the story. Either incidental or integral regulatory fit could enhance this process through self-validating critical thoughts (cf. Brinol, Petty & Barden, 2007; Brinol, Petty, Valle, et al., 2007), reducing transportation and story-consistent beliefs.

When Transportation Likelihood is Constrained to be High

When transportation likelihood is constrained to be high, aspects of the person and situation should make story-divergent thinking unlikely. Feelings of rightness and enjoyment from incidental or integral regulatory fit could – if attributed to the story – help people stay experientially engaged with a story when they encounter minor story flaws, maintaining transportation and enhancing story-consistent beliefs. With that said, if a story is of poor quality overall or if a single, devastating flaw becomes salient, counterarguing or disputing of the narrative could be intense - and it could be enhanced by incidental or integral regulatory fit.

CONCLUSION

In this chapter, my primary goal has been to put current research on regulatory fit and persuasion into the larger contexts of elaboration and transportation likelihood. I laid groundwork by describing what regulatory fit is, how it is operationally defined, and how it can affect judgments. Then I reviewed current research on how regulatory fit affects persuasion through advocacy messages and through narratives, noting where interpretational ambiguities exist. Next I speculated about how effects of regulatory fit on persuasion might differ according to elaboration or transportation likelihood and according to whether the regulatory-fit experience results from an initial event or from engagement with the persuasive communication. In drawing connections between different methods of varying regulatory fit and different ways of engaging with advocacy messages and narratives, my hope is to spur new directions for theorizing and research on regulatory fit and on persuasion. I also anticipate that insights gained from such new research could extend understanding of social judgment beyond prevention-promotion regulatory fit, persuasion, and transportation.

ACKNOWLEDGMENTS

Thanks go to Erin Abshere, Nathaniel Baum, Melissa Ball, Jolie Baumann, Emily Clark, Christine Dosch, Colin Flynn, Audrey Harkness, Christine Klemann, Jessica Nuzzetti,

Melahat Ozses, Rebecca Ramirez, Jennifer Rodgers, Lisa Schlessinger, and Adam Weber for help collecting the data in Vaughn (2006) and Vaughn (2007). Special thanks go to John Luginsland for comments on an earlier version of the chapter.

REFERENCES

Aaker, J. L., & Lee, A. Y. (2001). "I" seek pleasures and "we" avoid pains: The role of self-regulatory goals in information processing and persuasion. *Journal of Consumer Research, 28*, 33-49.

Aaker, J. L., & Lee, A. Y. (2006). Understanding regulatory fit. *Journal of Marketing Research, 43*, 15-19.

Avnet, T., & Higgins, E. T. (2003). Locomotion, assessment, and regulatory fit: Value transfer from "how" to "what." *Journal of Experimental Social Psychology, 39*, 525-530.

Avnet, T., & Higgins, E. T. (2006). How regulatory fit affects value in consumer choices and opinions. *Journal of Marketing Research, 43*, 1-10.

Berger, R. (Ed.). (1956). *The best short stories*. New York: Scholastic.

Bianco, A. T., Higgins, E. T., & Klem, A. (2003). How "fun/importance" fit impacts performance: Relating implicit theories to instructions. *Personality and Social Psychology Bulletin, 29*, 1091-1103.

Bilandzic, H. (2006). The perception of distance in the cultivation process: A theoretical consideration of the relationship between television content, processing experience, and perceived distance. *Communication Theory, 16*, 333-355.

Bless, H., Clore, G. L., Schwarz, N., Golisano, V., Rabe, C., & Wolk, M. (1996). Mood and the use of scripts: Does happy mood really lead to mindlessness? *Journal of Personality and Social Psychology, 71*, 665-679.

Bless, H., & Schwarz, N. (1999). Sufficient and necessary conditions in dual-mode models: The case of mood and information processing. In S. Chaiken & Y. Trope (Eds.), *Dual-process theories in social psychology* (pp. 423-440). New York, NY: Guilford.

Bodenhausen, G. V., Mussweiler, T., Gabriel, S., & Moreno, K. N. (2001). Affective influences on stereotyping and intergroup relations. In J. P. Forgas (Ed.), *The handbook of affect and social cognition* (pp. 319-343). Mahwah, NJ: Erlbaum.

Brinol, P., & Petty, R. E. (2003). Overt head movements and persuasion: A self-validation analysis. *Journal of Personality and Social Psychology, 84*, 1123-1139.

Brinol, P., Petty, R. E., & Barden, J. (2007). Happiness versus sadness as a determinant of thought confidence in persuasion: A self-validation analysis. *Journal of Personality and Social Psychology, 93*, 711-727.

Brinol, P., Petty, R. E., Valle, C., Rucker, D. D., & Becerra, A. (2007). The effects of message recipients' power before and after persuasion: A self-validation analysis. *Journal of Personality and Social Psychology, 93*, 1040-1053.

Brown, D. (2003). *The Da Vinci code*. New York, NY: Doubleday.

Busselle, R., & Bilandzic, H. (2008). Fictionality and perceived realism in experiencing stories: A model of narrative comprehension and engagement. *Communication Theory, 18*, 255-280.

Cacioppo, J. T., & Petty, R. E. (1982). The need for cognition. *Journal of Personality and Social Psychology, 42,* 116-131.

Cacioppo, J. T., Harkins, S. G., & Petty, R. E. (1981). The nature of attitudes and cognitive responses and their relationships to behavior. In R. Petty, T. Ostrom, & T. Brock (Eds.), *Cognitive responses in persuasion* (pp. 31–54). Hillsdale, NJ: Erlbaum.

Camacho, C. J., Higgins, E. T., & Luger, L. (2003). Moral value transfer from regulatory fit: What feels right *is* right and what feels wrong *is* wrong. *Journal of Personality and Social Psychology, 84,* 498-510.

Cacioppo, J. T., Petty, R. E., & Sidera, J. A. (1982). The effects of a salient self-schema on the evaluation of proattitudinal editorials: Top-down versus bottom-up processing. *Journal of Experimental Social Psychology, 18,* 324-338.

Cesario, J., Grant, H., & Higgins, E. T. (2004). Regulatory fit and persuasion: Transfer from "feeling right." *Journal of Personality and Social Psychology, 86,* 388-404.

Cesario, J., & Higgins, E. T. (2008). Making message recipients "feel right": How nonverbal cues can increase persuasion. *Psychological Science, 19,* 415-420.

Cesario, J., Higgins, E. T., & Scholer, A. A. (2008). Regulatory fit and persuasion: Basic principles and remaining questions. *Social and Personality Psychology Compass, 2,* 444-463.

Chaiken, S. (1987). The heuristic model of persuasion. In M. P. Zanna, J. M. Olson, & C. P. Herman (Eds.), *Social influence: The Ontario symposium* (Vol. 5, pp. 3–39). Hillsdale, NJ: Erlbaum.

Chaiken, S., Liberman, A., & Eagly, A. H. (1989). Heuristic and systematic processing within and beyond the persuasion context. In J. S. Uleman & J. A. Bargh (Eds.), *Unintended thought* (pp. 212-252). New York, NY: Guilford.

Chen, S., & Chaiken, S. (1999). The heuristic-systematic model in its broader context. In S. Chaiken & Y. Trope (Eds.), *Dual-process theories in social psychology* (pp. 73-96). New York, NY: Guilford.

Clore, G. L. (1992). Cognitive phenomenology: Feelings and the construction of judgment. In L. L. Martin & A. Tesser (Eds.), *The construction of social judgment* (pp. 133-163). Hillsdale, NJ: Erlbaum.

Clore, G. L., Gasper, K., & Garvin, E. (2001). Affect as information. In J. P. Forgas (Ed.), *Handbook of affect and social cognition* (pp. 121-144). Mahwah, NJ: Erlbaum.

Crowe, E., & Higgins, E. T. (1997). Regulatory focus and strategic inclinations: Promotion and prevention in decision-making. *Organizational Behavior and Human Decision Processes, 69,* 117-132.

Csikszentmihalyi, M. (1990). *Flow: The psychology of optimal experience.* New York: Harper & Row.

Dal Cin, S., Zanna, M. P., & Fong, G. T. (2004). Narrative persuasion and overcoming resistance. In E. S. Knowles & J. A. Linn (Eds.), *Resistance and persuasion* (pp. 175-191). Mahwah, NJ: Erlbaum.

Eagly, A. H., & Chaiken, S. (1993). *The psychology of attitudes.* New York: Academic Press.

Escalas, J. E. (2004). Imagine yourself in the product: Mental simulation, narrative transportation, and persuasion. *Journal of Advertising, 33,* 37-48.

Escalas, J. E. (2007). Self-referencing and persuasion: Narrative transportation versus analytical elaboration. *Journal of Consumer Research, 33,* 421-429.

Evans, L. M., & Petty, R. E. (2003). Self-guide framing and persuasion: Responsibly increasing message processing to ideal levels. *Personality and Social Psychology Bulletin, 29*, 313-324.

Forster, J., Higgins, E. T., & Idson, L. C. (1998). Approach and avoidance strength during goal attainment: Regulatory focus and the "goal looms larger" effect. *Journal of Personality and Social Psychology, 75*, 1115-1131.

Freitas, A. L., & Higgins, E. T. (2002). Enjoying goal-directed action: The role of regulatory fit. *Psychological Science, 13*, 1-6.

Freitas, A. L., Liberman, N., & Higgins, E. T. (2002). Regulatory fit and resisting temptation during goal pursuit. *Journal of Experimental Social Psychology, 38*, 291-298.

Gardner, W. L., Gabriel, S., & Hochschild, L. (2002). When you and I are "we," you are not threatening: The role of self-expansion in social comparison. *Journal of Personality and Social Psychology, 82*, 239-251.

Gasper, K., & Clore, G. L. (2002). Attending to the big picture: Mood and global versus local processing of visual information. *Psychological Science, 13*, 34-40.

Gilbert, D. T. (1991). How mental systems believe. American Psychologist, 46, 107-119.

Green, M. C., & Brock, T. C. (2000). The role of transportation in the persuasiveness of public narratives. *Journal of Personality and Social Psychology, 79*, 701-721.

Green, M. C., & Brock, T. C. (2002). In the mind's eye: Transportation-imagery model of narrative persuasion. In M. C. Green, J. J. Strange, & T. C. Brock (Eds.), *Narrative impact: Social and cognitive foundations* (pp. 315-341). Mahwah, NJ: Erlbaum.

Green, M. C., & Brock, T. C. (2005). Persuasiveness of narratives. In T. C. Brock & M. C. Green (Eds.), *Persuasion: Psychological insights and perspectives* (2nd ed., pp. 117-142). Thousand Oaks, CA: Sage.

Green, M. C., Garst, J., & Brock, T. C. (2004). The power of fiction: Determinants and boundaries. In L. J. Shrum (Ed.), *The psychology of entertainment media: Blurring the lines between entertainment and persuasion* (pp. 161-176). Mahwah, NJ: Erlbaum.

Higgins, E. T. (1997). Beyond pleasure and pain. *American Psychologist, 52*, 1280-1300.

Higgins, E. T. (2000). Making a good decision: Value from fit. *American Psychologist, 55*, 1217-1230.

Higgins, E. T. (2005). Value from regulatory fit. *Current Directions in Psychological Science, 14*, 209-213.

Higgins, E. T. (2006). Value from hedonic experience *and* engagement. *Psychological Review, 113*, 439-460.

Higgins, E. T., Bond, R. N., Klein, R., & Strauman, T. (1986). Self-discrepancies and emotional vulnerability: How magnitude, accessibility, and type of discrepancy influence affect. *Journal of Personality and Social Psychology, 51*, 5-15.

Higgins, E. T., Friedman, R. S., Harlow, R. E., Idson, L. C., Ayduk, O. N., & Taylor, A. (2001). Achievement orientations from subjective histories of success: Promotion pride versus prevention pride. *European Journal of Social Psychology, 31*, 3-23.

Higgins, E. T., Idson, L. C., Freitas, A. L., Spiegel, S., & Molden, D. C. (2003). Transfer of value from fit. *Journal of Personality and Social Psychology, 84*, 1140-1153.

Hong, J., & Lee, A. Y. (2008). Be fit and be strong: Mastering self-regulation through regulatory fit. *Journal of Consumer Research, 34*, 682-695.

Idson, L. C., Liberman, N., & Higgins, E. T. (2000). Distinguishing gains from nonlosses and losses from nongains: A regulatory focus perspective on hedonic intensity. *Journal of Experimental Social Psychology, 36*, 252-274.

Koenig, A. M., Cesario, J., Molden, D. C., Kosloff, S., & Higgins, E. T. (in press). Incidental regulatory fit and the processing of persuasive appeals. *Personality and Social Psychology Bulletin.*

Lavine, H., & Snyder, M. (1996). Cognitive processing and the functional matching effect in persuasion: The mediating role of subjective perceptions of message quality. *Journal of Experimental Social Psychology, 32*, 580-604.

Lee, A. Y., & Aaker, J. L. (2004). Bringing the frame into focus: The influence of regulatory fit on processing fluency and persuasion. *Journal of Personality and Social Psychology, 86*, 205-218.

Lee, A. Y., Aaker, J. L., & Gardner, W. L. (2000). The pleasures and pains of distinct self-construals: The role of interdependence in regulatory focus. *Journal of Personality and Social Psychology, 78*, 1122-1134.

Lockwood, P., Jordan, C. H., & Kunda, Z. (2002). Motivation by positive or negative role models: Regulatory focus determines who will best inspire us. *Journal of Personality and Social Psychology, 83*, 854-864.

Mazzocco, P. J., Green, M. C., & Brock, T. C. (2007). The effects of a prior story-bank on the processing of a related narrative. *Media Psychology, 10*, 61-90.

Nisbett, R. E., & Ross, L. (1991). *Human inference: strategies and shortcomings in social judgment.* Englewood Cliffs, NJ: Prentice-Hall.

Ouschan, L., Boldero, J. M., Kashima, Y., Wakimoto, R., & Kashima, E. S. (2007). Regulatory Focus Strategies Scale: A measure of individual differences in the endorsement of regulatory strategies. *Asian Journal of Social Psychology, 10*, 243-257.

Petty, R. E., Brinol, P., & Tormala, Z. L. (2002). Thought confidence as a determinant of persuasion: A self-validation analysis. *Journal of Personality and Social Psychology, 82*, 722-741.

Petty, R. E., & Cacioppo, J. T. (1986). The elaboration likelihood model of persuasion. In L. Berkowitz (Ed.), *Advances in experimental social psychology* (Vol. 19, pp. 123-205). New York: Academic Press.

Petty, R. E., & Wegener, D. T. (1998). Matching versus mismatching attitude functions: Implications for scrutiny of persuasive messages. *Personality and Social Psychology Bulletin, 24*, 227-240.

Petty, R. E., & Wegener, D. T. (1999). The elaboration likelihood model: Current status and controversies. In S. Chaiken & Y. Trope (Eds.), *Dual-process theories in social psychology* (pp. 37-72). New York, NY: Guilford.

Pham, M. T., & Avnet, T. (2004). Ideals and oughts and the reliance on affect versus substance in persuasion. *Journal of Consumer Research, 30*, 503-518.

Rapp, D. N. (2008). How do readers handle incorrect information during reading? *Memory and Cognition, 36*, 688-701.

Reber, R., & Schwarz, N. (1999). Effects of perceptual fluency on judgments of truth. *Consciousness and Cognition, 8*, 338-342.

Reber, R., Schwarz, N., & Winkielman, P. (2004). Processing fluency and aesthetic pleasure: Is beauty in the perceiver's processing experience? *Personality and Social Psychology Review, 8*, 364-382.

Richter, T., Schroeder, S., & Wohrmann, B. (2009). You don't have to believe everything you read: Background knowledge permits fast and efficient validation of information. *Journal of Personality and Social Psychology, 96*, 538-558.

Schwarz, N., & Bless, H. (1992). Constructing reality and its alternatives: Assimilation and contrast in social judgments. In L. L. Martin and A. Tesser (Eds.), *The construction of social judgments* (pp. 217-245). Hillsdale, NJ: Erlbaum.

Schwarz, N., & Bless, H. (2007). Mental construal processes: The inclusion/exclusion model. In D. A. Stapel & J. Suls (Eds.), *Assimilation and contrast in social psychology* (119-141). New York, NY: Psychology Press.

Schwarz, N., & Clore, G. (1983). Mood, misattribution, and judgments of well-being: Informative and directive functions of affective states. *Journal of Personality and Social Psychology, 45*, 513-523.

Schwarz, N., & Clore, G. L. (2007). Feelings and phenomenal experiences. In A. W. Kruglanski & E. T. Higgins (Eds.), *Social psychology: Handbook of basic principles* (2nd ed., pp. 385-407). New York: Guilford.

Semin, G. R., Higgins, E. T., de Montes, L. G., Estourget, Y., & Vallencia, J. F. (2005). Linguistic signatures of regulatory focus: How abstraction fits promotion more than prevention. *Journal of Personality and Social Psychology, 89*, 36-45.

Shah, J., Brazy, P. C., & Higgins, E. T. (2004). Promoting us or preventing them: Regulatory focus and manifestations of intergroup bias. *Personality and Social Psychology Bulletin, 30*, 433-446.

Shah, J., Higgins, E. T., & Friedman, R. S. (1998). Performance incentives and means: How regulatory focus influences goal attainment. *Journal of Personality and Social Psychology, 74*, 285-293.

Sheehan, P. W. (1967). A shortened form of Betts' questionnaire upon mental imagery. *Journal of Clinical Psychology, 23*, 386-389.

Snyder, M., & DeBono, K. G. (1985). Appeals to images and claims about quality: Understanding the psychology of advertising. *Journal of Personality and Social Psychology, 49*, 586-597.

Summerville, A., & Roese, N. J. (2008). Self-report measures of individual differences in regulatory focus: A cautionary note. *Journal of Research in Personality, 42*, 247-254.

Tellegen, A., & Atkinson, G. (1974). Openness to absorbing and self-altering experiences ("absorption"), a trait related to hypnotic susceptibility. *Journal of Abnormal Psychology, 83*, 268-277.

Thomas, J., Thomas, D., & Hazuka, T. (Eds.). (1992). *Flash fiction: Very short stories.* New York: W. W. Norton.

Trafimow, D., Triandis, H., C., & Goto, S. G. (1991). Some tests of the distinction between the private self and the collective self. *Journal of Personality and Social Psychology, 60*, 649-655.

Vallacher, R. R., & Wegner, D. M. (1989). Levels of personal agency: Individual differences in action identification. *Journal of Personality and Social Psychology, 57*, 660-671.

Vaughn, L. A. (2006). [The effect of integral regulatory fit on mental engagement with experimentally effective but not-transporting narratives]. Unpublished raw data.

Vaughn, L. A. (2007). [How Freitas and Higgins' (2002, Experiment 2) regulatory-fit manipulation affects subjective processing fluency]. Unpublished raw data.

Vaughn, L. A. (2009). *Regulatory fit as a "go" signal for high-level, inclusive processing.* Manuscript submitted for publication.

Vaughn, L. A., Baumann, J., & Klemann, C. (2008). Openness to Experience and regulatory focus: Evidence of motivation from fit. *Journal of Research in Personality, 42,* 886-894.

Vaughn, L. A., Harkness, A. R., & Clark, E. K. (in press). The effect of subjective experiences of regulatory fit on trust. *Personal Relationships.*

Vaughn, L. A., Hesse, S. J., Petkova, Z., & Trudeau, L. (2009). "This story is right on": The impact of regulatory fit on narrative engagement and persuasion. *European Journal of Social Psychology, 39,* 447-456.

Vaughn, L. A., Malik, J., Schwartz, S., Petkova, Z., & Trudeau, L. (2006). Regulatory fit as input for stop rules. *Journal of Personality and Social Psychology, 91,* 601-611.

Vaughn, L. A., O'Rourke, T., Schwartz, S., Malik, J., Petkova, Z., & Trudeau, L. (2006). When two wrongs can make a right: Regulatory nonfit, bias, and correction of judgments *Journal of Experimental Social Psychology, 42,* 654-661.

Wang, J., & Calder, B. J. (2006). Media transportation and advertising. *Journal of Consumer Research, 33,* 151-162.

In: Psychology of Persuasion
Editors: J. Csapó and A. Magyar, pp.101-120

ISBN: 978-1-60876-590-4
© 2010 Nova Science Publishers, Inc.

Chapter 4

ARGUING WITH DEATH: DIALOGUES WITH PERSONIFIED DEATH IN GERMAN-SPEAKING LITERATURE SINCE THE ENLIGHTENMENT

Christine Steinhoff

Braunschweig, Germany

ABSTRACT

This chapter deals with a peculiar kind of persuasive communication: the fictitious argument between a human being and personified death. This old literary motif shows a person who is about to die arguing with an anthropomorphic death figure. As the choice of German-speaking texts discussed here exemplifies, the dialogic and rhetorically structured way of dealing with the mortal threat has been living on well into Modern times. Various classical strategies of persuasion have been adapted to this particular scenario, trying to give the respective conceptions of life and death a vivid and convincing voice.

INTRODUCTION

Death is one of the basic conditions of human existence. Despite all progress of human civilisation, death remains a problem not to be overcome. Since the beginning of history, the personification of death has been a common attempt to grasp the incomprehensible. Death has been conceptualized as a person with supernatural, but also many human characteristics. Attributed body and speech, death suddenly appears as an entity one can deal with. In many societies this anthropomorphic concept of death has led to tales of people trying to bribe, to persuade, to play a trick on or to physically fight death in order to retain their lives.

This chapter deals with the tales of *verbal* attempts at influencing death. The dialogue between a person and personified death has been a popular literary motif from early on until today.[1] It usually shows a human being who is about to die arguing with a personalized death figure. The doomed people draw on various rhetorical devices to convince death to spare their lives, whereas death, on the other hand, tries to legitimate his doing by an equally skilful argumentation. With these fictitious conversations between a human person and a death figure, a dialectic way has been found to deal with the essential conflict between life and death. Human beings are thus making use of their specifically human faculty of speech in order to handle their specifically human problem: their notion of death.

In German-speaking literature, the most elaborate example of such a literary dispute between man and death is Johannes von Tepl's prose work "Der Ackermann aus Böhmen", written around 1400. Here, the speaker does not argue about his own death, but about his young wife's decease and human mortality in general. After a succession of 32 speeches, with death and the ploughman alternately putting forward their arguments, God himself resolves the dispute in the 33rd chapter, adjudging victory to death.

While the dialogue with personified death was a current motif in the late Middle Ages and often included as explanatory text in the pictorial representations of the *danses macabres*[2] coming into fashion at the time, its appearance in German-speaking countries was not at all limited to this period, but survived even through the enlightenment until today. With the rise of the individual, the experience of death has become more private, personal and thus possibly more fearful, the medical progress making death at the same time appear less inevitable than before. Focussing on earthly life rather than on the hereafter, the self-confident, enlightened individual does not humbly accept his/her death any longer. It may be on this background, that the intimate dispute between a person and personified death has survived as a literary motif. Despite its naiveness, the tale of an argument with death is compatible with and often reflects Modern attitudes towards death.

This chapter analyzes the rhetorics of these fictitious discussions between human being and death. How is death addressed, what kinds of arguments, what kind of linguistic register are used against him? How is death depicted, what kind of language does he use and what is his line of reasoning? In order to give an overview over the variety and the continuity of this motif, this study draws on very diverse literary works ranging from the 18th to the 20th century. While only a small choice of German-speaking texts can be discussed in detail, the examples include all three genres, both in prose and in verse, and cover both serious and comic, well known and less known variants. Thus, an impression can be given of how this remarkable kind of dialogue has been imagined since the enlightenment until today.

MATTHIAS CLAUDIUS: DER TOD UND DAS MÄDCHEN

In German-speaking literature, the most famous example of a dialogue between a human being and personified death is probably Matthias Claudius' small poem "Der Tod und das Mädchen", first published in 1775 and later set to music by Franz Schubert. In the history of

---

1 An early example is the debate between death and Apollo in Euripides' drama "Alkestis" (438 BC). See for a brief overview over ancient and medieval examples of disputes with personified death Seeba: Kritik des ästhetischen Menschen, pp. 168-171.
2 In the narrow sense, a dance of death means the medieval depiction of death as a dancer leading the representatives of all social classes in a final, macabre dance to their graves. In a wider sense, this term refers to all kinds of personifications of death.

this motif, the encounter between a young woman and death is a special subcategory, which has developed its own line of tradition in literature and the arts. At first only one element among others in the medieval *danses macabres*, the depiction of death approaching a girl soon became popular as a motif on its own.[3] In Baroque art, pictures of the death and the maiden relate to the concepts of *memento mori* and *vanitas* central to the time, with the young girl serving as a symbol of the criticized vanity. On a more general level, the image of a woman at child-bearing age of course lends itself to symbolize life and birth, and the most shocking and spectacular contrasting of the two opposed principles of evolution – growth and decay – can be achieved by showing a blooming girl in touch with a skeleton. Apart from this elementary meaning, most treatments of the motif also carry sexual undertones and often represent the male fantasy of the beauty being raped or molested by the beast, in this case the grim reaper.

In an attempt to overcome the melancholic preoccupation with mortality of the Baroque, the optimistic age of the enlightenment struggled for a positive image of death.[4] Matthias Claudius, who was in this regard a typical child of his times, repeatedly tries to picture death as a kind "Freund Hain" in his work. The edition of his collected works begins with a dedication addressed to death, which shows, though, that this affirmative attitude towards death takes quite an effort:

> 's soll Leute geben, heißen starke Geister, die sich in ihrem Leben den Hain nichts anfechten lassen, und hinter seinem Rücken wohl gar über ihn und seine dünnen Beine spotten. Bin nicht starker Geist; 's läuft mir, die Wahrheit zu sagen, jedesmal kalt über'n Rücken wenn ich Sie ansehe. Und doch will ich glauben, daß Sie 'n guter Mann sind, wenn man Sie genug kennt [...]. (Dedikation, p. 11)

While Gotthold Ephraim Lessing tries to evoke a positive image of death by referring back to the ancient concept of death as the brother of sleep, dismissing the medieval idea of death as a grim reaper,[5] Claudius tries to merge both ideas. He sticks to the picture of death as a skeletal figure, but tries to give it a more friendly appeal:

> Die Alten soll'n ihn anders gebildet haben; als 'n Jäger im Mantel der Nacht, und die Griechen: als 'n „Jüngling der in ruhiger Stellung mit gesenktem trüben Blicke die Fackel des Lebens neben dem Leichname auslöscht". Ist'n schönes Bild, und erinnert einen so tröstlich an Hain seine Familie und namentlich an seinen Bruder; [...] bin aber doch lieber beim Knochenmann geblieben. So steht er in unsrer Kirch', und so hab' ich 'n mir immer von klein auf vorgestellt [...] Er ist auch so, dünkt mich, recht schön, und wenn man ihn lange ansieht, wird er zuletzt ganz freundlich aussehen. (Dedikation, p. 11)

In Claudius' poem "Der Tod und das Mädchen", the death figure also wavers between dread and comfort, between the frightful skeleton assaulting a young girl and the tender brother of sleep offering sweet eternal slumber. As there is no context given, just the dialogue of the

---

[3] See for an overview over this European tradition from the Middle Ages until the present day Kaiser: Der Tod und die schönen Frauen.

4 Walter Rehm describes this struggle in the literary and philosophical discourses of the enlightenment in his book "Der Todesgedanke in der deutschen Dichtung vom Mittelalter bis zur Romantik", pp. 244-279.

[5] Cf. Gotthold Ephraim Lessing: Wie die Alten den Tod gebildet.

two, death's character can only be concluded either from the girl's frightened reaction or death's contradicting self-description. Whose words are justified, remains uncertain.

The poem is short and concentrated, focussing exclusively on the verbal struggle between the two antagonists. It is left open where and how they meet, what happens before and afterwards. The girl is not given a name or a further description. She is simply introduced as "Das Mädchen" as opposed to "Der Tod", the definite articles making the two appear as general personifications of youth, beauty and life on the one hand, and the negation of these on the other hand. Thus stripped of all diverting details, the quick succession of the girl's speech and death's rejoinder becomes one of the most intense examples of a dispute between a human being and death:

Der Tod und das Mädchen

Das Mädchen
Vorüber! Ach, vorüber!
Geh wilder Knochenmann!
Ich bin noch jung, geh Lieber!
Und rühre mich nicht an.

Der Tod
Gib deine Hand, du schön und zart Gebild!
Bin Freund, und komme nicht, zu strafen.
Sei gutes Muts! ich bin nicht wild,
Sollst sanft in meinen Armen schlafen!

In a condensed way, the girl's speech reflects different persuasive strategies, ranging from pleading, to flattering, to arguing. She begins with a breathless, elliptic plea, which concentrates all her fear and desperation into one single word: "Vorüber". She repeats it twice, before managing to speak a full sentence. The inserted "ach" is a direct emotional utterance, enforcing the urgence of her plea. The girl then seems to slightly calm down and starts giving death clear instructions: the imperative "geh" is repeated twice, and finally culminates in the repulsing *noli-me-tangere*-formula "rühre mich nicht an". This self-confidently asserts the girl's power over her body, at the same time evoking the image of the sensitive touch-me-not flower which seems to shyly shrink away from physical touch. This image supports the stanza's title "Das Mädchen", rendering clear that it is, in sharp contrast to the death figure, a young, unexperienced maiden who speaks.

The girl addresses death in two contrary ways. She at first accuses him of being uncontrolled, ugly and intimidating ("wilder Knochenmann"), which appears to be her frank and spontaneous reaction to death's apparition. At second thought, she seems to realize that a friendly address might be more helpful and switches to the flattering "Lieber". Calling death kind of course also expresses the wish that he might act accordingly and behave kindly towards her.

The girl justifies her demand to be spared with just one, but grave argument: "Ich bin noch jung". Implied here is the common idea of humans having a natural right to a certain life span, which makes death either 'timely' or 'untimely', depending on the dying person's age. In the fictitious discussions with death, the argument that death is coming at an unjust time belongs to the standard repertoire – even of older people, who argue that they are still not old 'enough'.

Whereas the girl's stanza consists of short, interrupted sentences and exclamations, which show her great anxiety and unreflected youth, death's counter-speech sounds completely different. His sentences are long, complete, and hypotactically structured, and his verse has a more even and steady metre than the girl's one. From this way of speaking alone, his calm superiority is made obvious.

Death's main rhetorical strategy is to carefully refute every single part of the girl's speech. Mirroring the antithetical structure at the basis of the poem – girl versus skeleton , his part of the dialogue presents an antithesis to most of the girl's utterances. Her "geh" he counters with "komme", her "rühr mich nicht an" with "gib deine Hand", her desperate "ach" with the encouraging "sei gutes Muts", her reproach of being a "wilder Knochenmann" with the negation "Ich bin nicht wild". He adds an even more explicit counterpoint describing his doings as "sanft": "sollst sanft in meinen Armen schlafen".

Addressed as "wilder Knochenmann" himself, the death figure chooses an address which sounds like a friendly, flattering compliment: "du schön und zart Gebild". The term "Gebild" compares the girl to a beautiful piece of art.[6] Nevertheless, it may also imply that she is, in the end, not much more than the "Knochenmann": a "Gebild" (construction) of bones, however nicely these may be arranged.

The death figure tries to assert a positive self-image, negating several common conceptions of death, more than are explicitly stated in the girl's speech. He claims not only to be "nicht wild", but even to be a friend rather than an enemy ("bin freund"), and that his task is not, as it says in the New Testament (Romans 6:23), to punish: "komme nicht, zu strafen".

Apart from establishing a trustworthy and friendly image, death tries to win the girl's consent by promising her that she is going to sleep safely and soundly in his arms: "Sollst sanft in meinen Armen schlafen!" As in the dedication already quoted, Claudius here blends the two conceptions of death as a frigthful skeleton and death as the brother of Hypnos, the ancient god of sleep.

In Claudius' poem, dying appears as a physical contact with personified death, starting with taking the hand, and leading up to an embrace, the closest form of contact between two bodies. As in other depictions of death and the maiden, this has erotic implications, and death's luring words "Gib deine Hand, du schön und zart Gebild!" might as well be the words of a lustful seducer or rapist. Apart from this, the image of the girl being embraced by death in the midst of life also recalls a famous line from an old church song: "Mitten wir im Leben sind von dem Tod umfangen". This saying, later made popular by Martin Luther, also uses the physical metaphor of death clasping life.

It remains open whether the encounter ends in a fatal embrace or not. But only to a certain extent: death clearly appears as the winner of the dispute. His words exceed those of the girl both in quantity and quality, and, most important: he literally and probably also figuratively has the final say. The girl is not given the chance to answer, she seems to have been silenced. The ending of the dialogue might thus as well mark the ending of her life.

---

[6] Cf. the entry "Gebild" in Pierer's Universal-Lexikon, p. 28.

Franz Von Kobell:
Die G'schicht Von' Brandner-Kasper

The fictitious encounter with personified death can take various forms, ranging from dance to fight. Besides the verbal argument, another wide-spread motif is the gamble with death, popularized by Ingmar Bergman's film "The Seventh Seal" (1956), which shows a knight challenging death to a chess match. In Franz von Kobell's "Die G'schicht von' Brandner-Kasper" the two motifs are combined: Kasper, the protagonist, puts up a good verbal fight, before switching over to a different strategy, that of cheating death in a game of cards. Death, too, has to eventually come up with other than just verbal techniques to persuade Kasper, who proves to be deaf to all argumentation.

Franz von Kobell's "Die G'schicht von' Brandner-Kasper" was first published in 1871 and has later gained popularity by various free adaptations in novel, drama and film.[7] Apart from its consoling outcome, it is probably the strong humanization of death, producing both humorous and comforting effects, which has made the story so attractive. The attribution of human qualities to death is always potentially funny, due to the striking discrepancy between this personalized concept of death and the common experience of death as neither human nor humane at all. In Kobell, a rather humorous picture of death is drawn by furnishing him with several human weaknesses and problems: Kobell's death drinks and gambles, he has got trouble with his boss, he wants to be liked by everybody, and suffers from his bad image.

In the history of the motif, death has been given different linguistic registers in talking to humans, ranging from elaborate verse as in Hugo von Hofmannsthal's "Jedermann" to Austrian colloquial speech as in Ferdinand Raimund's "Hobellied". Sometimes he is even shown using dialect: in Alfred Döblin's novel "Berlin Alexanderplatz", for instance, he speaks the Berlin dialect. The death figure in Franz von Kobell's "Die G'schicht von' Brandner-Kasper" speaks Bavarian, another detail making him appear comically human.

Humanized to that extent, Kobell's death lacks authority. He is not the superhuman power whose talking to man is an act of mercy: he needs to convince Kasper, who otherwise would refuse to die. Compared to Matthias Claudius' "Der Tod und das Mädchen", the dialogue between death and human being here takes a completely different course.

From the very beginning, death is on the defensive. First of all, he does not simply walk in, but politely knocks on the door and waits until Kasper calls him in. When he finally enters, Kasper rather aggressively asks of him what on earth he wants: "Was geit's, was willst?" (p. 362) Death introduces himself and kindly suggests that Kasper go with him: "Kasper, i bi' der Boanlkramer[8] und ho'Di'frag'n woll'n, ob D'nit ebba mit mir geh' willst?" (p. 362) Kasper is not frightened at all. He gives a plain answer, which is no: "na' Bruader, i' mag nit mitgeh'" (p. 362). Being seventy-five, he refrains from arguing that he is too young for dying, but he explains that life is still too much a pleasure to him as to be given up easily: "g'fallt ma' no' ganz guat auf der Welt." (p. 362) Death reacts rather helplessly to Kasper's refusion, stating that it is no use, some day or other he will have to fetch Kasper: "aber hol'n muaß i' Di' do' amal" (p. 362). He seems to have immediately given up his plan to make Kasper go with him at once. How about spring-time, he alternatively suggests, "was moa'st

---

[7] Cf. the plays by Josef Maria Lutz and Kurt Wilhelm, Kurt Wilhelm's novel and the films by Josef von Báky (1949) and Joseph Vilsmaier (2008).

[8] "Boanlkramer" is a Bavarian name for personified death. Translated literally, it means 'merchant of bones'.

ebber in' Fruajahr?" (p. 362). But Kasper does not even agree to a postponed death. Death proposes one season after the other, from spring to winter, but Kasper always has some arguments ready at hand to explain why the respective season is not the adequate time for dying: it is either too hot or too cold, too much to do, or there are too many seasonal events not to be missed, like harvest or hunting. He self-confidently puts forward his arguments, making death's suggestions appear as absolutely inacceptable impositions: "Ja was fallt Dir denn ei', ha' narret, soll' i d' Hirschbrunft hint'lass'n, und die Klopfeter und 's Oktoberschieß'n, waar' nit aus!" (p. 363) Death is not up to Kasper's argumentative power. After he is through with all four seasons, he does not know what else to suggest, and finally falls back on the old topos that living for good is not a solution either: "Ja willst denn Du ewi' leb'n? Dees thuat's nit, Kasper" (p. 363).

Kasper then offers an alternative plan himself: he wants death to grant him another fifteen years. Arguing by analogy, he refers to his father who was allowed to live up to his ninetieth birthday as well. Before death can think of an answer to this cheeky proposition, Kasper changes his strategy and draws on other than just verbal means to persuade death:

> Aber i' glaab', es is g'scheiter als die Rederei da, wann D' mit mir a' Glaasl Kersch'ngeist trinkst, i' hon an' recht an' guat'n und Du schaugst ja so elendi' aus und sper, daß Dir a' Glaasl g'wiß guat thoa' werd' und a' paar Kirternudl hon i' aa' no' dazua. (p. 363)

Kasper waits until death is slightly sozzled and then talks him into letting a game of cards decide. Kasper cheats and wins the game. Death resigns: "I' ko' nix macha" (p. 364). Kasper triumphantly wishes him farewell.

Back in heaven, when St Peter learns of his failure, death is scolded. He defends himself by arguing that heaven is a crowded place anyway and that it does not make much difference whether Kasper arrives late. But St Peter does not accept this, fearing to disorder his bureaucratic system, which allots a specific lifespan to every human being. Death is sent back to earth with the order to definitely take Kasper to heaven this time, if he does not want to lose his job as 'boanlkramer'.

Death is worried about his image. He has given Kasper his word not to come back before he is ninety. If he does not keep it, people might think even worse of him as they do anyway: "es mag mi' a' so koa' Mensch auf der Welt und wann's aufkimmt, daß i' an' schlecht'n Kerl g'macht ho', na' derf i' mi' ninderscht mehr segn lass'n." (p. 366) Death has learned that verbal argument is not the way to get the better of Kasper. He is quite desperate, "g'walti verdroß'n" (p. 365), but finally he comes up with another strategy: persuasion not through telling, but through showing.

He again calls on Kasper, who is not at all pleased to see him again: "Ja was willst denn Du?" (p. 366) Death claims to be on the way to a place from where it is possible to look into paradise and asks whether Kasper wants to take the opportunity to have a look. At first, Kasper refuses, stating again how much he likes being at his own place, but when death promises to drive him home again after an hour, he eventually consents. Confronted with the beautiful sight of paradise, Kasper begins to change his mind. When meeting his relatives again, his decision is made: "i' bleib' da und will nix mehr wiss'n vo' der Welt d'runt und sag' Herr vergelt's Gott tausendmal, daß ma' die Gnad' wor'n is, daß i' daher kemma bi'." (p.

367) By his demonstration, death has finally managed to convince Kasper to renounce his earthly life of his own free will.

As in most of the other literary examples of struggles between death and human being, the death figure wins out in the end. But here dying is not imagined as yielding to a higher power: it is shown as a choice made out of conviction. In Franz von Kobell, death's attempt at persuasion really proves successful. At last, Kasper is convinced and voluntarily agrees to death's suggestion. At no point being helplessly at death's mercy, Kobell's protagonist offers a comforting fiction, not only of dying as a transition to a better form of being, but of dying as a voluntary act.

HUGO VON HOFMANNSTHAL: DER TOR UND DER TOD

Death is a ubiquitous topic in the literature written around 1900. The current notion of living at a *fin de siècle*, at the end of a century, already indicates a preoccupation with transitoriness and the end of time, and the finiteness of life is thematized in various forms both in literature and the arts. One of these forms is again the encounter between human being and personified death. Allegorical personifications of death appear especially in the works of Hugo von Hofmannsthal, who revived the medieval morality play and its characteristic device of personification in his "Jedermann" and, later on, in "Das Salzburger Große Welttheater". With regard to the motif of *arguing* with death, Hofmannsthal's early lyrical drama "Der Tor und der Tod" is of particular interest, as it evolves around a dialogue between the protagonist and personified death.

"Der Tor und der Tod", written and first published in 1893, deals with a man who only learns to overcome his estrangement from life at the moment of death. Claudio, the protagonist, is designed as the type of the highly self-reflective and educated aesthete who rather contemplates than lives his life. The play begins with a long soliloquy, in which Claudio laments his incapability to take part in normal life: to live through the usual ups and downs, to work, to relate to others, to belong and be involved. He pictures himself as being condemned to experience his life as if he was reading a book: "Stets schleppte ich den rätselhaften Fluch / [...] / Mein Leben zu erleben wie ein Buch" (p. 203f.). He spent his whole life waiting for his real life to begin, never making direct experiences, but observing everything from a distance. All his perception is mediated through art, making him see a sunset, as happens at the beginning of the play, as a painted masterpiece. He thus fails to ever feel alive and describes his senses as being dead: "Ich hab mich so an Künstliches verloren, / daß ich die Sonne sah aus toten Augen / Und nicht mehr hörte als durch tote Ohren" (p. 203). At this stage of Claudio's self-reflection, when he presents himself as dead in life, personified death appears in order to fetch him.

The dialogue between Claudio and death runs through different phases. It begins with an introductory phase, in which death introduces himself and Claudio articulates and then overcomes his first shock. After death has revealed his intention, an argumentative phase sets off, in which Claudio draws on various persuasion tactics in order to convince death of sparing him: he presents rational arguments and backs them with physical evidence, he makes concessions and promises to change, he tries to gain death's pity by a pathetic outburst. Death at first stays rather reserved, not being in the need of justifying his doing, before being provoked to action. His means of rebutting Claudio's argumentation are so effective that Claudio immediately has to give in, the dialogue ending with a concluding phase, in which both Claudio and death reflect the results of their encounter.

The introductory phase of the dialogue strongly recalls Matthias Claudius' "Der Tod und das Mädchen".[9] Like the girl in Claudius' poem, Claudio rather uncontrolledly expresses his fear, stammering short, incoherent sentences, and he anxiously begs death to go away again, using the simple imperative "Geh!" several times, which, as in the girl's case, demonstrates unreflected panic:

> Geh weg! Du bist der Tod. Was willst du hier?
> Ich fürchte mich. Geh weg! Ich kann nicht schrein.
> (*Sinkend*)
> Der Halt, die Luft des Lebens schwindet mir!
> Geh weg! Wer rief dich? Geh! Wer ließ dich ein? (pp. 208f.)

Claudio's repeated inquiry about the cause of death's sudden apparition ("Wer rief dich? [...] Wer ließ dich ein?") draws the reader's/audience's attention to the fact that it was Claudio himself who, expressing his weariness of life, unconsciously called for death. By his appearance alone, though, death at this early stage already effects a change in Claudio. The ever non-chalant dandy, who has until then suffered from indifference and lack of feeling, is suddenly overwhelmed by emotion. The reason for his passionate reaction is the incomprehensibility of the event: "Wie packt mich sinnlos namenloses Grauen!" (p. 208). Being "sinnlos" and "namenlos", the experience goes beyond Claudio's book-learning. For the first time, Claudio is confronted by something which cannot be compared to anything. He is therefore unable to keep his usual distance, but has to face up to the situation.

Like the death figure in Matthias Claudius' poem, Hofmannsthal's death repudiates the accusation of being frightful and tries to correct his bad image: "Steh auf! Wirf dies ererbte Graun von dir! / Ich bin nicht schauerlich, bin kein Gerippe!" (p. 209). While death in "Der Tod und das Mädchen" explicitly opposes the concept of death as punishment, the death figure in Hofmannsthal's play implicitly contradicts this notion as well by claiming to be akin to Dionysos, the god of wine and ecstasy, and Venus, the goddess of love: "Aus des Dionysos, der Venus Sippe, / Ein großer Gott der Seele steht vor dir." (p. 209).[10]

Finally a bit more at ease, Claudio greets death and asks for his purpose. The given answer is plain: "Mein Kommen, Freund, hat stets nur einen Sinn!" (p. 209). Death's intention now being explicit, Claudio begins to argue against it. An asymmetrical debate sets off, in which Claudio passionately puts forward his arguments and carefully counters death's replies, using many direct persuasive appeals such as "Merk" (p. 209), "Oh, du sollst sehn" (p. 211), "Denn schau, glaub mir" (p. 212), and "Da schau" (212), whereas death reacts cooly, not once appealing to Claudio's understanding or directly referring to his words.

Claudio's main argument is that he has not lived yet: "Ich habe nicht gelebt." (p. 208). Implied here is the idea of death presupposing life: only who has lived must die. Claudio

---

9 Hinrich C. Seeba also shows some similarities to an earlier example of a literary controversy between life and death, the anonymous "Dialogus mortis cum homine" (probably 12th century) . Cf. Seeba, Kritik des ästhetischen Menschen, pp. 172ff.

10 Richard Alewyn describes Hofmannsthal's death figure as a Romantic synthesis of ancient and Christian thought. Cf. Alewyn, Über Hugo von Hofmannsthal, p. 75.

logically concludes that he, having not lived, is not subject to death. Death does not object to the major premise of this syllogism, that life is a precondition of death, but he contradicts Claudio's notion of not having had a life.

Death has introduced himself as surrounding everything that is 'ripe': "Wenn in der lauen Sommerabendfeier / Durch goldne Luft ein Blatt herabgeschwebt, / Hat dich mein Wehen angeschauert, / Das traumhaft um die reifen Dinge webt" (p. 209). In order to make his statement more convincing, Claudio carefully takes up death's imagery, comparing himself to a leaf which is not yet ready to fall: "Bei mir hats eine Weile noch dahin! / Merk: eh das Blatt zu Boden schwebt, / Hat es zur Neige seinen Saft gesogen! / Dazu fehlt es viel: Ich habe nicht gelebt!" (p. 210).

Death remains unimpressed, answering just one sentence, which negates Claudio's sense of exceptionality: "Bist doch, wie alle, deinen Weg gezogen!" (p. 210). Again, Claudio's reply relates directly to death's metaphoric words. Formulating an antithesis to death's picture of 'making one's way', he describes how he has been blindly driven through time, opposing the image of a dark, uncontrolled flood to the image of a clear-cut way: "Wie abgerißne Wiesenblumen / Ein dunkles Wasser mit sich reißt / So glitten mir die jungen Tage, / Und ich habe nie gewußt, daß das schon Leben heißt." (210). Claudio pleads diminished responsibility due to ignorance. He argues that, if this was already meant to be life, he was not given the capacity to recognize and experience it as such.

Death contradicts: "Was allen, ward auch dir gegeben" (p. 210). He explains what the ability to live a life, which was granted to Claudio as well as to all other humans, consists of: "Im Innern quillt euch allen treu ein Geist, / Der diesem Chaos toter Sachen / Beziehung einzuhauchen heißt / Und euren Garten draus zu machen / Für Wirksamkeit, Beglückung und Verdruß. / […] Man bindet und man wird gebunden […]" (p. 211).

This time, Claudio does not try to disprove death's proposition. Changing his strategy from *confutatio* to *concessio*, he affirms death's concept of life and promises to live accordingly: "Ich will nicht länger töricht jammern, […] Jetzt fühl ich – laß mich – daß ich leben kann! […] Ich dränge mich in jede Lust und Pein […]" (p. 211). In order to show his compliance, he literally refers back to death's "Man bindet und man wird gebunden": "gebunden werden – ja! – und kräftig binden" (p. 211). Claudio aims at a deal: if he is allowed to live on, he offers to change his attitude towards life in return, no longer disregarding, but cherishing it. But death does not seem to be interested in this deal, the stage direction attributing a motionless face, "ungerührte Miene" (p. 211), to him.

As death does not say anything, Claudio draws on the classical strategy of *praemunitio*: he anticipates his antagonist's arguments, "Du meinst, ich hätte doch geliebt, gehaßt …" (p. 212), and tries to refute them in advance. He shows some letters, claiming that they prove his complete incapability to be emotionally involved:

Da schau, ich kann dir zeigen: Briefe, sieh,
Mit Schwüren voll und Liebeswort und Klagen;
Meinst du, ich hätte je gespürt, was die –
Gespürt, was ich als Antwort schien zu sagen?! (p. 212)

Death still not reacting, Claudio grows desperate. Overwhelmed by emotion, he throws the letters at death's feet: "Da! Da! und alles andre ist wie das: / Ohn Sinn, ohn Glück, ohn Schmerz, ohn Lieb, ohn Haß!" (p. 212) It is this switching from logos to pathos, appealing to death's pity rather than his rational insight, which finally makes death lose his temper. Provoked by Claudio's outburst, death becomes emotional himself and calls him a fool: "Du Tor! Du schlimmer Tor, ich will dich lehren, / Das Leben, eh dus endest, einmal ehren." (p. 212). Although, as the short subclause "eh dus endest" implies, Claudio's fate is sealed anyway, death now wants him to recognize at all costs that every human being is given the capacity to live a fulfilled life and that it was only him who has not used this potential: "[…] lern, daß alle andern diesen Schollen / Mit lieberfülltem Erdensinn entquollen, / Und nur du selber schellenlaut und leer." (p. 212)

Since Claudio is not to be convinced by verbal argument, death falls back on other means which he, as a supernatural being, can dispose of. As Claudio tries to support his argument with a physical proof (the letters), death similarly demonstrates the truth of his words by *evidentia*. He brings three dead persons back to life, Claudio's mother, his lover and his close friend, and has them give an account of their lives. The stories they tell all function as counterexamples to Claudio's vita, being full of love and pain and other normal human experiences. They testify the truth of death's statement "Was allen, ward auch dir gegeben" (p. 210), as they are people Claudio could have related to, experiencing the usual "Man bindet und man wird gebunden […]" (p. 211). These authentic testimonies cannot be argued against, and Claudio has to give in at last. He accepts death's lesson, only complaining about its lateness: "Warum, du Tod, / Mußt du mich lehren erst das Leben sehen, / Nicht wie durch einen Schleier, wach und ganz, / Da etwas weckend, so vorübergehen?" (p. 219). In his final reflections, he nevertheless draws a positive conclusion. Fighting with death, he for the first time has developed a sense of being alive. At least for this short time, death has enabled him to fully experience life:

> In eine Stunde kannst du Leben pressen,
> Mehr als das ganze Leben konnte halten,
> […]
> Kann sein, dies ist nur sterbendes Besinnen,
> Heraufgespült vom tödlich wachen Blut,
> Doch hab ich nie mit allen Lebenssinnen
> So viel ergriffen, und so nenn ichs gut!
> Erst, da ich sterbe, spür ich, daß ich bin. (p. 219f.)

Claudio dies with the feeling to have at last overcome his remoteness and desintegration.

Death shakes his head upon Claudio's positive reinterpretation of his decease. Coming back to his former remark about the human ability to make sense of everything, "diesem Chaos toter Sachen / Beziehung einzuhauchen" (p. 211), he wonders at the interpretative power of human beings: "Wie wundervoll sind diese Wesen, / Die, was nicht deutbar, dennoch deuten, / Was nie geschrieben wurde, lesen, / Verworrenes beherrschend binden / Und Wege noch im Ewig-Dunkeln finden." (p. 220) With this concluding comment from death's superior point of view, the winner expressing some respect for his subordinates, the play ends.

"Der Tor und der Tod" is an example of an argument between death and man in which arguing for death does not mean to argue against life. Instead, Hofmannsthal's death is a didactic advocate of life. The debate between him and Claudio centers on the question of 'ripeness', Claudio claiming not to be ready yet and death proving to him that he has had his share. In the course of the argument, death aims at convincing Claudio to accept his death. But interestingly, death nevertheless argues in favour of life. The discussion is not, as is often the case, a controversy between life and death, with the human being representing the claims of life. On the contrary, Claudio despises life, whereas death demonstrates its richness. In Hofmannsthal's play, death postulates to cherish life during lifetime, because to him *everybody* is ripe for death one day, whether they have lived to the full or not: "Doch alle r e i f, fallt ihr in meinen Arm." (p. 211)

HANS HENNY JAHNN: NEUER LÜBECKER TOTENTANZ

The first half of the 20th century was characterized by war. In the arts, the experience of the first as well as the second world war resulted in a wide range of pictures personifying the atrocities of war in all-destroying death figures, a famous example being Ernst Barlach's "Aus einem neuzeitlichen Totentanz" (1916).[11] In literature, allegorical death figures recur as well, for instance in Rolf Hochhuth's "Sommer 14. Ein Totentanz" (reflecting the first world war) or in Wolfgang Borchert's "Draußen vor der Tür" (reflecting the second world war).

The new phenomenon of martial mass murder made possible by technological advancement led to new depictions of personified death. Thomas Theodor Heine's picture "Der Schwarze Tod" (1918), for instance, shows death as a spreader of poison-gas. In two plays of the time, Ernst Toller's "Die Wandlung" (1919) and Hans Henny Jahnn's "Neuer Lübecker Totentanz" (first written in 1930, revised in 1953), death appears split up into two separate figures: old and new death, "Friedenstod" and "Kriegstod", as they are called in Toller. In these literary works an innovative variant of the dialogue with personified death emerges: the discussion between two different deaths who argue about their legitimation and role in human society.

In his play "Neuer Lübecker Totentanz", Hans Henny Jahnn is nevertheless not only concerned with violent death, but also with the more general idea of death as an inevitable human condition. Recalling Martin Heidegger's pessimistic post-war concept of human life as "Sein zum Tode"[12], Jahnn presents life as aiming toward death, as a prolonged mode of dying: "Für jeden, der einmal erscheint, ist auch der Abtritt schon bereit" (p. 148). His play ends with a dialogue between the two death figures and a mother, in which the latter is made recognize this concept as an inexorable law.

The mother, simply called "Mutter" in the play, is not an individualized, but a representative character, standing for the parental generation. Her son, as well, is generalizingly referred to as "der junge Mensch" and represents the generation to follow. The controversial dialogue between mother and death is thus meant as an exemplary conflict common to all mankind.

At this point of the play, the two deaths, the old and the new one, "der Tod" and "der feiste Tod", cooperate and are hardly to differentiate.[13] They are shown at what is presented

---

11 Cf. for further exemaples: Thema Totentanz, pp. 167-249.
12 Michael Walitschke gives an overview over the biblical and philosophical concepts of 'being born only to die' which Jahnn might have derived his idea from. Cf. Walitschke: Hans Henny Jahnns Neuer Lübecker Totentanz, pp. 199ff.
13 For a detailed discussion of Jahnn's two death figures and their relationship to each other, see Walitschke, Hans Henny Jahnns Neuer Lübecker Totentanz, pp. 117-138.

as their 'natural' work, in contrast to the new death's perverted mass murder of young people. Their fetching away of the old in order to make way for the young is to be understood as 'how it should be' and is designed as a critical foil to the violent deaths shown before in the play.

Death figures are generally shown as being superior to humans. They usually know more and they have the power to end human life. This common asymmetry in the dialogue with death is here even increased as the mother is confronted with two death figures at the same time: it is two against one. Jahnn thus very much emphasizes the human helplessness in view of death.

In spite of their superiority, the deaths begin their conversation with the mother as if it were an open-end dialogue whose outcome was not yet determined to be the mother's death. They do make very clear what they want – "Du sollst mit uns gehen" (p. 145) – but they also claim that there is no hurry and that the pros and cons of their friendly "suggestion" could be thoroughly discussed, as if the mother had any choice:

> Der FEISTE TOD Wir sind gekommen, um dir einen guten Vorschlag zu machen.
> MUTTER Das unheimliche Gespräch läßt sich vertraulich an.
> TOD Du sollst mit uns gehen.
> MUTTER Wohin?
> TOD Es soll nichts Plötzliches geschehen.
> Der FEISTE TOD Es soll das Für und Wider erwogen werden. (p. 145)

The mother's reaction is sceptical. She has immediately identified whom she is talking to: "Tiere kennen den ewigen Gegner nicht. Ich spüre ihn" (p. 145). She mistrusts the familiar way in which the deaths approach her ("Das unheimliche Gespräch läßt sich vertraulich an", p. 145) and immediately asks "Wohin?" (p. 145) when they suggest to go with them. The deaths do not answer her question. Like the death figure in Matthias Claudius' poem, they try to soothe their female opponent by presenting themselves as warm and nonviolent: "Unsere Glieder sind warm von der Sonne. Wir sind von der Gewalttätigkeit abgedrängt." (p. 145) But the mother is not easily deceived. Instead, it is only the recognition of her hopeless situation that keeps her from shouting for help: "Ich könnte schreien. Ich müßte schreien. Aber ich würde nicht erwachen. Hier ist eine neue Wirklichkeit heraufgestiegen, die ich nicht mehr bekämpfen kann." (p. 145)

After their introduction, the deaths move on to explain and justify why the mother is to go with them. They refer to a "Gesetz der Nachfolge" (p. 146), a law of eternal succession, which forces every generation to finally make way for a new generation. According to this argumentation, the individual life is part of a greater scheme, in which death is a necessary and useful stage: the ending of one life, but also the beginning of another life. The two death figures apply this argument to the mother's personal situation. In spite of generally talking about 'generations', they try to convince the mother by relating to her own son: "Es geht um deinen Sohn. Um das Glück deines Sohnes. Du sollst mit uns gehen, damit er glücklich wird." (p. 145)

When the mother refuses to consent, the deaths become more explicit. If she remained alive, breaking the law of succession, her son would have to go back to non-existence: "Dein Sohn müßte abtreten, wenn du bleiben wolltest. Er würde einschrumpfen zum

Niedagewesenen, wenn das Gesetz der Nachfolge aufhörte." (p. 146) The deaths also fall back on the classical rhetorical strategy of questioning the adversary's competence. They reproach her of not thinking carefully ("Du beschwerst dich nicht mit gründlichen Gedanken, ehe du antwortest", p. 146) and deny her a proper knowledge of the world ("Dir ist im Weltenhaus noch vieles unenthüllt.", p. 146), implying that they have a much deeper insight into the course of life. On the other hand, they also appeal to her understanding and insight as an elderly woman: "Du bist gealtert und nicht ohne Erkenntnis geblieben" (p. 147).

The mother answers in the same style, attacking the deaths on a personal level. She acknowledges their wisdom, but at the same time criticizes that this wisdom is cruel and cold: "Ich hasse Weisheit, die nicht lächeln kann" (p. 146). She complains about the deaths' callous, abstract way of reasoning and compares them to a treacherous fever trying to overwhelm her: "Was für ein unechtes Fieber hat sich herangeschlichen; das mit Bildern geizig ist, aber mit kalten Vernunftworten Verschwendung treibt." (p. 146) She is not willing to yield to the impersonal rationality of an invisible "law", but wishes to receive concrete evidence for the necessity of her death.

At first, the deaths insist on her rational insight: "Du sollst mit Augen schauen. Mit der Vernunft jedoch mußt du vorweg begreifen." (p. 146) But similar to Franz von Kobell's protagonist, the mother is not to be convinced by rational argumentation only. As in "Die G'schicht' von' Brandner-Kasper", it is only when the deaths change their strategy from telling to showing, that their attempt at persuasion proves successful.

The mother repeatedly urges the deaths to give her a sign of the happiness they have promised for her son's life following her death: "Zeigt mit das Glück, das meinem Kind verheißen worden ist!" (p. 146), "Gebt mir Gewißheit, daß mein Kind nicht verdirbt!" (p. 147). The deaths finally do grant her a concrete sight of the way the cycle of life is going to continue in her case: they let her glimpse at her son hugging a young girl and declaring his love to her. Now, the mother can see what kind of bliss is intended for her son: "Glück heißt die gute Leidenschaft in jungen Jahren" (p. 146), as the deaths have explained before. She has to realize that her son loves another, younger woman now, and that she is going to be replaced. At this sight, she immediately and explicitly gives in, calling all further argumentation superfluous: "Ich bin überwunden. Es ist gar nichts mehr zu sagen. Es ist alles gesagt." (p. 147) The term she choses for her change of mind – "überwunden" – sounds like a surrender after a physical fight. This is not willing acceptance, but resignation. She calls the "Glück" she has seen in her son "brünstiges Verlangen" and opposes it to "Dauer", a permanence she obviously had wished for, but now resigns from: "Glück ist ein Wort wie brünstiges Verlangen. Ein anderes Wort heißt Dauer. Gleichviel." (p. 147) The deaths correct her terminology, making once more clear that it was only an example of an overruling law which she has seen: "Gesetz klingt unerbittlicher; dennoch, es ist ein inhaltsvolleres Wort." (p. 148) They approve of her acquiescence: "Die Einkehr kommt bei dir sehr schnell." (p. 148)

At the end of Jahnn's play, the mother, who is about to fall and has to be supported by the two death figures, shows that she has learned her lesson well. In a final, sad soliloquy, she explicates the "law" the deaths have taught her, describing the eternal succession of generations. Remarkably, though, her sentences still end with question marks, showing that she has understood, but not accepted this harsh law:

Hier ist doch Licht? Auf diesem Weg ging doch mein Sohn vorbei mit einer Braut? Und andre Menschenpaare wandern vorüber? Und wieder andre folgen? Das ist in diesem Jahre so? Im nächsten auch? Und weiter durch die Zeiten? Die Blumen blühn im Mai, und vor dem Winter quellen Früchte an allen Pflanzen?[14] Für jeden, der einmal erscheint, ist auch der Abtritt schon bereit, das Stichwort, das ihn wegfegt? Zeit ist stets eines Wesens Zeit?
Ich hab' begriffen. Mein in meinem Schoß gezeugter Sohn zeugt weiter in einem jüngeren Schoß. Doch einmal noch will ich die Straße entlanggehen, auf der er mir entschwand. Ich werde ihn ganz fern erkennen. Gebt euren Arm mir. Wir wandern bis nach Mitternacht. – Alle gehen die gleiche Straße – ob sie stolpern oder aufrecht bleiben.
(p. 148)

This résumé sounds bitter. The possible comfort which lies in the notion of an endless cycle of birth and death – the idea of life going on beyond the individual's life – is not stressed here, but rather the degradation of the individual and the low status of a single life which are also implied by this concept.

ROBERT GERNHARDT: DER LETZTE GAST

In the second half of the 20th century, after the post-war era, literature concerned with death increasingly focusses on death caused by fatal disease. Realistic representations of physical decline owing to illness become more and more common.[15] Due to the authors' wish to grasp the process of dying in all its clinical and psychological reality, the personification of death is getting rarer. Nevertheless, anthropomorphic death figures still do occur, as for instance in Lotte Ingrisch's play "Wiener Totentanz" (1971), which deals with more general questions of life and death. But even an author like Robert Gernhardt, who died from cancer himself and dedicated major part of his late work to the poetic reflection of this experience, repeatedly made use of personified conceptions of death. The attribution of human characteristics to death always has a comic potential, which is of course attractive for a humorous writer such as Robert Gernhardt.
In Gernhardt's "Die K-Gedichte", published in 2004, which centre on his cancerous disease, death appears in some poems as a personified antagonist who, as a "Vielergestalt" (p. 34), brutally fights life.[16] His earlier work "Lichte Gedichte" (1997) includes poems in which death is talked to. One of these, a poem entitled "So", takes up the same argumentation used by Franz von Kobell's Brandner Kasper. Just as Kasper enumerates the advantages of each season, arguing that none is the adequate time for dying, the speaker here has for every month of the year an argument ready at hand: "Nicht jetzt im Januar, einmal noch Schnee sehn. / Nicht jetzt im Februar, einmal noch Frost spürn. / Nicht jetzt im März, noch einmal das Tauen. / [...]" (p. 201) The basic idea is the same: there is no just time for death. Each period

---

[14] In the first version of the play, the following sentences were included at this point: "Das ist ein Ablauf? Das ist die Ordnung? Das ist die Folge des Gesetzes?" (p. 105).
[15] A famous example which was highly influential on German authors is Simone de Beauvoir's "Une mort très douce", in which Beauvoir tells the story of her mother's fatal disease. German-speaking examples are discussed in: Motté: Der Mensch vor dem Tod in ausgewählten Werken der Gegenwartsliteratur.
[16] Cf. "7. Juni. Rückblick und Ausblick" and "Freund Z oder Beerdigung im Juni".

of the year has its merits and is worth living. The biblical saying "To everything there is a season" (Kohelet 3:1) is clearly refuted. Death is rejected as at all times inacceptable.

In a late poem, though, it is made unmistakably clear that death is not to be overcome. This idea is put in a very simple form, showing death as an ever-victorious, relentless person: "Tod wird durch nichts erweicht: / Siegt." (Später Spagat, p. 42) Another poem describes death as a person who cannot be discussed with: "Nicht durch Worte zu erweichen, / muß man ihn durch Taten hindern" (K-Gedichte, p. 67). Here, the argument with death so often imagined in literature is explicitly exposed as utopian: it is not words, but only deeds, that is medical help, which might have some influence.[17]

In his sonnet "Der letzte Gast", Gernhardt does imagine a dialogue with death, but this one differs very much from the vital discussions usually shown. Here, the human being does not argue against, but in favour of death:

Der Letzte Gast

Im Schatten der von mir gepflanzten Pinien
will ich den letzten Gast, den Tod, erwarten:
„Komm, tritt getrost in den betagten Garten,
ich kann es nur begrüßen, daß die Linien

sich unser beider Wege endlich schneiden.
Das Leben spielte mit gezinkten Karten.
Ein solcher Gegner lehrte selbst die Harten:
Erleben, das meint eigentlich Erleiden.“

Da sprach der Tod: „Ich wollt' mich grad entfernen.
Du schienst so glücklich unter deinen Bäumen,
daß ich mir dachte: Laß ihn weiterleben.
Sonst nehm ich nur. Dem will ich etwas geben.
Dein Jammern riß mich jäh aus meinen Träumen.
Nun sollst du das Ersterben kennenlernen.“

Inverting the common pattern, Gernhardt here makes the human being argue that death is to be welcomed. The lyrical I's main argument is that life means suffering: "Erleben, das meint eigentlich Erleiden." Not death, but life is personified as a "Gegner", as an antagonist in a cruel game. Whereas in Kobell man and death gamble for life, with death as man's opponent, the image of a game of cards is here applied to the relationship between human being and life. Man is involved in an unfair gamble with life, and here it is him who is cheated: "Das Leben spielte mit gezinkten Karten." Disappointed of treacherous life, the lyrical I warmly invites death to come in: "Komm, tritt getrost in den betagten Garten, / ich kann es nur begrüßen, daß die Linien / sich unser beider Wege endlich schneiden." Death is called a "Gast", a welcome visitor. The protagonist wants to ally with death against the life which treated him so badly.

---

[17] Cf. Gernhardt's poem "Ach", in which the lyrical I tries to talk to death, but is silenced by him: "– ach! Ich soll hier nichts mehr sagen? / Geht in Ordnung! Bin schon" (Lichte Gedichte, p. 206).

The human speech ends with the two quatrains of the sonnet. The beginning of the two tercets marks a turning point. Now, death is speaking, and his speech forms the antithesis to the first part of the poem. Suprisingly, death claims that he was actually about to spare his victim, who, in his eyes, led such a happy life that he did not want to take it away from him: "Ich wollt' mich grad entfernen. / Du schienst so glücklich unter deinen Bäumen, / daß ich mir dachte: Laß ihn weiterleben." After this confrontation of the protagonist's thesis ("unhappy life, ought to be ended") and the death's antithesis ("happy life, ought not to be ended"), a conclusion is drawn in the last two sentences. Death explains that the protagonist's moaning about the unfairness of life has made him change his plans. If man does not consider life worthwhile, he is to be taught how much worse than life death is: "Dein Jammern riß mich jäh aus meinen Träumen. / Nun sollst du das Ersterben kennenlernen." By its similar morphological structure, the word "ersterben" refers back to the words "erleben" and "erleiden" carelessly identified by the lyrical I. Thus contrasted with "ersterben", "erleiden" suddenly appears as less bad and "erleben" appears as something positive. The lyrical I's argumentation is proven incorrect.

It remains uncertain whether death is serious when claiming that he was on the verge of going away again or whether he is just making a cruel joke in order to teach the protagonist how mistaken he is. The message of the poem is nevertheless clear: while causing a lot of suffering, life is still to be cherished and not to be carelessly thrown away.

CONCLUSION

The personification of death allows the conflict between life and mortality to take the form of a verbal discussion, which, at first sight, does not differ from a debate between one human being and another. Classical persuasion tactics are used, beginning with a *captatio benevolentiae* on the side of death, whose first rhetorical strategy is often to correct his negative image and establish personal credibility (*ethos*). The human being, as well, tries to win death's sympathy and pity, flattering him and pointing out his/her deplorable situation. Besides these strategies of *conciliare* and *movere*, rational arguments are brought forward. There are certain *topoi* often referred to in the argumentation, such as the necessity to make room for a new generation, eternal life not being an alternative and death as transition to a better form of existence, on the one hand, and the merits of life and the untimeliness of death, either due to lack of age or lack of mental ripeness, on the other hand. Both parts support their arguments by examples or evidence (*exempla, evidentia*), at the same time also making concessions (*concessio*) and trying to arrange a deal, such as postponing death to a later point of time. The often stated hidden continuity of ancient rhetorics can thus be verified for this type of dialogue as well, although its rhetoricity has become less obvious since the 18th century. Due to the general decline of the rhetoric tradition, the adaptation of classical rhetorical devices has become more subtle since then and is no longer shown as openly as in "Der Ackermann aus Böhmen", for instance.

While displaying various features which are common to argumentative communication, the argument between human being and personified death still remains a particular kind of dialogue. The discussion is always existential. The outcome of the controversy is a matter of life and death; the humans argue for their lives. This vital importance makes the debate very tense, and, as it concerns every human being, draws the reader's special interest. Connected to this essential dimension is a basic asymmetry. For the human being, it is usually a forced communication, becoming necessary with the unexpected appearance of death. Death, on the other hand, actively seeks the contact, but, being superior to man, is not in the need of justifying his doing. It usually appears as an act of mercy that he takes the time to discuss the matter at all. The outcome of the dialogue is also mostly clear: whatever arguments the human being may produce, death wins out in the end. There are, of course, exceptions to the rule. In Kobell, the death figure is at pains to convince the stubborn protagonist to consent, and there are also some examples where the discussion with death turns out well, as in Matthias Claudius' poem "Nach der Krankheit 1777", which shows an ill man successfully persuading death to spare him. But differing from what is expected, these suspensions of the common roles almost automatically produce comic effects and appear less serious.

Certain persuasive tactics are specific to this kind of dialogue, whereas others are more or less precluded. An exclusive element is death's ability to draw on strategies which exceed human possibilities. Reflecting the notion that the meaning of life and death is beyond rational comprehensibility, the death figures are sometimes shown to switch from telling to showing, making use of their superhuman faculties. In Kobell, Hofmannsthal and Jahnn, for instance, the deaths provide a very special kind of *evidentia*: they grant a glimpse at paradise or they magically make people appear and illustrate the truth of their arguments. On the side of the human being, certain persuasive strategies appear useless, depending on how humanized the death figure is: the less humanized, the harder he seems to be persuaded. The claim of *tua res agitur*, for instance, the classical strategy of demonstrating that the matter to be discussed is of personal concern to the opponent, is usually not relevant in this kind of dialogue, as personified death is mostly imagined as being only to a small extent subject to human conditions.

Apart from these common characteristics, the depictions of the dialogue of course vary from author to author and from time to time, reflecting personal or contemporary conceptions of death and life. The optimistic naivety of Kobell's tale thus forms a sharp contrast to the bleak resignation of Jahnn's interpretation of the motif, for instance, and Hofmannsthal's story of death teaching to overcome the aestheticist estrangement from life is rather specific to the literature of the *fin de siècle*, whereas Claudius' attempt to reduce death's frightfulness can be seen as a typical feature of the 18th century. The choice of genre also has its impact on the depiction of the dialogue. The drama lends itself to a vivid, rhetorically refined alternation of speech and counter-speech, whereas the epic form embeds the dialogue in descriptive passages, giving room for further background information, e.g., on what is in the back of the mind of the protagonist while talking. The poem requires a concentration of the conflict, reducing the argumentation and enhancing the rhetorical relevance of each single word.

While the contexts and intentions differ in detail, the dialogue with death is usually presented for didactic purposes. Although literary didacticism has had its popular and unpopular phases in the course of history, the advisory impetus seems to have always accompanied this motif. The old concepts of *memento mori* and *carpe diem*, the advice to cherish life with regard to its finiteness, belongs to the common intentions. As Robert Gernhardt's poem "Der letzte Gast" shows, this characteristic message has been living on until the present day. The argumentative conversation with personified death serves as an instrument to impart the intended instruction in a dialectic format, avoiding a straightforward lecture. The rhetorics of the literary dialogue between human being and death are thus part of an overriding rhetorical strategy: the one which directs from the text to the reader, teaching the recipient in a dialogic way a lesson about life and death.

REFERENCES

Alewyn, Richard (1958): *Über Hugo von Hofmannsthal*. Göttingen: Vandenhoeck and Ruprecht.

Claudius, Matthias (1989[7]). *Dedikation*. In Sämtliche Werke. Nach dem Text der Erstausgaben (*Asmus* 1775-1812) und den Originaldrucken (Nachlese) samt den 10 Bildtafeln von Chodowiecki und den übrigen Illustrationen der Erstausgaben. Mit Nachwort und Bibliographie von Rolf Siebke, Anmerkungen von Hansjörg Platschek sowie einer Zeittafel (pp. 11-12). Darmstadt: Wissenschaftliche Buchgesellschaft.

Claudius, Matthias (1989[7]). *Der Tod und das Mädchen*. In ibidem (pp. 86-87).

Gernhardt, Robert (2004). *K-Gedichte*. Frankfurt am Main: Fischer Taschenbuch Verlag.

Gernhardt, Robert (1997). *Lichte Gedichte*. Zürich: Haffmanns Verlag.

Gernhardt, Robert (2008). *Später Spagat. Gedichte*. Frankfurt am Main: Fischer Taschenbuch Verlag.

Hofmannsthal, Hugo von (1952). Der Tor und der Tod. In: H. von Hofmannsthal, *Gedichte und Lyrische Dramen* (pp. 199-220). Frankfurt am Main: S. Fischer Verlag.

Jahnn, Hans Henny (1965). Neuer Lübecker Totentanz. In: H. H. Jahnn, *Dramen II* (pp. 105-250). Frankfurt am Main: Europäische Verlagsanstalt. (2nd version)

Jahnn, Hans Henny (1994). Neuer Lübecker Totentanz. In: U Bitz and U Schweikert (Eds.), *Hans Henny Jahnn. Dramen II*. Hamburg: Hoffmann and Campe. (1st version)

Kaiser, Gert (1995). *Der Tod und die schönen Frauen. Ein elementares Motiv der europäischen Kultur*. Frankfurt am Main, New York: Campus Verlag.

Motté, Magda (1989). Der Mensch vor dem Tod in ausgewählten Werken der Gegenwartsliteratur. In: H. H. Jansen (Ed.), *Der Tod in Dichtung, Philosophie und Kunst* (pp. 487-502). Darmstadt: Steinkopff Verlag.

Pierer's Universal-Lexikon der Vergangenheit und Gegenwart oder Neuestes encyclopädisches Wörterbuch der Wissenschaften, Künste und Gewerbe (1859). Vierte, umgearbeitete und stark vermehrte Auflage, Siebenter Band: Gascognisches Mer – Hannok. Altenburg: Verlagsbuchhandlung von H.A. Pierer.

Rehm, Walter. (1967[2]). *Der Todesgedanke in der deutschen Dichtung vom Mittelalter bis zur Romantik*. Darmstadt: Wissenschaftliche Buchgesellschaft.

Seeba, Hinrich C. (1970). *Kritik des ästhetischen Menschen. Hermeneutik und Moral in Hofmannsthals "Der Tor und der Tod"*. Bad Homburg v. d. H., Berlin, Zürich: Verlag Gehlen.

Tauber, Walter (1989). Franz von Kobell 'Die G'schicht' von' Brandner-Kasper'. In W. Tauber (Ed.), *Aspekte der Germanistik. Festschrift für Hans-Friedrich Rosenfeld zum 90. Geburtstag* (pp. 361-377). Göppingen: Kümmerle.

Thema Totentanz. Kontinuität und Wandel einer Bildidee vom Mittelalter bis heute. Katalog zur Ausstellung vom 5. Oktober bis 9. November 1986. Mannheim: Mannheimer Kunstverein.

Walitschke, Peter (1994). *Hans Henny Jahnns Neuer Lübecker Totentanz: Hintergründe – Teilaspekte – Bedeutungsebenen.* Stuttgart: M and P, Verlag für Wissenschaft und Forschung.

In: Psychology of Persuasion
Editors: J. Csapó and A. Magyar, pp.121-131

ISBN: 978-1-60876-590-4
© 2010 Nova Science Publishers, Inc.

Chapter 5

SMALL INVESTMENT, BIG RETURN: THE ART OF THE PEP TALK

Tiffanye M. Vargas

The University of Texas San Antonio, TX, USA

ABSTRACT

Within the sports arena, coaches and athletes routinely look for ways to improve performance. While most of these attempts tend to focus on physical practice, the roles of the mind, and psychological factors such as self-efficacy, have become increasingly important. Self-efficacy has long been a strong predictor of athletic performance (Feltz, 1988, 1994) and may perhaps be one of the keys to enhanced competitive performance. While verbal persuasion is a source of self-efficacy, one often overlooked aspect of this efficacy source is the pep talk. The pep talk is the coach's final opportunity to help set athletes up for success prior to competition. It is possible that an effective pep talk has the ability to persuade athletes to feel more efficacious (Vargas-Tonsing and Bartholomew, 2006), to appropriately channel facilitative emotions (Vargas-Tonsing, 2009), and to start competition with positive expectations for success (Vargas-Tonsing and Short, 2008). Thus, this overlooked form of verbal persuasion can help create the springboard for a positive cycle of performance. By design, the pep talk leads to feelings of functional emotions and high efficacy which then impacts performance. The improved performance further enhances these positive feelings which should, in turn, continue to enhance performance; thus establishing a positive cycle. It is clear that the pep talk is one small aspect of verbal persuasion with potential for great impact. This chapter will explore the research and theory within this area and make recommendations for the content and delivery of pep talks.

REVIEW OF LITERATURE

Within the sports arena, coaches and athletes routinely look for ways to improve performance. While most of these attempts tend to focus on repeated physical practice, the often overlooked coaching tool of verbal persuasion, and how a coach influences his/her athletes using this tool, has become increasingly important and effective.

Self-Efficacy

Albert Bandura introduced the concept of self-efficacy in 1977, defining it as an individual's belief in his/her ability to complete a specific task. This theory postulates that an individual's efficacy beliefs will determine if coping behaviors are initiated, the amount of effort expended, and how long effort will be sustained when faced with obstacles and aversive experiences. Based on the theoretical tenets of self-efficacy theory, an athlete's perceptions of efficacy are influenced by four principal sources of information: performance accomplishments, vicarious experiences, verbal persuasion, and emotional arousal. Of the four principal sources of information for self-efficacy, performance accomplishments are considered the most influential (Bandura, 1977, 1997). Performance accomplishments, which are based on personal mastery experiences, effect feelings of self-efficacy through the cognitive processing of these past experiences. When events are viewed as successful, future expectations are raised; when events are perceived as failures, efficacy expectations drop. This is especially true when mistakes/failures occur early in the event (Bandura, 1977, 1997). Repeated successes will likely result in strong feelings of efficacy, which lessen the negative effect of future, and occasional, failures.

While considered less influential than performance accomplishments, verbal persuasion is also able to influence efficacy beliefs. Ness and Patton (1979) examined the role of verbal persuasion in a weight lifting task. Participants were told they would either be lifting more weight than they were, or less weight than actuality. Participants, who were told that they would be lifting less weight than they actually did, outperformed the opposing group even though all were actually lifting the same resistance. Later research replicated these findings and showed that false positive feedback increased future bench press performance (Fitzsimmons, Landers, Thomas, and van der Mars, 1991). Wise, Posner and Walker (2004) also examined the effects of verbal persuasion on bench press efficacy. While they confirmed previous findings of the positive influence of verbal messages, they also further validated the characteristics of the influential speaker. The amount of influence wielded through verbal persuasion often depends on the credibility, prestige, expertise, and trustworthiness of the speaker (Feltz and Lirgg, 2001; Wise, Posner, Walker, 2004). Successful coaches are generally thought to encompass these qualities.

The Sports Coach and Verbal Persuasion

Of the original four efficacy sources, verbal persuasion is perhaps the most convenient and readily available tool for coaches, especially in the few remaining moments prior to a game. In addition to verbal persuasion's convenience and availability, athletes consider verbal persuasion to be one of the most effective methods coaches can use to enhance athletes' feelings of efficacy (Vargas-Tonsing, Myers, and Feltz, 2004). Coaches have ranked verbal persuasion highly for both frequency of use and for effectiveness with athletes (Gould, Hodge, Peterson, and Giannini, 1989; Weinberg and Jackson, 1990). Coaches are able to utilize verbal persuasion to provide positive sport-specific feedback that not only aids athletes in their ability to understand how to be successful and utilize positive attributional styles, but also to persuade them that success is possible. Furthermore, by providing athletes with informational feedback through the review of individual and collective strengths, the coach is articulating his/her confidence in the skill of both individual players and the team as a whole.

There are additional forms of verbal persuasion that coaches can use; however, an often underemphasized form of coaches' verbal persuasion is that of the pre-game speech. While these speeches have made their way into pop culture and Hollywood movies (e.g., Miracle and Braveheart), these same speeches have long lived in infamy within the sporting world. Coaches such as Vince Lombardi and Knute Rockne have become part of coaching lore as a result of their powerful use of verbal persuasion and pre-game speeches (e.g., Win one for the Gipper) and further anecdotal evidence continues to point to the effectiveness of this persuasive tool. For example, prior to the Notre Dame 27-23 victory over the University of Michigan, Notre Dame linebacker Pete Bercich noted "I was never so emotionally charged for a game" following the speech from his assistant head coach (http://www.irishlegends.com/pages/calender/9.asp). Many American collegiate coaches have noted the importance of these speeches and the need to prepare in advance to truly impact athletes (Berkowitz, 2003).

This particular form of verbal persuasion is unique in that it represents the coach's final opportunity to impact athletic performance; these words are often some of the last that an athlete hears prior to beginning play. It is possible that an effective pep talk has the ability to persuade athletes to feel more efficacious (Vargas-Tonsing and Bartholomew, 2006), to appropriately channel facilitative emotions (Vargas-Tonsing, 2009), and to start competition with positive expectations for success (Vargas-Tonsing and Short, 2008). Thus, this overlooked form of verbal persuasion can help create the springboard for a positive cycle of performance. By design, the pep talk can lead to feelings of functional emotions and high efficacy which then impacts performance. The improved performance further enhances these positive feelings which should, in turn, continue to enhance performance; thus establishing a positive cycle.

It is clear that the pep talk is one small aspect of verbal persuasion with potential for great impact. However, what is still unknown is how to gain maximum impact with this technique. For instance, some coaches use their final moments prior to competition to remind athletes of lessons learned during practices or of game strategy while others design pre-game speeches that play on an athlete's emotion hoping to inspire them towards great performances.

Information/Strategy and the Pre-Game Speech

Coaches are an important source of external information for athletes. What they say, when they say it, and how often they say it, can significantly alter the learning and development of athletes. In fact, the time spent presenting appropriate explanations and demonstrations have been shown to be positively associated with achievement (Silverman, Tyson, and Morford, 1988) as well as feedback that was descriptive, corrective, or a combination of feedback. (Silverman, Tyson, and Krampitz, 1992). Markland and Martiken (1988) found that successful coaches were significantly different from less successful coaches in the types of feedback given to their athletes. Undoubtedly, the information presented by a coach to athletes is critical for performance.

Madden (1995) found that coaches often used verbal persuasion to offer solutions and commentaries on performance to athletes. Such information from coaches is often related to increases in athletes' efficacy levels (or perceived competence) in themselves and their team (Allen and Howe, 1998) as well as promoting positive and reducing negative cognitions (Anshel, 1990). Informative feedback from coaches may suggest to athletes that they are capable of better performances and that future performance will be successful (Horn, 1985). Athletes use information from coaches to determine ability, effort and expectations of success (Amorose and Weiss, 1998) and informational feedback can help athletes focus and serve as a reminder of game strategy (Theodorakis, Weinberg, Natsis, Douma, and Kazakas, 2000). Information is important to athletes, so much so that McCarty (1986) also noted that a lack of information can inhibit performance.

Clearly, informative feedback from coaches within a pre-game speech may be an important source of efficacy information for athletes. Initial research certainly suggests this to be the case. In 2009, Vargas-Tonsing surveyed 151 competitive soccer players on a day of competition. Participants were asked to complete an efficacy scale upon their arrival to the soccer field, and to retake the efficacy scale immediately following their coach's pre-game speech. The soccer players were also asked to indicate their perceptions of information and emotion present within the pre-game speech. The results of this study found a change in athletes' perceptions of efficacy from Time 1 to Time 2 that was significantly influenced by athletes' perceptions of the informational content within the pre-game speech. This is not surprising as athletes often link their perceptions of ability with informational feedback received from their coaches (Amorose and Weiss, 1998). However, it is important to note that the athletes reported higher perceptions of informative speeches, and that the event in which they were surveyed was a regular season game.

Another study surveyed the efficacy beliefs of 90 former competitive soccer players following a taped pre-game speech (Vargas-Tonsing and Bartholomew, 2006). Each of these athletes were told to pretend that they were in the state championship game and asked to review statistics of their imaginary team and their competitors. Following a one minute perusal of these statistics, these soccer players listened to one of three speeches. The first speech served as a control and discussed what uniform to wear, where to stand during the line-up announcement, etc. The strategic speech offered information about the opponent along with game strategy and the emotional plea speech attempted to focus the athlete on playing with pride and other related emotions. Contrary to Vargas-Tonsing (2009), the results from this study did not show an increase in efficacy for athletes listening to either the strategic or the control speech. While the results from these two studies differed, it is possible that another variable impacted athletes' efficacy needs. Vargas-Tonsing (2009) surveyed athletes on a day of regular competition whereas Vargas-Tonsing and Bartholomew (2006) asked athletes to imagine a championship game. It is possible that the event impacts athletes' preferences for pre-game speech content.

Vargas-Tonsing and Guan (2006) asked 208 collegiate basketball, soccer, football and volleyball athletes to indicate their preference for informational and emotional content within pre-game speeches according to various situations. Situations included a championship game, tournament play, when facing an unknown opponent, when considered the underdog, and when playing teams that they had previously been victorious and been defeated by both small and large margins. Results found that athletes desired high levels of information within the pre-game speech when facing an unknown opponent and when facing an opponent to whom they had narrowly lost to in a previous meeting. Gender differences were also found with female athletes preferring more informational content than their male counterparts. This finding may be attributed to females greater responsiveness to evaluative feedback (Roberts, 1991; Roberts and Nolen-Hoeksma, 1994), their tendency to utilize feedback to gain information regarding their competence (Allen and Howe, 1998) and their ability to be successful (McCarty, 1986; Roberts, 1991; Roberts and Nolen-Hoeksma, 1994). Lenny (1977) suggested that the feedback females receive provides an increase of confidence which moderates their tendency to undermine their possibility of success.

While research is limited regarding pre-game speeches, findings seem to suggest that the perceived informational content of a coach's speech may be a salient source of efficacy information on which athletes judge the strength of their self-efficacy. However, while coaches use verbal persuasion to provide information to athletes, they also provide inspirational messages and encouragement (Bandera, 1997). Thus, perhaps emotion within a pre-game speech also has an impact on athletes' performances as emotional and physiological states are also sources of efficacy beliefs; as such, emotions are also theoretically linked to performance (Bandura, 1977, 1986, 1997; Feltz et al., 2008).

Emotion and the Pre-Game Speech

Research literature suggests that emotions consist of three main elements: physiological changes, action tendencies, and subjective experiences (Deci, 1980; Vallerand and Blanchard, 2000). Physiological changes include such symptoms as increases in heart rate and blood pressure, as well as other changes in the autonomic system. Action tendencies include what is sometimes referred to as the core element of emotion, for example, the tendency to run away when frightened. Subjective experiences, possibly the most fundamental (Leventhal, 1974), refers to what an individual will consciously experience when confronted with an emotional episode (Vallerand and Blanchard, 2000). Through these three elements, it is possible to convey a working definition of the term emotion:

"An emotion is a reaction to a stimulus event (either actual or imagined). It involves change in the viscera and musculature of the person, is experienced subjectively in characteristic ways, is expressed through such means as facial changes and action tendencies, and may mediate and energize subsequent behaviors (Deci, 1980, p. 85)."

Interestingly, this definition seems to imply that emotion can drive behavior, a very powerful concept for coaches and verbal persuasion. Fridja (1986) proposed the idea that action tendencies are inherent in emotion and would lead individuals either towards or away from an object. It has also been suggested that emotions would dictate an individual to attend to immediate concerns and needs (Izard, 1993). More than a decade earlier, Weiner (1977) suggested that motives were largely determined by emotions as well as that specific emotions were linked to specific motives. For example, the emotion of anger would lead to an aggressive play style. Research findings have supported the linkage between emotion and motivational consequences and behavior. Since Bandura's (1977) initial conception of the four sources of efficacy, additional sources have been proposed, including one's emotional state (Maddux and Meier, 1985). Maddux and Meier (1985) believed that positive affect, such as happiness and exhilaration, was more likely to enhance efficacy perceptions than was a negative affect such as sadness or anxiety. Consistent with previous sources of self-efficacy, Scanlan, Stein, and Ravizza (1989) found that positive affective states are associated with elite performers' desire to continue to perform and exert effort. Conversely, negative affective states are related to dropping out of sport (Gould, Feltz, Horn, and Weiss, 1982), decreased performance (Burton, 1988) as well as low personal performance expectancies (Burton and Martens, 1986).

Prior to competing, athletes expectations are often based on the appraisals they make of the situation they are facing. Athletes base these appraisals on the extent to which they view the situation as a challenge (challenge appraisal), the extent to which they view the situation as harmful (harm appraisal) and the extent to which they view the situation as a threat (threat appraisal) (Lazarus, 1999). The intensity of their appraisals can impact their emotions. Cerrin (2003) found that athletes most often associate competition with the terms "threat" or "challenge." She also found that athletes associating competitions with "challenge" reported lower levels of negative emotions and higher levels of interest and enjoyment. Interestingly, the term "challenge" was positively associated with athletes perceiving their emotional state as functional. Emotions appear to offer athletes information on the subjective importance of an event, on their perceived ability to cope with the event, and on the action tendency associated with this event (Fridja, 1986; Green and Sedikides, 1999). However, athletes may not understand emotions or their resultant behavior. Therefore, it is essential that coaches help athletes perceive and control emotion. This is critical for achieving desired performance.

A case study of a coach and his professional hockey team across a competitive season revealed that the coach carefully managed athletes' emotions through various forms of verbal persuasion, culminating with a pre-game speech (Gallmeier, 1987). The coach's speech addressed feelings of readiness, courage, and pride, feelings that may not only help motivate athletes, but that may also help increase athletes' challenge appraisal. The intensity of their appraisals can impact their emotions. Athletes, who experience worry and anxiousness due to perceived threat or harm, will be less likely to perform well. Therefore, coaches should carefully choose words and phrases within the pre-game speech to direct athletes towards a more challenged focused outlook resulting in potentially more facilitative emotions, increased efficacy and improved performance. Coaches' who are able to effectively focus their athletes on these emotions associated with challenge appraisal may gain that needed edge in competition.

The pre-game speech can be used to gain this desired edge in competition. This form of verbal persuasion serves as a "stimulus event" and can possibly be used to invoke desired emotions within athletes. Interestingly, emotional words are responded to more accurately than neutral words (Eviator and Zaidel, 1991) and highly affect-arousing words are better recalled than less emotional words (Bock, 1987). This suggests that in using an emotionally charged pre-game speech, athletes are likely to react and remember the emotional pleas more so than any proffered information. Thus, if a coach can use emotionally charged words to create the appropriate stimulus for the athlete, the athlete should report enhanced emotional arousal and self-efficacy, which should, in turn, improve performance. This is consistent with Vargas-Tonsing and Bartholomew's (2006) research which found that while information within pre-game speeches did not impact perceptions of efficacy, exposing athletes to emotional pleas within pre-game speeches enhanced efficacious beliefs, and increased athletes' predicted margins of victory in an imagined championship game situation.

Vargas-Tonsing's (2009) research on competitive soccer players also explored the impact of emotion on self-efficacy. As previously mentioned, athletes' perceptions of informational, as opposed to emotional, content predicted feelings of efficacy. However, while there did not appear to be a direct impact on efficacy through emotions, the results did indicate that athletes' perceptions of information within the speech did predict changes in functional emotions (e.g., charged, determined and energetic). In other words, athletes perceiving a more informational speech reported higher levels of emotions often considered optimal for soccer (Hanin, 2000). As well, there was a positive relationship between these functional emotions and athletes' reported efficacy. It was conjectured that perhaps these athletes showed this increase in functional emotions as a result of an increase in efficacy (even though the self-efficacy changes were not statistically significant). Essentially, athletes perceiving higher levels of informational content may have also perceived cues regarding their ability (Amorose and Weiss, 1998), which then increased their feelings of efficacy. Lazarus (1991) believed that confidence can generate emotion and is, in fact, often linked with emotion. This would appear to be consistent with social cognitive theory, which suggests that the relationship between efficacy and emotion may be reciprocal (Bandura, 1986). With such a reciprocal relationship, coaches may be able to increase optimal emotions in athletes by increasing feelings of efficaciousness through informational feedback, or, by increasing optimal emotions in athletes, coaches may be able to increase feelings of efficacy. This may offer coaches two different techniques to achieve the same goal.

CONCLUSION

Individuals hoping to effectively utilize the pre-game speech should recognize that research is currently limited; however, the available research has provided some much needed insight into this form of verbal persuasion allowing for recommendations. To begin, it is important to note that the majority of athletes find the pre-game speech to be effective and to have a positive impact on performance. Thus, the pre-game speech should not be ignored and coaches should take the time to prepare speeches in advance and to make them meaningful according to the situation. Breakey, Jones, Cunningham and Holt (in press) found that athletes prefer coaches use shorter and more meaningful messages within the speech. Anecdotal evidence from a study conducted by Vargas-Tonsing and Short (2008) also noted athletes to disengage from the coach following his repeated use of a seemingly meaningless metaphor, when athletes' positions were never discussed (e.g., the goalkeeper), and when the speech was too long. This same study queried athletes for suggestions on making their coach's speech better as well. Athletes responded by noting the importance of the delivery, suggesting the use of more emotion (e.g., speak from the heart, if he was intense) and slightly more information (e.g., more positional talk, what to do and how to do it). Certainly this is not surprising to Kuchenbecker (2003) who suggested that without emotions, it is impossible to excite and push players to a higher level of performance. This idea is particularly interesting as critics of the pre-game speech often suggest that when a coach uses this technique to "pump-up" athletes, the coach is actually at risk for pushing some athletes beyond their optimal arousal and potentially towards a performance decline (Duffy, 1981; Mack, 1999). Rather, perhaps pre-game speeches have the potential to benefit these very athletes. It is possible that an emotional pre-game speech might serve athletes by redirecting worrisome thoughts towards more facilitating emotions as the adverse effects of anxiety on an individual's performance are often due to worry rather than to emotionality (Deffenbacher, 1980; Morris, Davis, and Hutchings, 1981). This concept would seem consistent with athletes' preferences for more emotion within a pre-game speech prior to a championship game (Vargas-Tonsing and Guan, 2007).

Research on pre-game speeches is limited, and there is much more information that is still needed. While this particular chapter has focused on emotion and information, it is possible that additional categories of speech content exist. As well, this chapter focused on pre-game speeches as a form of verbal persuasion, and thus a source of efficacy. However, it is important to note that the pre-game speech may act through various mechanisms on the athletes' performance, of which efficacy beliefs and emotions are but two aspects. Pre-game speeches may also influence performance by impacting other motivational processes such as goal attainment. By offering information on goal progress, the coach helps sustain motivation in athletes, thus promoting performance (Schunk, 1995). Pre-game speeches may also encourage a sense of shared purpose amongst the team which helps to promote team unity and cohesion; cohesion can help lead to a successful performance (Carron and Chelladurai, 1981; Shangi and Carron, 1987). It is also possible that pre-game speeches may help focus athletes on more task/performance oriented behavior, which can promote higher effort (Burton, 1989; Duda, 1988), including when faced with difficult goals (Dweck, 1975). Future research should begin to incorporate and examine the role of these various constructs as impacted by the coach's pre-game speech in addition to the continued role of efficacy.

REFERENCES

Allen, J.B., and Howe, B.L. (1998). Player ability, coach feedback, and female adolescent athletes perceived competence and satisfaction. *Journal of Sport & Exercise Psychology, 20*, 280-299.

Amorose, A.J., and Weiss, M.R. (1998). Coaching feedback as a source of information about perceptions of ability: A developmental examination. *Journal of Sport & Exercise Psychology, 20*, 395-420.

Anshel, M. H. (1990). *Sport psychology*. Scottsdale, AZ: Gorsuch Scarisbrick.

Bandura, A. (1977). Self-efficacy: Toward a unifying theory of behavioral change. *Psychological Review, 84*, 191-215.

Bandura, A. (1986). *Social foundations of thought and action: A social cognitive theory.*Englewood Cliffs, NJ: Prentice-Hall, Inc.

Bandura, A. (1997). *Self-efficacy: The exercise of control.* New York: W.H. Freeman and Company.

Berkowitz, K. (2007, May). The Eloquent Edge, Coaching Management. Retrieved August 6, 2007, from http://www.momentummedia. com/articles/cm/cm1104/edge.htm

Breakey, C., Jones, M.I., Cunningham, C., and Holt, N.L. (in press). Female athletes' perceptions of a coach's speeches. *International Journal of Sports Sciences and Coaching*

Bock, M. (1987). The influence of emotional meaning on the recall of words processed for form or self-reference. *Psychological Research, 48,* 107-112.

Burton, D. (1988). Do anxious swimmers swim slower? Re-examining the elusive anxiety-performance relationship. *Journal of Sport & Exercise Psychology, 10,* 45-61.

Burton, D. (1989). Winning isn't everything: Examining the impact of performance goals on collegiate swimmers' cognitions and performance. *Sports Psychologist,3,* 105-132.

Burton, D., and Martens, R. (1986). Pinned by their own goals: an exploratory investigation into why kids drop out of wrestling. *Journal of Sports Psychology, 8,* 183-197.

Carron, A.V., and Chelladurai, P. (1981). Cohesion as a factor on sports performance.*International Review of Sport Sociology, 16,* 21-41.

Cerin, E. (2003). Anxiety versus fundamental emotions as predictors of perceived functionality of pre-competitive emotional states, threat, and challenge in individual sports. *Journal of Applied Sport Psychology, 15,* 223-238.

Deci, E.L. (1980). *The psychology of self-determination.* Lexington, MA: Heath, Lexington.

Deffenbacher, J.L. (1980). Worry and emotionality in test anxiety. In I.G.Sarason (Ed.), *Test Anxiety: Theory, research, and applications.* Hillsdale NJ: Lawrence Erlbaum Associates, Inc.

DiCicco, T. (2002). Feedback is the breakfast of champions: Communicating with your team. In T. DiCicco, C. Hacker, and C. Salzberg (Eds.), *Catch them being good.*(pp.119-132). New York: Penquin.

Duda, J.L. (1988). The relationship between goal perspectives, persistence, and behavioral intensity among male and female recreational sports participants. *Leisure Sciences, 10,* 95-106.

Dweck, C.S. (1975). The role of expectations and attributions in the alleviation of learned helplessness. *Journal of Personality and Social Psychology, 31,* 674-685.

Eviator, Z., and Zaidel, E. (1991). The effects of word length and emotionality on hemispheric contribution to lexical decision. *Neuropsychologia, 29,* 415-428.

Feltz, D.L., and Lirgg, C.D. (2001). Self-efficacy beliefs of athletes, teams and coaches. In Singer, R.N., Hausenblas, H.A., and Janelle, C.M. (Eds.), *Handbook of sport psychology* (pp. 340-361). New York: John Wiley and Sons, Inc.

Feltz, D.L., Weiss, M. (1982). Developing self-efficacy through sport. *Journal of Physical Education, Recreation and Dance, 53,* 24-36.

Fitzimmons, P.A.; Landers, D.M.; Thomas, J.R.; Van der Mars, H. (1991) *Research Quarterly for Exercise and Sport, 62,* 424-431

Fridja, N. (1986). *The emotions.* Cambridge: Cambridge University Press. Gallmeier, C.P. (1987). Putting on the game face: The staging of emotions in professional hockey. *Sociology of Sport Journal, 4,* 347-362.

Green, J.D., and Sedikides, C. (1999). Affect and self-focused attention revisited: The role of affect orientation. *Personality and Social Psychology Bulletin, 25,* 104-119.

Gould, D., Feltz, D., Horn, T., and Weiss, M.R. (1982). Reasons for discontinuing involvement in competitive youth swimming. *Journal of Sport Behavior, 5,* 155-165.

Gould, D., Hodge, K., Peterson, K., and Giannini, J. (1989). An exploratory examination of strategies used by elite coaches to enhance self-efficacy in athletes. *Journal of Sport & Exercise Psychology, 11,* 128-140.

Hanin, Y.L. (2000). Soccer and emotion: Enhancing or impairing performance? In J. Bangsbo (Ed.), *Soccer and Science* (pp. 69-89). Copenhagen, Denmark: Copenhagen University.

Horn, T.S. (1985). Coaches' feedback and changes in children's perceptions of their physical competence. *Journal of Educational Psychology, 77,* 174-186.

Irish Legends. (n.d.). Retrieved August 8, 2007, from http://www.irishlegends.com/Pages/calendar/9.asp

Izard, C. E. (1993). Four systems for emotion activation: Cognitive and non-cognitive processes. *Psychological Review, 100,* 68-90.

Kuckenbecker, R. (2003). Halftime talk: Use your time wisely. *Success in Soccer, 6,* 24-29.

Lazarus, R.S. (1999). *Stress and emotion: A new synthesis.* London: Free Association Books.

Leventhal, H. (1974). Emotion: A basic problem for social psychology. In C. Nemeth (Ed.), *Social Psychology-classic and contemporary integrations* (pp. 1-51). Chicago: Rand McNally.

Madden, C.C. (1995). The nature and relative importance of coaching communications in Australian rules football. *International Journal of Sport Psychology, 26,* 524-540.

Maddux, J.E., and Meier, L.J. (1985). Self-efficacy and depression. In J.E. Maddux (Ed.), *Self-efficacy, adaptation, and adjustment: Theory, research and application* (pp. 143-172). New York: Plenum Press.

Markland, R., and Martinek, T.J. (1988). Descriptive analysis of coach augmented feedback given to high school varsity female volleyball players. *Journal of Teaching in Physical Education, 7,* 289-301.

McCarty, P.A., (1986). Effects of feedback on the self-confidence of men and women. *Academy of Management Journal, 29,* 840-947.

Morris, L.W., Davis, M.A., and Hutchings, C.H. (1981). Cognitive and emotional components of anxiety: Literature review and a revised worry-emotionality scale. *Journal of Educational Psychology, 73,* 541-555.

Ness, G.R., and Patton, R.W. (1979). The effects of beliefs on maximum weight lifting performance. *Cognitive Therapy and Research, 3,* 205-211.

Roberts, T., (1991). Gender and the influence of evaluations on self-assessments in achievement settings, *Psychological Bulletin, 109,* 297-308.

Roberts, T., and Nolen-Hoeksema, S. (1994). Gender comparisons in responsiveness to others'evaluations in achievement settings, *Psychology of Women Quarterly, 18,* 221-240.

Scanlan, T., Stein, G.L., Ravizza, K. (1989). An in-depth study of former elite figure skaters II: Sources of enjoyment. *Journal of Sport & Exercise Psychology, 11,* 65-83.

Schunk, D.H. (1995). Self-efficacy, motivation, and performance. *Journal of Applied Sport Psychology, 7,* 112-137.

Shangi, G., and Carron, A.V. (1987). Group cohesion and its relationship with performance and satisfaction among high school basketball players. *Canadian Journal of Sport Sciences, 12,* 1-20.

Silverman, S., Tyson, L., and Krampitz, J. (1992). Teacher feedback and achievement in physical education: Interaction with student practice. *Teaching and Teacher Education, 8,* 333-344.

Silverman, S., Tyson, L. and Morford, L.M. (1988). Relationship of organization, time and student achievement in physical education. *Teaching and Teacher Education, 4,* 247-257.

Theodorakis, Y., Weinberg, R., Natsis, P., Douma, I., and Kazakas, P., (2000). The effects of motivational versus instructional self-talk on improving motor performance. *The Sport Psychologist, 14*, 253-272.

Vallerand, R. and Blanchard, C. (2000). The study of emotion in sport and exercise: Historical, definitional, and conceptual perspectives. In Y. Hanin (Ed.), *Emotions in Sport* (pp. 3-37). Champaign, IL: Human Kinetics.

Vargas-Tonsing, T.M. (2009). An exploratory examination of the effects of coaches' pre-game speechs on athletes' perceptions of self-efficacy and emotion. *Journal of Sport Behavior, 32*, 92-111.

Vargas-Tonsing, T.M. and Bartholomew, J.B. (2006). An exploratory study of the effects of pre-game speeches on team-efficacy beliefs. *The Journal of Applied Social Psychology, 36*, 918-933.

Vargas-Tonsing, T.M., and Guan, J. (2007). Athletes' preferences for informational and emotional pre-game speech content. *International Journal of Sports Sciences and Coaching, 2*, 171-180.

Vargas-Tonsing, T.M. and Short, S. (2008). Athletes' perceptions of coaches' pre-game speeches. Manuscript submitted for publication.

Vargas-Tonsing, T.M., Myers, N.D., and Feltz. (2004). Coaches' and athletes perceptions of efficacy enhancing techniques. *The Sport Psychologist, 18*, 397-414.

Weiner, B. (1977). Attribution and affect: Comments of Sohn's critique. *Journal of Educational Psychology, 69*, 506-507.

Weinberg, R., and Jackson, A. (1990). Building self-efficacy in tennis players: A coach's perspective. *Journal of Applied Sport Psychology, 2,* 164-174.

In: Psychology of Persuasion
Editors: J. Csapó and A. Magyar, pp.133-148

ISBN: 978-1-60876-590-4
© 2010 Nova Science Publishers, Inc.

Chapter 6

A VIRTUAL AGENT AS PERSUASIVE TECHNOLOGY

Kaoru Sumi[*,1,2] *and Mizue Nagata*[3]

[1] Hitotsubashi University, Kunitachi, Tokyo, 186-8601 Japan
[2] National Institute of Information and Communications Technology
Seika-cho, Soraku-gun, Kyoto, 619-0289 Japan
[3] Jumonji University, Niiza, Saitama, 352-8510 Japan

ABSTRACT

As a first step towards development of intelligent system using a virtual agent that proactively interacts with a user and changes user's intension according to the user's circumstances, we examine how to react with the user under several emotional situations. We set up scenarios that evoked emotional feelings in a user and controlled the agent's reaction in order to evaluate the user's impression of the agent. In this experiment, we made 96 patterns of content, which were a combination of emotional scenarios, facial expressions, and words used by the agent. The test subjects accessed the content and answered a questionnaire on the Web. After discussing the experimental results, we derive a rule for the agent's reaction favorable to the user on the basis of facial expressions and words.

1. INTRODUCTION

Nowadays, there are many systems that use virtual agents to mediate between a user and the system (e.g. company reception systems, recommender systems). Among commercial products, Microsoft agent [1] is well known to users as a medium to present the Windows desktop. Character agents make the user feel the presence of an assistant to access the system and also give him or her a feeling of affinity with the system.

According to Media Equation [2], people treat computers, television, and new media as real people and places, thereby making the users uncomfortable if an agent behaves in a

---

[*] kaoru.sumi@acm.org.

disagreeable manner. In the field of persuasion technology research [3] it is said that if a user recognizes the presence of something in a computer, he or she will respond to it according to the normal social rules. However, there are still many things that we do not know about how an agent's response affects a user during their interaction.

In the development of intelligent systems, it is important to consider how best a feeling of affinity with the system and show the presence of the system that has human-like intelligent functions such as recommendation or persuasion. Therefore, evaluating the interpersonal impressions conveyed by agents is very important.

Our research group has started to develop intelligent dialogue system that proactively interacts with a user according to the user's circumstances. As a first step, we examine how to react with the user under several emotional situations through the experiment.

We performed an experiment to evaluate how the facial expressions of an agent and the words used by the agent affected users during agent-user interaction. In this paper, we report on our evaluation of the user's impression of agents in emotion-arousing scenarios set up to see how users react to various patterns of agent reactions. In particular, after setting up situations that evoke feelings of "joy", "anger", "sadness", "disgust", "fright", and "surprise" and matching up the agent's reaction with the combination of facial and verbal expressions, we asked users about their impressions of the agent.

2. RELATED RESEARCH

There have been some studies using character agents as the interface of a system. For example, there are many systems such as e-mail filtering systems [4], matching support systems [5], systems for recommending information on Web pages [6], systems for guidance in virtual space [7], and speech dialogue systems [9][10][11]. However, it is not known how and there has been no evaluation of how the agents affect the users. For the purpose of persuading users, systems that use an agent that acts as an authority have been developed [2]. However, interactive patterns of the combination of the agents' facial expressions and words have not yet been evaluated.

The situation in which a message and its contradiction are both presented simultaneously is called a double-bind situation [12]. There has been research on information processing by the memory and the feelings perceived by humans in double bind situation. However, it is not clear what impression the speaker conveying the messages of double-bind situation gives to the receiver.

3. EXPERIMENT ON IMPRESSIONS OF REPLIES FROM THE AGENT

We planned an experiment to examine how the impression that the user gets from the agent's answer is affected by the combination of facial and word expressions. It was intended to clarify the impression that the agent gave the user by answering when interacting with the user in an emotion-arousing scenario.

3.1. Experimental Method

We chose six kinds of feelings. From the total of 216 combinations, covering multiple feelings that the user felt (6 patterns) and the facial expressions for the agent's interaction with the user (6 patterns) and word expressions used by the agent (6 patterns), we selected 96 patterns in this experiment. These covered 16 patterns in each feeling: empathetic words and consistent facial expressions, nonempathetic words and consistent facial expressions, word consistent and facial inconsistent, and word inconsistent and facial consistent. This is because the conditions of nonempathetic and both inconsistent word and facial expressions are nonsensical in normal communication. This is the condition where the word and facial expressions are inconsistent, which is the condition for double bind communication, but it can be considered as either word or facial being empathetic to the user. The case of nonempathetic condition and inconsistent word and facial expressions can be considered as pathological.

A total of 1236 people, 568 male and 668 female (AV. age 38.0, SD age 11.5), were assigned 96 contents. More than ten users were assigned to each content. The analysis sheet is given in Appendix A.

Experimental Materials

1. Six kinds of emotion-arousing scenarios
"Joy", "anger", "sadness", "disgust", "fright", and "surprise" scenarios were selected as scenarios with a high concordance rate in a preliminary experiment as emotion-arousing scenarios for each emotion. These scenarios were described by a male reader reading in a neutral manner.

2. Agent
A female character agent was used to react to the user's emotion.
-Facial expressions
Faces representing "joy", "anger", "sadness", "disgust", "fright", and "surprise" were selected as faces with a high concordance rate in a preliminary experiment as emotional faces. These facial expressions are shown in Figure 1.
-Word expressions
The agent dialog was read by a female reader with emotions conveyed. At first, as empathetic dialogue, "I think so, too" or "I don't think so" as nonempathetic dialog were spoken. Then, emotionally, the dialogue of "that's nice", "that's aggravating", "that's sad", "that's disgusting", "that's scary", and "that's a big surprise" were spoken.

3. Impression evaluation task
In this experiment, we use nine factors: three factors for interpersonal impression evaluation [13] were "affable-inaffable", "serious-unserious", "conversable-inconversable" and original six factors

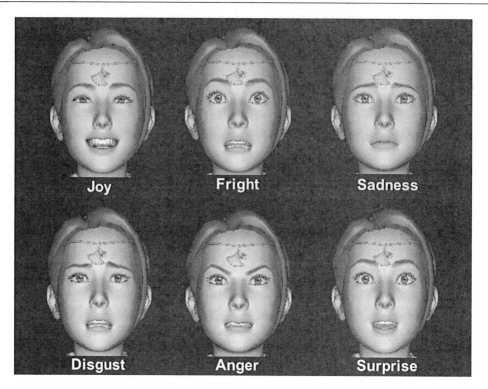

Figure 1. Facial expressions of the agent.

"reliable-unreliable",   "gentle-bitter",   "egotistic-humble",   "empathetic-unempathetic",
"authoritative-unauthoritative", and "offensive-inoffensive".

Content

We prepared 96 contents to cover the combination of emotions that a user feels, the facial expressions of the agent, and the word expressions used by the agent. These contents were developed using the Bot3D Engine [14], which displays an agent on web pages. The Bot3D Engine is an embedded engine for developing software using the Web3D plug-in and ActiveX component. Users can use the 3D agent program only to access web pages that have the program embedded.

Procedure

The examination was conducted in the form of a questionnaire on the Web. The content was displayed on user's own PC monitor after the user accessed the target URL.

1.   Inputting the user's attributes
The users were asked about their sex, age, marital status, occupation, intended purpose of using the PC, and for how long they had been using a PC.

2.   Instruction
Next, the following teaching sentences were presented.
"This examination aims to discover what emotions people feel in various cases. There is no correct answer, so please say exactly what you think and feel. This examination is not a

test of your personal abilities. The answers will be analyzed statistically and private information will not be released. First, please consider the given scenario and then select from the alternatives the emotions that you feel. Next, an animated character will respond to your selected answer. Please answer the question by giving your impression of the character. Your answer should relate only to this scenario. Please do not include feeling from previous scenarios, but think scenario by scenario."

3. Content presentation
Each user was presented with one of 96 contents. One of the emotion-arousing scenarios was read by a male voice. It then asked: "What kind of emotion do you feel?" and prompted the user to select from the alternatives "joy", "anger", "sadness", "disgust", "fright", and "surprise". On the other hand, the female agent on the screen responded with facial and word expressions.

4. Evaluation of the impression given by the agent
Users were asked: "How do you feel about this person? Please answer using the degrees listed in the questionnaire." Five conditional moods in nine answers, "conversable-inconversable", "reliable-unreliable", "gentle-bitter", "egotistic-humble", "empathetic-unempathetic", "authoritative-unauthoritative", "offensive-inoffensive", "serious-unserious", "affable-inaffable" were given and the user selected a suitable answer. The order of the terms was kept constant throughout the questions.

3.2. Evaluation of Agent Impressions by Factor Analysis

A total of 1236 men and women participated in the research. At first, a total of 3400 people were surveyed, but the emotions given in the answers of 2164 were different from the intended emotions for the emotion-arousing scenarios, so we excluded these data. The data were factor analyzed using the principal factor method and a promax rotation.

Table 1. The result of factor analysis

	I	II	III	IV	Commonality
1st factor Friendliness					
Q 1 conversable-inconversable	1.05	-0.09	-0.15	-0.07	0.75
Q 5 empathetic-unempathetic	0.62	0.17	0.04	0.04	0.62
Q 9 affable-inaffable	0.48	0.12	0.38	-0.01	0.80
2nd factor Modesty					
Q 4 humble-egotistic	-0.09	0.82	-0.02	-0.02	0.57
Q 7 no offensive-offensive	0.11	0.71	0.06	-0.03	0.70
3rd factor Sincerity					
Q 8 serious-unserious	-0.16	0.09	0.74	0.11	0.51
Q 3 gentle-bitter	0.41	0.01	0.46	-0.11	0.64
4th factor Trustworthiness					
Q 6 authoritative-unauthoritativ	-0.14	-0.06	0.09	0.72	0.48
Q 2 reliable-unreliable	0.45	0.05	-0.06	0.53	0.62
Factor contribution	3.78	3.33	3.39	1.12	

Four factors were included: (1) friendliness, (2) modesty, (3) sincerity, and (4) trustworthiness. The reasons for choosing these four factors were that the earlier cumulative eigenvalue including the four factors was more than 80% and there was a decline in eigenvalue between the 4th and 5th factors (Table 1).

-First factor: friendliness
Q1(conversable-inconversable),
Q5(empathetic-unempathetic), and Q9(affable-inaffable) indicated higher positive factor loading. The values of Pearson's product-moment correlation coefficient between three questions were r=0.64 (p<0.01) between Q1 and Q5, r=0.70 (p<0.01) between Q5 and Q9 and r=0.66 (p<0.01) between Q1 and Q9.
-Second factor: modesty
Q4(egotistic-humble) and Q7(offensive-no offensive) indicated higher positive factor loading. Pearson's product-moment correlation coefficient between two questionnaires were r=.61(p<.01).
-Third factor: sincerity
Q8(serious-unserious) and Q3(gentle-bitter) indicated higher positive factor loading. Pearson's product-moment correlation coefficient between two questions was r=0.51 (p<0.01).
-4th factor: trustworthiness
Q6(authoritative-unauthoritative) and Q2(reliable–unreliable) indicated higher positive factor loading. Pearson's product-moment correlation coefficient between two questions was r=0.40 (p<0.01).

3.3. Classification of Content by Cluster Analysis

The scores for friendliness, modesty, sincerity, and trustworthiness were defined as the combined value of all the questions for each factor. The data were cluster analyzed using Ward's method, where the dependent variables were the four scores. These four scores were standardized as Z-scores. The average scores of the eight clusters are shown in Figure 2, and the average scores for nine questions are shown in Figure 3.

The main effect of the cluster was dominant at all scales. This is a result of one factor analysis of variance with the scale score as the dependent variable and the cluster as the independent variable for each cluster. (Here, the scales for the factors were: friendliness $F(7, 1235)=41.3$, p<0.01; modesty $F(7, 1235)=37.9$, p<0.01; sincerity $F(7, 1235)=33.7$, p<0.01; and trustworthiness $F(7, 1235)=18.3$, p<0.01).

Our consideration of the characteristics of each cluster, including the result for Student-Newman-Keulsis, is as follows
- First cluster: reliable friend
This cluster is the most intermediate image of a man among all the eight clusters. After the 8th cluster, its characteristics were high friendliness, modesty, and sincerity. Meanwhile, after the 5th cluster, trustworthiness was higher.

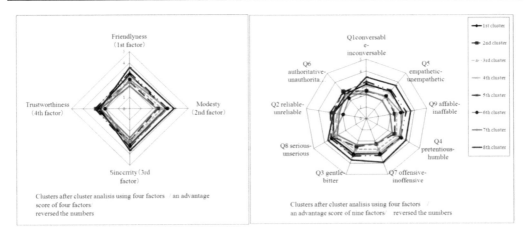

Figure 2. The average scores of clusters   Figure 3. The average scores for nine questions

- Second cluster: arrogant boss

After the 7th cluster, this cluster is second worst in friendliness and sincerity. Here, modesty was the lowest of all, which is similar to the 7th cluster, and trustworthiness was the highest, which is similar to the 5th cluster.

-Third cluster: fulsome offensive acquaintance

After the 7th cluster, this cluster is second worst in friendliness and sincerity. Modesty was the second lowest of all after the 7th and 2nd clusters, while trustworthiness was intermediate.

-4th cluster: friend on nodding terms

Friendliness was intermediate. However, modesty and sincerity were second highest after the 8th cluster. Trustworthiness was intermediate or rather low.

-5th cluster: reliable boss

Friendliness, modesty, and sincerity were high after the 8th cluster, and trustworthiness was the highest.

-6th cluster: younger person on nodding terms

After the 7th cluster, this cluster is second worst in unfriendliness and trustworthiness. Modesty and sincerity were intermediate.

-7th cluster: alarming wicked people

This had the worst friendliness and worst sincerity. Modesty was lowest, similar to the second cluster. Trustworthiness was also rather low. It could be said that this conveyed the worst impression of all.

-8th cluster: congenial chummy friend

This had the highest friendliness, modesty, and sincerity. Trustworthiness was intermediate. It could be said that this was the best impression.

Likewise, considering the conformation of the eight clusters, they can be combined into upper-level clusters. We defined the 8th, 5th, and 1st clusters as "favorable impressions"; the 4th and 6th clusters as "intermediate impressions"; and the 2nd, 3rd, and 7th clusters as "unfavorable impressions".

3.4. Analysis by Each Emotion

We examined the data for each emotion of the users to investigate what the user's impression would be when the agent gave a certain reaction.

From a chi-square analysis of three upper clusters and six emotions, we found that the bias of the content number was significant ($\chi2(10)=25.0$, $p<0.01$), signifying that the emotions and upper clusters were related to each other.

From residual analysis, when the user's emotion was "surprise", the expectation value of being classified into a favorable impression was significantly large while that of it being classified into an unfavorable or intermediate impression was significantly small. When the user's emotion was "anger", the expectation value of being classified into a favorable impression was significantly small, whereas when the user's emotion was "sadness", the expectation value of being classified into an intermediate impression was significantly large.

According to these analyses, (1) the user has a greater tendency to form a favorable impression when his/her emotion is "surprise", (2) the user has a greater tendency to not form a favorable impression when the user's emotion is "anger", and (3) the user has a greater tendency to create an intermediate impression when his/her emotion is "sad".

From the results of a chi-square analysis of two conditions for which facial expressions were synchronized to the user's emotion and three upper clusters, we found that the bias of content number was not significant ($\chi2(2)=2.4$, n.s.), so the facial expression condition was synchronized with the user's emotion and the upper clusters were not related to each other.

However, the conditions of words was synchronized with the user's emotion and the upper clusters were related to each other because from the results of the chi-square analysis of the two conditions where word expressions were synchronized with the user's emotion and the three upper clusters, the content number bias was significant ($\chi2(2)=24.6$, $p<0.01$). From the results of residual analysis, for the condition where word expressions were synchronized with the user's emotion, the expectation value of it being classified into a favorable impression was significantly large and that of it being classified into an unfavorable one was significantly small. On the other hand, when the words were not synchronized with the user's emotion, the expectation value of it being classified into a favorable impression was significantly small and the expectation value of it being classified into an unfavorable one was significantly large.

According to these analyses, the synchronization of the agent's words with the user's emotion has a major impact on the impression of the agent as perceived by the user. However, the synchronization of facial expressions of the agent with the user's emotion does not have a major impact on the creation of an impression.

Next, we examined the data to see whether the user's impression of the agent obeyed some rules of combination between the agent's words and facial expressions.

1. Case where the user's emotion was "joy" (Table 2)

Essentially, the condition wherein the agent's word expressions were synchronized with the user's emotion led to a more favorable impression. Among such conditions, favorable impressions were obtained when the agent's facial expression was "surprise" , "sadness", or "fright". The reason for this could be that these facial expressions were recognized as "joy" because they are more empathetic than the facial expression for "joy" itself. On the other hand, user emotions of "anger" and "disgust" led to unfavorable impressions. This might be because these facial expressions negate the emotion of "joy".

Among the conditions wherein the agent's word expressions were not synchronized with the user's emotion, combining "sadness" words led to an intermediate impression, whereas combining "surprise", "disgust" and "anger" words led to unfavorable impressions.

2. Case where the user's emotion was "surprise" (Table 2)

When the user's emotion was "surprise", the user had a greater tendency to create favorable impressions of the agent by its nature. It could be that the scenario of "surprise" itself tends to create several emotional aspects. Reacting to "sadness" or "disgust" as both facial and word expressions creates an unfavorable impression via the user's "surprise" emotion.

3. Case where the user's emotion was "fright" (Table 2)

Essentially, the condition where the agent's word expressions were synchronized with the user's emotion led to more favorable impressions. Among such conditions, agent facial expression of "sadness" and "disgust" led to favorable impressions. The reason for this could be that these facial expressions are recognized as "fright" and are more empathetic than the facial expression of "fright" itself. On the other hand, user emotions of "anger" and "joy" led to intermediate impressions. The reason might be that these facial expressions were recognized as "fright" because of an overwhelming big facial motion conveyed by this facial expression.

Among the conditions where the agent's word expressions were not synchronized with the user's emotion, combining "joy" or "sadness" words with facial expressions led to intermediate impressions, while combining "surprise", "disgust", and "anger" words led to unfavorable impressions.

4. Case where the user's emotion was "anger" (Table 3)

When the user's emotion was "anger", it was difficult to create a favorable impression. Essentially, the condition where the agent's word expressions were synchronized with the user's emotion led to more favorable impressions. Among such conditions user emotion of "sadness" and "fright" led to unfavorable impressions. Among the conditions where the agent's word expressions were not synchronized with the user's emotion, combining "sadness" and "fright" led to intermediate impressions. Cases not mentioned above led to unfavorable impressions.

5. Case where the user's emotion was "disgust" (Table 3)

Essentially, the condition where the agent's word expressions were synchronized with the user's emotion led to more favorable impressions.

Reacting to "fright" or "disgust" word expressions led to intermediate impressions. Among the conditions where the agent's word and/or facial expressions were not

Table 2. The user's impression of the agent

Emotion "Joy"

Impression	Cluster	I Friendliness	II Modesty	III	IV Trust	ID	Code
Favorable impression	8th cluster / Congenial chummy friend	◎	◎	◎	△	D-13	Jo Su Jo
						C-11	Jo Fr Jo
	5th cluster / Reliable boss	○	○	○	◎	D-14	Jo Sa Jo
	1st cluster / Reliable friend	○	○	○	○	B-09	Jo Jo Fr
						E-01	Jo Jo Jo
						F-08	Jo Su Su
Intermediate impression	4th cluster / Friend on nodding terms	△	○	○	△	A-16	Jo Jo Sa
						D-07	Jo Ag Jo
						E-02	Jo Sa Sa
	6th cluster / Junior fellow on nodding terms	×	△	△	××		
Unfavorable impression	2nd cluster / Arrogance boss	×	××	×	◎		
	3rd cluster / Fulsome offensive acquaintance	×	×	×	△	B-05	Jo Jo Su
						D-10	Jo Dt Jo
	7th cluster / Alarming wicked people	××	××	××	××	B-12	Jo Jo Dt
						B-15	Jo Jo Ag
						F-03	Jo Fr Fr
						F-04	Jo Dt Dt
						F-06	Jo Ag Ag

Emotion "Fright"

Impression	Cluster	I Friendliness	II Modesty	III	IV Trust	ID	Code
Favorable impression	8th cluster / Congenial chummy friend	◎	◎	◎	△	C-04	Fr Sa Fr
	5th cluster / Reliable boss	○	○	○	◎	C-06	Fr Dt Fr
	1st cluster / Reliable friend	○	○	○	○	B-01	Fr Fr Fr
						D-16	Fr Su Fr
Intermediate impression	4th cluster / Friend on nodding terms	△	○	○	△	C-05	Fr Ag Fr
						C-14	Fr Jo Fr
						E-03	Fr Jo Jo
	6th cluster / Junior fellow on nodding terms	×	△	△	××	E-12	Fr Sa Sa
Unfavorable impression	2nd cluster / Arrogance boss	×	××	×	◎	A-07	Fr Fr Dt
						A-08	Fr Fr Ag
	3rd cluster / Fulsome offensive acquaintance	×	×	×	△	A-09	Fr Fr Jo
						A-10	Fr Fr Sa
						B-02	Fr Fr Su
						E-13	Fr Ag Ag
						F-11	Fr Su Su
	7th cluster / Alarming wicked people	××	××	××	××	E-15	Fr Dt Dt

Emotion "Surprise"

Impression	Cluster	I Friendliness	II Modesty	III	IV Trust	ID	Code
Favorable impression	8th cluster / Congenial chummy friend	◎	◎	◎	△		
	5th cluster / Reliable boss	○	○	○	◎	A-03	Su Su Dt
						A-05	Su Su Jo
						A-06	Su Su Sa
						C-12	Su Ag Su
						C-15	Su Sa Su
						C-16	Su Fr Su
						E-08	Su Jo Jo
						E-11	Su Fr Fr
	1st cluster / Reliable friend	○	○	○	○	A-01	Su Su Su
						A-02	Su Su Fr
						A-04	Su Su Ag
						C-09	Su Dt Su
						C-13	Su Jo Su
						E-10	Su Ag Ag
Intermediate impression	4th cluster / Friend on nodding terms	△	○	○	△		
	6th cluster / Junior fellow on nodding terms	×	△	△	××		
Unfavorable impression	2nd cluster / Arrogance boss	×	××	×	◎		
	3rd cluster / Fulsome offensive acquaintance	×	×	×	△	E-07	Su Sa Sa
						E-14	Su Dt Dt
	7th cluster / Alarming wicked people	××	××	××	××		

Table 3. The user's impression of the agent

Emotion "Disgust"

Impression	Cluster	I Friendliness	II Modesty	III	IV Trust	No.	Expression
Favorable impression	8th cluster / Congenial chummy friend	◎	◎	◎	△		
	5th cluster / Reliable boss	○	○	○	◎	C-01	Dt Dt Dt
						E-05	Dt Sa Sa
	1st cluster / Reliable friend	○	○	○	○	C-02	Dt Ag Dt
						C-08	Dt Sa Dt
						D-09	Dt Fr Dt
Intermediate impression	4th cluster / Friend on nodding terms	△	○	○	△	B-07	Dt Dt Fr
						C-10	Dt Jo Dt
	6th cluster / Junior fellow on nodding terms	×	△	△	× ×	D-06	Dt Fr Dt
						Γ-15	Dt Fr Fr
Unfavorable impression	2nd cluster / Arrogance boss	×	× ×	×	◎	A-11	Dt Dt Ag
						E-16	Dt Ag Ag
	3rd cluster / Fulsome offensive acquaintance	×	×	×	△	A-12	Dt Dt Jo
						A-13	Dt Dt Sa
						B-03	Dt Dt Su
						E-04	Dt Jo Jo
						Γ-14	D L3u 3u
	7th cluster / Alarming wicked people	× ×	× ×	× ×	× ×		

Emotion "Anger"

Impression	Cluster	I Friendliness	II Modesty	III	IV Trust	No.	Expression
Favorable impression	8th cluster / Congenial chummy friend	◎	◎	◎	△		
	5th cluster / Reliable boss	○	○	○	◎		
	1st cluster / Reliable friend	○	○	○	○	D-01	Ag Ag Ag
						D-02	Ag Dt Ag
						D-12	Ag Su Ag
Intermediate impression	4th cluster / Friend on nodding terms	△	○	○	△	A-14	Ag Ag Sa
						B-08	Ag Ag Fr
						C-07	Ag Jo Ag
	6th cluster / Junior fellow on nodding terms	×	△	△	× ×	E-09	Ag Sa Sa
						F-13	Ag Fr Fr
Unfavorable impression	2nd cluster / Arrogance boss	×	× ×	×	◎	B-11	Ag Ag Fr
	3rd cluster / Fulsome offensive acquaintance	×	×	×	△	B-04	Ag Ag Su
						D-05	Ag Fr Ag
						C-03	Ag Sa Ag
						E-06	Ag Jo Jo
						F-16	Ag Dt Dt
	7th cluster / Alarming wicked people	× ×	× ×	× ×	× ×	A-15	Ag Ag Jo
						F-10	Ag Su Su

Emotion "Sadness"

Impression	Cluster	I Friendliness	II Modesty	III	IV Trust	No.	Expression
Favorable impression	8th cluster / Congenial chummy friend	◎	◎	◎	△	D-08	Sa Dt Sa
	5th cluster / Reliable boss	○	○	○	◎	B-16	Sa Sa Jo
	1st cluster / Reliable friend	○	○	○	○	F-01	Sa Sa Sa
						F-02	Sa Jo Jo
Intermediate impression	4th cluster / Friend on nodding terms	△	○	○	△	B-06	Sa Sa Fr
						D-03	Sa Ag Sa
						D-04	Sa Fr Sa
						D-11	Sa Jo Sa
						D-15	Sa Su Sa
	6th cluster / Junior fellow on nodding terms	×	△	△	× ×	B-10	Sa Sa Fr
						F-12	Sa Fr Fr
Unfavorable impression	2nd cluster / Arrogance boss	×	× ×	×	◎		
	3rd cluster / Fulsome offensive acquaintance	×	×	×	△	B-13	Sa Sa Dt
	7th cluster / Alarming wicked people	× ×	× ×	× ×	× ×	B-14	Sa Sa Ag
						F-05	Sa Dt Dt
						F-07	Sa Su Su
						F-09	Sa Ag Ag

Jo: Joy
Fr: Fright
Su: Surprise
Dt: Disgust
Ag: Anger
Sa: Sadness

* Right side of content number describes user's emotion, agent's facial expression, and word expression.

[shaded] emotion and word consistent (face non-consistent)
emotion and face consistent (word non-consistent)
emotion/face and word non-consisymt
all consistent

synchronized with the user's emotion, "joy", "surprise", and "anger" led to unfavorable impressions.

6.   Case where the user's emotion was "sadness" (Table 3)

This condition had a greater tendency to create intermediate impressions. In particular, the condition where the agent's word expressions were synchronized with the user's emotion led to a greater tendency for intermediate impressions. Among the conditions where the agent's word expressions were not synchronized with the user's emotion, combining "anger" led to intermediate impressions, while combining "disgust" and "anger" led to unfavorable impressions.

4. DISCUSSION

We conducted the experiment on how the user felt about the agent's reaction by setting up an emotion-arousing scenario for the user. Four factors were extracted by using factor analysis. Eight clusters were indicated by cluster analysis by using four factors as the dependent variable. Favorable, intermediate, and unfavorable impressions fell in category of higher-level clusters among these eight clusters. Therefore, we focused on the relationship between agent reaction and the higher clusters.

The synchronization of the agent's words with the user's emotion has a major impact on the impression of the agent as perceived by the user. However, the synchronization of facial expressions of the agent with the user's emotion does not have a major impact on the creation of an impression.

First, we predicted that words and facial expressions reflected on the emotions aroused by the scenario would lead to the most favorable impression, so we set these data as the control group. In fact, there were more favorable impressions than those obtained for the control group. For example, the words and facial expressions were "joy" when the user's emotion was "joy" for the control group. It is very interesting that when the user's emotion was "joy", the agent's words for "joy" with facial expressions of "surprise", "sadness", or "fright" were most favorable. On the other hand, when the user's emotion was "fright", the agent's words for "fright" with facial expressions of "disgust" or "sadness" were the most favorable.

These facial expressions were recognized as the emotion conveyed by the words and were more empathetic and somewhat meaningful emotions. For example, when the user's emotion was "joy", the agent's words of "joy" with facial expressions of "surprise" or "fright" might have been recognized as the agent being exaggeratedly surprised at the "joy" scenario. When the user's emotion was "joy", the agent's words of "joy" with facial expressions of "sadness" might have been recognized as the agent being highly pleased from the heart at the "joy" scenario. When the user's emotion was "fright", the agent's words of "fright" with facial expressions of "sadness" might have been recognized as the agent grieving deeply at the user's "fright" scenario. When the user's emotion was "fright", the agent's words of "fright" with facial expressions of "disgust" might have been recognized as the agent feeling deep hate at the user's "fright" scenario.

Through these observations, we concluded that there is a rule for facial expressions: in a certain scenario, synchronizing foreseen emotion of the user caused by the situation will make a favorable impression. For example, when the user has the emotion of "joy", he/she wants someone to be surprised or highly pleased. Then, showing surprised or highly pleased face expression make the user feels favorable impression. When the user has the emotion of "fright", he/she wants someone to grieve deeply or disgust. Then, showing grieved or disgust face expression make the user feels favorable impression. Users want the agent to ooze synchronized their foreseen emotion by hearing the news instead of simply showing synchronized reaction according to emotion at present time.

The ability to do this is known as the emotional intelligence quotient (EQ) [15], which is a measure of the ability to understand the feelings of the partner and maintain human relations well.

This facial expression rule is a kind of EQ rules as we can often see service-minded persons show their sympathy with very sad face when they on hearing bad news. In this case, the emotional situation was "disgust", their word is "disgust" with facial expressions of "sad". These patterns are consistent with the cluster of favorable impressions in the result of the experiment. These persons favorably impress, as we often see them employed as salesmen having some technical know-how in order to make themselves look good. We often see this type of person in our country and they are accepted as favorable. However, this facial expression might be considered as a specific feature of Japanese culture. It needs more examination, taking into account diverse nationalities.

This facial expression rule is a technique of foreseeing the other's emotion and the agent can behave proactively by reading the other's feelings.

5. CONCLUSION

As a purpose of developing intelligent system using virtual agent which interacts with a user proactively according to the user's circumstances, we evaluated the user's impression of agents by setting up an emotion-arousing scenario and observed how the users reacted to various patterns of agent reactions. The results of the experiment reveal the rule for creating an agent which reacts proactively using facial expressions.

REFERENCES

[1] Microsoft: Developing for Microsoft Agent , Microsoft Press, Redmond, WA(1998).
[2] Reeves, Byron and Clifford Nass The Media Equation: How People Treat Computers, Television, and New Media Like Real People and Places, Cambridge University Press, 1996.
[3] B.J.Fogg: Persuasive Technology –Using Computers to Change What We Think and Do-, Elsevier, 2003.
[4] Pattie Maes: Agent that Reduce Work and Information Overload, Communications of the ACM, Vol.37, No.7, pp.31-40, ACM, 1994

[5]   Yasuyuki Sumi and Kenji Mase: Interface agents that facilitate knowledge interactions between community members, H. Prendinger and M. Ishizuka eds., Life-Like Characters: Tools, Affective Functions, and Applications, pp.405-427, Springer, January, 2004.

[6]   E. André, J. Müller, and T. Rist. WebPersona: A Life-Like Presentation Agent for the World-Wide Web. In Proc. of the IJCAI-97 Workshop on Animated Interface Agents: Making them Intelligent, Nagoya, 1997.

[7]   Stacy Marsella, Jonathan Gratch and Jeff Rickel: Expressive Behaviors for Virtual World, Life-Like Characters, Helmet Prendinger and Mitsuru Ishizuka Eds.,pp.163-187, Springer, 2004.

[8]   Kitamura, Y., Nagata, N., Ueno, M., and Nagamune, M.: Toward Web Information Integration on 3D Virtual Space. In F. Kishino et al. (Eds.), Entertainment Computing - ICEC2005, Lecture Notes in Computer Science 3711, Berlin et al.: Springer-Verlag, 445-455, 2005.

[9]   Nagao, K., Takeuchi, A. : Speech dialogue with facial displays: Multimodal human-computer conversation, Proc. ACL-94, pp.102-109 (1994).

[10] S.Seto, H.Kanazawa, H.Shinchi, Y.Takebayashi: Spontaneous speech dialogue system TOSBURG II and its evaluation, International Symposium on Spoken Dialogue, ISSD-93, Vol.15, Issue 3-4, pp.41-44 (1993.10).

[11] Shin-ichi Kawamoto, Hiroshi Shimodaira, Tsuneo Nitta, Takuya Nishimoto, Satoshi Nakamura, Katsunobu Itou, Shigeo Morishima, Tatsuo Yotsukura, Atsuhiko Kai, Akinobu Lee, Yoichi Yamashita, Takao Kobayashi, Keiichi Tokuda, Keikichi Hirose, Nobuaki Minematsu, Atsushi Yamada, Yasuharu Den, Takehito Utsuro, Shigeki Sagayama: Galatea: Open-source Software for Developing Anthropomorphic Spoken Dialog Agents, Life-Like Characters, Helmet Prendinger and Mitsuru Ishizuka Eds.,pp.163-187, Springer, 2004.

[12] Bateson, G., Jackson, D. D., Jay Haley and Weakland, J., "Toward a Theory of Schizophrenia", Behavioral Science, vol.1, 1956, 251-264, 1956

[13] Ikuo Daibo: Sansya kan communication ni okeru taijininsyo to genngo katudousei, jikkenn shinri gaku kenkyu,18, 21-34, 1978 (in Japanese)

[14] Bot3D: http://www.atom.co.jp/bot/

[15] Daniel Goleman: Emotional Intelligence, Bantam Dell Pub Group, 1995.

Appendix: A (1/2)

Content No.	Condition	User's emotion	Agent's word expression	Agent's facial expression	Total	(male : female)	Average Age	(SD)
A-01	all consistent	surprise	surprise	surprise	12	7 : 5	38.1	10.8
B-01	all consistent	fright	fright	fright	35	14 : 21	37.1	13.1
C-01	all consistent	disgust	disgust	disgust	12	5 : 7	33.1	7.1
D-01	all consistent	anger	anger	anger	11	8 : 3	40.8	12.4
E-01	all consistent	joy	joy	joy	13	7 : 6	40.4	12.1
F-01	all consistent	sadness	sadness	sadness	11	9 : 2	37.0	8.6
A-02	emotion and face consistent (word non-consistent)	surprise	surprise	fright	11	6 : 5	36.8	10.6
A-03	emotion and face consistent (word non-consistent)	surprise	surprise	disgust	10	5 : 5	40.4	13.3
A-04	emotion and face consistent (word non-consistent)	surprise	surprise	anger	11	6 : 5	33.1	5.6
A-05	emotion and face consistent (word non-consistent)	surprise	surprise	joy	10	4 : 6	46.8	16.6
A-06	emotion and face consistent (word non-consistent)	surprise	surprise	sadness	12	6 : 6	38.3	13.1
A-07	emotion and face consistent (word non-consistent)	fright	fright	disgust	12	2 : 10	38.7	11.6
A-08	emotion and face consistent (word non-consistent)	fright	fright	anger	11	3 : 8	38.1	17.8
A-09	emotion and face consistent (word non-consistent)	fright	fright	joy	64	30 : 34	38.8	12.5
A-10	emotion and face consistent (word non-consistent)	fright	fright	sadness	24	12 : 12	35.9	9.9
B-02	emotion and face consistent (word non-consistent)	fright	fright	surprise	11	5 : 6	32.7	9.5

Appendix: A (2/2)

Content No.	Condition	User's emotion	Agent's word expression	Agent's facial expression	Total	(male	:	female)	Average Age	SD
A-12	emotion and face consistent (word non-consistent)	disgust	disgust	joy	11	(7	:	4)	37.5	(12.5)
A-13	emotion and face consistent (word non-consistent)	disgust	disgust	sadness	10	(5	:	5)	43.3	(11.5)
B-03	emotion and face consistent (word non-consistent)	disgust	disgust	surprise	13	(8	:	5)	33.9	(9.4)
B-07	emotion and face consistent (word non-consistent)	disgust	disgust	fright	11	(1	:	10)	44.5	(17.2)
B-04	emotion and face consistent (word non-consistent)	anger	anger	surprise	14	(10	:	4)	36.4	(12.4)
A-14	emotion and face consistent (word non-consistent)	anger	anger	sadness	28	(14	:	14)	39.0	(11.5)
A-15	emotion and face consistent (word non-consistent)	anger	anger	joy	11	(8	:	3)	39.8	(10.7)
B-08	emotion and face consistent (word non-consistent)	anger	anger	fright	10	(4	:	6)	41.2	(10.0)
B-11	emotion and face consistent (word non-consistent)	anger	anger	disgust	10	(7	:	3)	38.1	(14.3)
B-05	emotion and face consistent (word non-consistent)	joy	joy	surprise	14	(9	:	5)	39.9	(12.8)
B-09	emotion and face consistent (word non-consistent)	joy	joy	fright	10	(4	:	6)	34.9	(12.4)
B-12	emotion and face consistent (word non-consistent)	joy	joy	disgust	10	(3	:	7)	36.6	(12.2)
B-15	emotion and face consistent (word non-consistent)	joy	joy	anger	10	(4	:	6)	33.2	(8.8)
B-06	emotion and face consistent (word non-consistent)	sadness	sadness	surprise	11	(7	:	4)	42.1	(12.3)
B-10	emotion and face consistent (word non-consistent)	sadness	sadness	fright	11	(4	:	7)	37.3	(16.4)
B-13	emotion and face consistent (word non-consistent)	sadness	sadness	disgust	10	(4	:	6)	39.1	(13.6)
B-14	emotion and face consistent (word non-consistent)	sadness	sadness	anger	11	(6	:	5)	39.5	(7.9)
C-09	emotion and word consistent (face non-consistent)	surprise	disgust	surprise	18	(6	:	12)	41.2	(14.3)
C-12	emotion and word consistent (face non-consistent)	surprise	anger	surprise	11	(2	:	9)	34.8	(12.5)
C-13	emotion and word consistent (face non-consistent)	surprise	joy	surprise	13	(7	:	6)	36.5	(10.2)
C-15	emotion and word consistent (face non-consistent)	surprise	sadness	surprise	10	(4	:	6)	34.4	(9.6)
C-16	emotion and word consistent (face non-consistent)	surprise	fright	surprise	15	(6	:	9)	37.0	(12.4)
C-04	emotion and word consistent (face non-consistent)	fright	sadness	fright	10	(5	:	5)	38.9	(8.0)
C-05	emotion and word consistent (face non-consistent)	fright	anger	fright	11	(1	:	10)	37.1	(15.6)
C-06	emotion and word consistent (face non-consistent)	fright	disgust	fright	10	(5	:	5)	36.7	(8.2)
C-14	emotion and word consistent (face non-consistent)	fright	joy	fright	14	(8	:	6)	35.9	(10.1)
D-16	emotion and word consistent (face non-consistent)	fright	surprise	fright	10	(4	:	6)	37.7	(8.1)
C-02	emotion and word consistent (face non-consistent)	disgust	anger	disgust	13	(7	:	6)	39.2	(10.0)
C-08	emotion and word consistent (face non-consistent)	disgust	sadness	disgust	11	(5	:	6)	39.9	(16.4)
C-10	emotion and word consistent (face non-consistent)	disgust	joy	disgust	10	(4	:	6)	36.8	(12.7)
D-06	emotion and word consistent (face non-consistent)	disgust	fright	disgust	11	(6	:	5)	40.2	(11.4)
D-09	emotion and word consistent (face non-consistent)	disgust	surprise	disgust	12	(4	:	8)	40.0	(9.5)
C-03	emotion and word consistent (face non-consistent)	anger	sadness	anger	10	(6	:	4)	42.7	(17.2)
C-07	emotion and word consistent (face non-consistent)	anger	joy	anger	12	(3	:	9)	39.9	(11.6)
D-02	emotion and word consistent (face non-consistent)	anger	disgust	anger	15	(7	:	8)	42.8	(9.9)
D-05	emotion and word consistent (face non-consistent)	anger	fright	anger	12	(7	:	5)	32.7	(9.0)
D-12	emotion and word consistent (face non-consistent)	anger	surprise	anger	11	(7	:	4)	36.9	(11.6)
C-11	emotion and word consistent (face non-consistent)	joy	sadness	joy	10	(3	:	7)	43.9	(13.7)
D-07	emotion and word consistent (face non-consistent)	joy	anger	joy	12	(7	:	5)	39.9	(11.3)
D-10	emotion and word consistent (face non-consistent)	joy	disgust	joy	15	(3	:	12)	30.1	(10.1)
D-13	emotion and word consistent (face non-consistent)	joy	surprise	joy	10	(7	:	3)	37.6	(8.1)
D-14	emotion and word consistent (face non-consistent)	joy	fright	joy	10	(5	:	5)	34.6	(7.7)
B-16	emotion and word consistent (face non-consistent)	sadness	sadness	joy	12	(6	:	6)	39.6	(13.8)
D-03	emotion and word consistent (face non-consistent)	sadness	anger	sadness	10	(6	:	4)	36.3	(12.5)
D-04	emotion and word consistent (face non-consistent)	sadness	fright	sadness	11	(4	:	7)	36.5	(16.2)
D-08	emotion and word consistent (face non-consistent)	sadness	disgust	sadness	11	(3	:	8)	38.1	(6.2)
D-11	emotion and word consistent (face non-consistent)	sadness	joy	sadness	11	(7	:	4)	35.8	(9.9)
D-15	emotion and word consistent (face non-consistent)	sadness	surprise	sadness	11	(6	:	5)	38.1	(8.3)
E-07	face and word consistent/emotion unconsistent	surprise	sadness	sadness	12	(2	:	10)	34.8	(5.5)
E-08	face and word consistent/emotion unconsistent	surprise	joy	joy	16	(4	:	12)	34.4	(4.0)
E-10	face and word consistent/emotion unconsistent	surprise	anger	anger	10	(6	:	4)	42.3	(13.0)
E-11	face and word consistent/emotion unconsistent	surprise	fright	fright	17	(7	:	10)	37.4	(8.3)
E-14	face and word consistent/emotion unconsistent	surprise	disgust	disgust	10	(7	:	3)	45.9	(9.1)
E-12	face and word consistent/emotion unconsistent	fright	sadness	sadness	13	(5	:	8)	39.7	(14.6)
E-13	face and word consistent/emotion unconsistent	fright	anger	anger	20	(10	:	10)	35.3	(7.8)
E-15	face and word consistent/emotion unconsistent	fright	disgust	disgust	13	(4	:	9)	31.8	(10.0)
F-11	face and word consistent/emotion unconsistent	fright	surprise	surprise	10	(5	:	5)	40.2	(10.9)
E-03	face and word consistent/emotion unconsistent	fright	joy	joy	12	(3	:	9)	40.0	(11.1)
E-04	face and word consistent/emotion unconsistent	disgust	joy	joy	10	(4	:	6)	33.7	(10.2)
E-05	face and word consistent/emotion unconsistent	disgust	sadness	sadness	10	(3	:	7)	42.2	(20.0)
E-16	face and word consistent/emotion unconsistent	disgust	anger	anger	15	(8	:	7)	35.3	(9.0)
F-14	face and word consistent/emotion unconsistent	disgust	surprise	surprise	11	(7	:	4)	42.7	(15.5)
F-15	face and word consistent/emotion unconsistent	disgust	fright	fright	11	(6	:	5)	41.4	(10.8)
E-06	face and word consistent/emotion unconsistent	anger	joy	joy	11	(7	:	4)	44.1	(13.2)
E-09	face and word consistent/emotion unconsistent	anger	sadness	sadness	11	(4	:	7)	34.6	(9.3)
F-10	face and word consistent/emotion unconsistent	anger	surprise	surprise	10	(2	:	8)	39.9	(7.4)
F-13	face and word consistent/emotion unconsistent	anger	fright	fright	12	(4	:	8)	38.8	(15.5)
F-16	face and word consistent/emotion unconsistent	anger	disgust	disgust	19	(8	:	11)	33.9	(11.7)
E-02	face and word consistent/emotion unconsistent	joy	sadness	sadness	14	(6	:	8)	38.6	(9.4)
F-03	face and word consistent/emotion unconsistent	joy	fright	fright	10	(5	:	5)	40.0	(7.6)
F-04	face and word consistent/emotion unconsistent	joy	disgust	disgust	16	(7	:	9)	37.5	(8.7)
F-06	face and word consistent/emotion unconsistent	joy	anger	anger	14	(3	:	11)	31.8	(6.6)
F-08	face and word consistent/emotion unconsistent	joy	surprise	surprise	13	(5	:	8)	41.7	(9.8)
F-02	face and word consistent/emotion unconsistent	sadness	joy	joy	10	(7	:	3)	41.9	(10.8)
F-05	face and word consistent/emotion unconsistent	sadness	disgust	disgust	12	(3	:	9)	37.0	(8.7)
F-07	face and word consistent/emotion unconsistent	sadness	surprise	surprise	11	(4	:	7)	36.3	(12.6)
F-09	face and word consistent/emotion unconsistent	sadness	anger	anger	11	(4	:	7)	34.7	(11.7)
F-12	face and word consistent/emotion unconsistent	sadness	fright	fright	10	(7	:	3)	39.2	(11.7)
Total					1236	(568	:	668)	38.0	(11.5)

In: Psychology of Persuasion
Editors: J. Csapó and A. Magyar, pp.149-169

ISBN: 978-1-60876-590-4
© 2010 Nova Science Publishers, Inc.

Chapter 7

GILBERT'S MULTIMODAL ARGUMENTATION MODEL AND THE PSYCHOLOGY OF PERSUASION IN ADVERTISEMENTS

M. Louise Ripley
York University, Toronto, Canada

ABSTRACT

A half century after Vance Packard's *The Hidden Persuaders* labelled advertising as immoral because of psychological techniques used to get us to buy, we are still seeking ways to determine when an ad crosses an ethical boundary. Most advertising persuades by argument. Michael Gilbert of York University maintains we need to examine three other modes of argumentation as well: emotional, physical, and intuitive. This chapter examines the application of Gilbert's Multimodal Argumentation Model to a series of advertisements, exploring how analyzing in all four modes can help a reader decide whether a particular ad violates his or her ethical principles.

INTRODUCTION

A half century ago, Vance Packard (1958) in his book *The Hidden Persuaders* labelled advertising as immoral because of psychological techniques used to convince us to buy products. We still seek ways to determine whether a particular advertisement oversteps an ethical boundary when it attempts to induce us to change our behaviour by reaching us with a particular kind of argument.

Most advertising persuades by argument and most of those arguments are logical. There is a built-in bias in our Western culture that says that a good argument is a logical one. We hear it frequently in conversations:

> "I'm not going to argue with you if you can't be logical".
> "We can't have this argument if you're going to get emotional on me".
> "'What you feel' is not a good argument; give me a good reason why I should do it".
> "If all you can say is that you've got a hunch, there's no point in arguing".

Michael Gilbert, in his theory of Multimodal Argumentation (1994) maintains that while argumentation traditionally is associated with logic and reasoning (Balthorp; 1979' O'Keefe, 1982; Willard, 1983 and 1989; van Eemeren and Grootendorst, 1989), there are four kinds of argument we must examine:

- o *Logical* (from the Latin *logica:* of reason) of or used in the science that deals with the canons and criteria of validity of inference and demonstration
- o *Emotional* (from the Latin *exmovere*: to move away, disturb) pertaining to or appealing to the affective aspect of consciousness
- o *Visceral* (from the Latin *viscus:* inner parts of the body) of, having the nature of, situated in, or affecting the internal organs of the body, especially the thorax and abdomen
- o *Kisceral* (from the Japanese ki: energy) "non-logical communication that is a synthesis of experience and insight" (Gilbert, 1994, 159)

Gilbert defines *argument* as, "a communicative interaction centred on a disagreement" (Gilbert, 1995, 5) and this chapter uses this definition. In an advertisement, the concept of disagreement is between the advertiser who believes the reader should buy the product and the reader who does not at first so believe.

This chapter examines the application of Gilbert's Multimodal Argumentation Model to a series of advertisements. It examines in turn the logical, emotional, visceral, and kisceral arguments present in each ad. It then explores how an analysis of these different kinds of arguments can help a viewer decide whether a particular ad violates his or her ethical principles by exposing possibly unseen but powerful arguments in the advertisement. This applies to advertisers producing an ad (with or without the help of an advertising agency) and to consumers interested in evaluating and understanding advertisements and their effect on us.

JUDGING ADVERTISEMENTS

Scholars of Consumer Behaviour estimated we are exposed to more than 5,000 advertisements (ads) in a day (Armstrong, Kotler, Cunningham, and Buchwitz, 2010, 234). Advertising is a powerful tool, made more powerful every day by the increasing ability of the advertiser to reach us on many psychological levels. Most people love ads. We love them so much that we watch entire television programmes dedicated to showing us the best and the worst of them, but they do have an effect on our behaviour as consumers. Most advertising aims at changing people's behaviour, touching them in some way that will cause them to do what the advertiser would like them to do. Thus it is necessary that we take some care with the question of ethics in advertising. What makes an ethical ad is not an easy question to answer. To help answer that question, we need to understand the arguments made by an advertisement.

Johnson (2000, p. 149) says that "preeminent among [the purposes of argument] is the function of persuading someone...of the truth of something...." He further states that a good argument must not only be rational, but must appear to be rational. This is perhaps even more important with the arguments and assumptions in ads because the advertiser only gets the one chance, as the reader sees (and the advertisers hopes reads) the ad for the first time. If the reader is turned off by what appears to be an irrational ad[1], or by assumptions clearly made by the advertiser that are out of line, the advertiser loses the chance to make the argument for the wisdom of purchasing the product. This is why it is necessary for the arguer to respond "even to criticisms known (or believed) to be misguided" (Johnson 2000, p. 164). It is why the copywriter must take care in reviewing assumptions behind the writing, why s/he must consider all potential objections and criticisms likely to be made against the ad, and respond by adjusting the content of the ad.

A major problem facing advertisers is determining whether a particular ad can be considered ethical. Morris Engel (2000) points out that if we are to succeed in analyzing the bombardment by the mass media of appeals to purchase particular products, we must know something about logic in order to better judge the ethics of an ad. Ethics is a relativist issue, depending upon the person making the decision. What may seem appropriate to the standards of conduct and judgment of one group may offend another. Given, however, the huge presence of advertising in our everyday lives and the post-Enron concern with more ethical performance in business, the ethics of the way in which advertising of products is done must be considered. We also need to remember the argument that advertising not only reflects what is prevalent but has a defining influence on what prevails in our society (Holbrook, 1987; Pollay, 1986). To consider ethics, we need to look beyond just the customarily examined logical argument in an advertisement.

The purpose of this chapter is not to provide a method of rating absolutely the ethics of a particular advertisement, but to open for consideration different psychological ways in which different people may react to an advertisement. It need not ultimately be a question of ethics. One may find an ad objectionable even though it does not violate any ethical standards. Too often we underestimate particularly the power of emotion when analyzing an advertisement's argument. This chapter examines specific ads first in the logical mode of argumentation, considering structures of Formal Deductive Logic, the issue of false premises, and some fallacies from the study of Informal Logic. It then uses Gilbert's (1994) model of Multi-Modal Argumentation to consider emotional, physical, or intuitive arguments made by the same ad which may cause it to be questionable or even unethical even though it may meet the stringent requirements of logical argumentation. This chapter argues for the existence and importance of emotional, physical, and intuitive arguments as well as logical ones, but makes the assumption, with Carozza (2002) as support, that an argument or component of an argument may be visual as well as verbal.

FORMAL DEDUCTIVE LOGIC

Working with Formal Deductive Logic and its syllogism, we need to be aware of the meaning of some basic terms. *Premises* are the reasons given in support of one's conclusion. *Truth* in the context of syllogisms asks, "Are the premises true or false?" *Inference* refers to the way the conclusion is derived from the reasons given. *Validity* asks whether the ad's argument follows the rules of logic. *Soundness* is assured when the argument has true premises and valid inferences.

---

1 unless the goal of the ad is to attract readers by its very appearance of irrationality, which some ads do

The best kind of syllogism to construct when analyzing an ad created by someone else is *First Figure, AAA Mood*. This means the syllogism has a universal affirmative major premise, a universal affirmative minor premise, and a conclusion that is also a universal affirmative. Finding a syllogism in this form to represent the argument of the ad gives the greatest benefit of doubt to the advertiser. It would constitute a "straw man" fallacy and be too easy and unfair to construct a syllogism for the purpose of analysis without good structure and then criticize the advertiser's logic as if the advertiser had used that argument.

The following are characteristics of a valid and an invalid argument.

- It is impossible for it to have true premises and a false conclusion
- If its premises are true, its conclusion must be true
- If its conclusion is false, it must have at least one false premise
- All of the information in the conclusion is also in the premises
- The probability of its conclusion, given its premises, is 1

Characteristics of an invalid argument

- It can have true premises and a false conclusion
- Even if its premises are true, it may have a false conclusion
- Even if its conclusion is false, it may have true premises
- There is information in the conclusion that is not in the premises
- Probability of its conclusion, given its premises, is less than 1
- (University of South Carolina)

We need to distinguish between Formal Deductive Logic and the term *logic* which we use often in everyday language. Michael Gilbert notes the term *logical* indicates "not merely a respect for orderliness of presentation, but also a subscription to a certain set of beliefs about evidence and sources of information" (Gilbert, 1994, 159). An ad may contain some logic in its everyday sense and still not have a readily visible sound logical syllogism. An ad might have some internal logic, which does not appear in the ad, leaving the reader to fill in the blanks. Almost every ad will make assumptions, about the intended target market, about the product, about the scene depicted in the advertisement. If one reads an ad carefully (or even views an ad with no words), one may see where the assumptions have been made and probably know what the advertiser is trying to say, but that does not necessarily constitute a *logical* argument.

GILBERT'S THEORY OF MULTI-MODAL ARGUMENTATION

One of the problems addressed by Gilbert's model is the too-frequent perception that *logical* means *right* and *emotional* means *wrong*. Any of the four modes of argumentation may be *right* for any particular use. What may be *wrong* is the use of any of the four modes of argumentation to unfairly or improperly make a covert argument for the purchase of a product. Thus an ad may meet all the requirements for a valid logical argument but still be questionable or even unethical when we examine its emotional, physical, or intuitive arguments in addition to its logical one. When an ad does this, we may label it *deceptive*.

A non-deceptive argument in this context is one which makes proper use of the chosen mode of argumentation, which makes no blatantly false claims, and which argues mainly from specific attributes of the product rather than from insinuated extraneous effects to be obtained by purchasing it. It is fairly easy to establish what makes an ad valid or invalid in the logical mode. The premises and conclusion are true, all information is in the premises, and the probability of its conclusion is 1. It would be presented in a way that is proper according to the standards of formal logic. The presentation would be orderly and would correctly use available evidence.

The more difficult task is to define what *valid* means in the case of an emotional, physical, or intuitive mode of argumentation. This is particularly difficult with emotional arguments. An emotional argument may be made by using emotionally charged words or by using a picture to invoke emotion. Gilbert maintains emotional arguments include elements of "degree of commitment, depth, and the extent of feeling, sincerity, and degree of resistance" (Gilbert, 1997, 84). For the purpose of this chapter, and recognizing that years of research may be needed to establish finally, if at all, correct answers, we assume that a valid emotional ad would target feelings appropriate to the product advertised and would not distort facts to increase emotion. A valid visceral ad would emphasize physical qualities of the product the purchaser could expect to experience and physical reactions s/he could be expected to have with the ad or the product. A valid ad in kisceral mode would require intuitive connections that are not outrageous leaps of faith to make the link between benefits implied by the ad and those attainable with the product.

This chapter examines a series of print ads which use these four modes of argumentation in non-deceptive and then in deceptive ways, and finally in ways that the author believes make the ad unethical. The ads examined could each be placed in more than one of the four categories. Indeed, most ads contain all four of Gilbert's components to at least some degree. The point is not to prove categorically that one ad belongs in one mode of evaluation, but rather to utilize Gilbert's theory of Multi-Modal Argumentation to illustrate ways in which an advertiser or agency might explore psychological reactions to an ad and then decide whether most consumers would deem the ad offensive or unethical. The point is to do this other than through analysis solely of the logical argument made by the ad. When using Multi-Modal Argumentation theory to analyze the suitability of ads, it is wise to consider all four modes of argumentation and use the combined results to help form a decision. Not everyone will agree on either the classification of the main argument (logical, emotional, visceral, or kisceral), or on interpretation of the parts of the argument. Ultimately each person working with the ads will make up his or her mind as to interpretation and results. Part of what makes advertising difficult and at the same time exciting is the question of how to settle on just the right words, pictures, and text to send the right message to the right people – the intended target market.

ANALYZING THE ADS

Non-Deceptive Ads

Logical Non-Deceptive Ad: Duo-Pro Pipes

A business-to-business ad for Duo-Pro containment piping shows white pipe-fittings against a blue background in the top third of the ad. Small bulleted paragraphs of print fill the lower two thirds of the page. Although the predominant thrust of the ad is logical, it also contains an appeal in each of the other modes of argumentation. It is difficult to find an emotional argument in this ad, but the first paragraph claims the piping is made for people "who care enough about quality, safety and reliability to invest in the industry's premium…piping system". This may evoke a hint of the famous greeting card company slogan ("When you care enough to send the very best…"). It may summon some emotional feeling in the reader for the care with which this product was manufactured. The ad contains a physical argument, as does any ad that contains any kind of visual element. We see the pipes. We may consider how they might feel in our hand, sensing the smoothness of the joints and the density of the material, and thus experience a physical argument for their quality. The blue background reminds us intuitively of water, and thus makes a kisceral (intuitive) argument for the importance of the pipes built to carry it. The major mode of argumentation in the Duo-Pro ad, however, is logical, appealing to our reasoning processes. Following classic syllogism structure,

All M are P.
All S are M.
Therefore All S are P.

The logical argument in this ad can be constructed as First Figure, AAA Mood:

All pipes that meet safety standards (M) are pipes of high quality (P).
All Duo-Pro pipes (S) are pipes that meet (and exceed) safety standards (M).
Therefore, all Duo-Pro pipes (S) are pipes of high quality (P).

This ad is non-deceptive in a number of other ways. The industry and company standards referred to will have been documented and may be checked by a potential buyer. The logic is clearly presented in a proper fashion, and speaks directly to the attributes of the product. We can accept both premises of the syllogism and its inferences, so by the laws of logic, we must accept the conclusion that Duo-Pro pipes are worth buying.

Emotional Non-Deceptive Ad: Mount Sinai Medical Centre

Emotion is a staple good in advertising, partly because an appeal to our emotion often breaks down or overrides logical counter-arguments we might make. Almost all ads contain at least some emotional appeal, but an ad for the Mount Sinai Medical Centre in New York City has emotion as its primary argument. The ad shows a black-and-white photograph of an ordinary woman holding a copy of the *New York Times* as she smiles out at us. The subtitle says, "Yesterday She Was Blind". The copy goes on to tell us that, using laser surgery, the doctors at Mount Sinai Medical Centre were able to restore her sight. The ad contains some appeal to logic; almost every ad does in some manner. The copy tells the woman's story and links the recovery of her sight directly to the medical centre's 135 years of experience. In fact, we could accuse the ad's argument of the logical fallacy of hasty generalization in assuming that if the hospital could cure one woman it can cure all.

The picture of her holding the newspaper makes a physical argument as we view what she is now able to see. We find the intuitive mode of argumentation in the leap from the headline that if she was blind yesterday, she can see today. Again we see all four modes of argumentation, but with emotional as the major mode.

The emotional argument in ads is perhaps the most difficult one to evaluate in terms of whether it is done properly and in a non-deceptive fashion. There are no laws of emotional argumentation as there are for Formal Deductive Logic. Gilbert identifies rules for emotional arguments as including "such factors as veracity, non-exaggeration, justification of evidence, avoidance of bias, consideration of alternatives, and so on" (Gilbert, 2004, 16). In this chapter we assume Gilbert's contention that, "there are [such things as] emotional arguments (Gilbert, 1995, 5) and that, "the utilization of emotion in arguments…is perfectly rational" (Gilbert, 2004, 2). We take Gilbert's definition of an emotional argument as "one in which the words used are less important than the feelings being expressed" (Gilbert, 1995, 8), because in advertisements we usually are looking at covert messages as well as overt ones.

The emotion appealed to in this ad does target feelings appropriate to the product advertised, and does not distort facts to increase emotion. Work is being done (Duran, 2009; Ripley, 2009) on what constitutes an emotional argument and how such arguments should be evaluated, but we are a long way from understanding how to analyze an emotional argument. Elkyam (2003) even questioned whether it is fair to "analyze" emotional arguments at all, as he argued, with a silent visual presentation of pictures taken during the aftermath of Hurricane Katrina, the incompetence of the American government's handling of that disaster.

Nevertheless, in this ad, we can verify some of the facts behind the emotional argument. While we have no proof of this specific event's occurrence, we do know there are many true stories of such cures by laser surgery.

Visceral Non-Deceptive Ad: Birds Eye Frozen Vegetables

Any ad that contains a picture or illustration automatically contains a visceral or physical argument. Even an ad containing only print may make a visual and thus visceral argument in its choice of font style, colour, and size. In an ad for Birds Eye International Recipes Bavarian Style, the full-page colour picture is the major argument. We experience a visceral reaction to an image of fresh crisp moist green beans and the almost luminous yellow "intriguing little German-style noodles". The addition of the "delicately seasoned sauce with sprinkles of parsley" should soon have the reader's stomach crying for a bite.

The ad uses some logical reasoning in its suggestion that, "We could have just given you the tenderest, tastiest, greenest green beans and stopped there....Instead we added spaetzle..." The ad uses emotion in describing this food as "the most unforgettable serving of beans that ever sat on the side of your plate," but the predominant mode of argumentation is physical. The ad is essentially non-deceptive. There is some puffery in the "unforgettable serving of beans" but the ad stresses attributes of the product, and the physical picture is a good representation of what you would expect to find in the package. Purchasing the product can provide proof that the picture does indeed fairly represent the finished product.

Kisceral Non-Deceptive Ad: Westvaco Packaging

Ads that focus on a kisceral mode of argumentation ask us to make a leap of faith and connection. In a dramatic business-to-business ad, Westvaco argues to convince its packaging customers that it is the right partner to present their client's food to the end user. The small amount of copy at the bottom of the ad makes the argument that Westvaco "people work hand in hand with yours throughout the development cycle".

The ad makes logical arguments, with a bit of emotion in the concept of people working hand-in-hand or the revisiting of childhood circuses, but what makes the ad work is the link between the partnership of the trapeze artists and the partnership offered by Westvaco. In the full-page colour ad, two male trapeze artists, dressed alike in leopard skin tights and white boots perform against the black ceiling of a circus tent, one catching the other by the wrists as he falls into space. We experience more than just the physical tension of the picture. We make that intuitive leap from the partnership integral to this life-or-death circus act to the partnership with a packaging company that will ensure success of a food product. The ad is non-deceptive because not only is the picture directly connected to the concept of partnership, but in the survival of a product in today's competitive markets, packaging can indeed be a life-or-death decision, either the death of a company that does not succeed in business, or the death of a customer who eats poorly packaged, spoiled food.

DECEPTIVE ADS

The previous four ads were all essentially non-deceptive. They made no outrageous claims. They stated nothing which could not fairly easily be shown to be true. Their arguments for the most part emphasized the direct qualities of the product rather than implied benefits. The next ads are going to push those boundaries a bit. There is something deceptive about the argument in each one, but none will be labelled as unethical.

Logical Deceptive Ad: Chrysler Lebaron Convertible

A 1987 ad for the US$17,000 Chrysler LeBaron convertible compares it to the US$106,000 Mercedes 500SL as if the only difference between them were the US$89,000 in price. The predominant mode of argumentation is logical:

All things that are otherwise identical to a higher-priced item are a better buy.
Chrysler is identical to the higher priced Mercedes.
Therefore Chrysler is the better buy.

The ad consists almost entirely of written copy with only a small colour picture of the two cars side by side at the top of the page. The picture is less than two inches high and nowhere near large enough to enable the reader to ascertain physical differences between the two cars. The headline quips, "Think of it as a Mercedes with a [US]$89,000 rebate". The copy only mentions one other difference, a star with five rather than three points.

The argument is deceptive. We can consider the first premise true, that between two things identical except for the price, the less expensive one will be the better buy. The second premise, however, is patently false so the conclusion cannot be derived from the premises. The argument is not labelled unethical because we expect and accept a certain amount of puffery in ads. It would be as absurd to insist no ad could ever employ exaggeration as it would to suggest that many people are going to be fooled into thinking a Chrysler is exactly the same as a Mercedes.

Emotional Deceptive Ad: Pepsi

There is something almost perverse in using logic to analyze an emotional argument, even though we do it, even in this chapter. Looking at an ad without a syllogism from Formal Deductive Logic requires us to look instead for assumptions underlying the ad's message. Pepsi provides an example of an ad constructed of pure emotion, with barely a word on the page. We see four little Asian girls in school uniforms sitting on the ground in what looks like it might be Thailand, a few schoolbooks, four bottles of Pepsi, and in the background across a muddy street, a Pepsi and Coke stand in front of some shops. The only English words in the ad are "Every Body Need (sic) a Friend," printed on a tote sack that bears a picture of a white Anglo-looking boy.

This ad's emotional jerk on our heartstrings makes a connection between schoolgirl friendships and exotic locales, and the sugared cola that competes with Coke for the world's largest distribution system. The ad makes no reference to any attributes of the drink – quality, taste, freshness, purity – only to its apparent ability to help one make friends. Nothing is presented to argue that drinking Pepsi will make you friends. The ad may not be unethical, but it is certainly deceptive given its reliance solely on the suggestion of promised benefits unrelated to product attributes.

Visceral Deceptive Ad: Tabu

An ad for Tabu perfume presents a full-page colour picture of a female artist clad in soft linens, paint brush still in her hand as she is embraced by the handsome long-haired male model whom she is in the act of recreating on her canvas. The only words on the page are, "Blame it on Tabu". The visceral sexual image promises that if a woman will only buy this fragrance, she too will be transformed into a talented artist whose Adonis will enfold her as she struggles to put just the right touch on what will clearly be this century's challenge to Rembrandt.

The ad is deceptive mainly because it relies for effect not upon qualities of the product but upon the physical reaction of lust and longing created by the picture. The ad commits the fallacy of false cause, suggesting because this one woman wearing Tabu entranced a handsome man, any woman wearing Tabu will be able to do the same. Again, however, we most likely will not rate the ad as unethical mainly because it is a perfume ad, and consumers expect a high level of overblown romance in such ads.

Kisceral Deceptive Ad: French Wine

An ad for French wines consists of a full-page picture of a man and a woman dressed in disheveled evening clothes kissing in the kitchen. Next to them is a partially consumed bottle of red wine. The copy, "Wild things happen in the *oui* hours…Say yes to wines from France," makes the leap of intuition that drinking alcoholic beverages will lead to the answer "yes" when the kissing starts.

We may find nothing wrong with a couple's sharing a glass of wine and then spending romantic time together. What makes the appeal deceptive is that it does not deal with real qualities of the product but rather hints at effects to be obtained by purchasing it. This ad too commits the fallacy of false cause, and perpetuates a possibly dangerous stereotype of using alcohol to induce the giving of sexual favours. This latter problem is mitigated slightly for some viewers by the fact that while the traditional seduction in ads usually involved man's overpowering woman, in this ad, clearly the woman is in charge.

UNETHICAL ADS

The preceding four ads were labelled deceptive because each was based on a fallacy, an untrue premise, benefits promised that are not directly related to product attributes, or an unfair use of logical, emotional, physical, or intuitive arguments. The use of questionable appeal in ads is not automatically unethical, and indeed the charm of many ads lies in their exaggeration or twisting of the truth. Some ads, however, push this too far. At some point we decide whether the components underlying an ad are truly unfair, damaging, or dangerous, and we consider labeling the ad *unethical*. In the standards of conduct and moral system of the author, these four preceding ads did not cross the line from deceptive to unethical, but not everyone agrees with this classification. In presentations in workshops and classrooms, the following comments have been heard:

> Chrysler: "Advertising of any automobile that pollutes our environment is unethical."
> Pepsi: "The proliferation of American products in the developing world is unethical."
> Tabu: "Using images of sexual domination of women to sell products is unethical."
> French Wine: "Stereotyping of the French as overly interested in sex is unethical."

We cannot disregard these statements, nor can anyone pretend to make final and absolute decisions on the ethics of any ad. Ethics does not test, sample, or evaluate *per se* (Hegel, 1977, 279); it accepts or rejects as a relativist proposition. What is proposed is a method for determining an ad's ethical acceptability to those who may be exposed to it, through examining modes of argumentation and the tendency to deceive. The final decision, however, will depend on who is making the judgment, for the benefit of which viewers, and under what circumstances. In the following section, the author has applied a judgment of *unethical* to four ads.

Logical Unethically Deceptive Ad: Ryka Running Shoes

An ad for Ryka running shoes shows a woman with a tear running down her face. The copy reads, "Sometimes the only way to work it out is to work it out". We also see two pictures of running shoes, a picture of a woman exercising, and in the centre, a picture of a pink rose. The copy continues, "When you buy a pair, Ryka will commit seven percent of its profits to the Ryka ROSE Foundation (Regaining One's Self-Esteem) to fund community-action programmes to end violence against women".

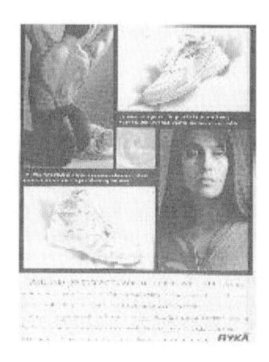

The surface-level syllogism is:

All firms that donate to a worthy cause are firms that deserve your business.
Ryka is a firm that donates to a worthy cause.
Therefore Ryka is a firm that deserves your business.

This argument is First Figure, AAA Mood. We can assume that most people could accept the premises. The syllogism is valid, but the argument is still deceptive because the benefits touted have little to do with the attributes of the product itself, a running shoe. This alone does not make the ad unethical. There is, however, a more subtle and dangerous covert argument:

All cases of pain in the world can be solved by buying a product.
Violence against women is a case of pain.
Therefore violence against women can be solved by buying a product (preferably ours).

As consumers in our consumption-based society become more sophisticated through media education and experience, more advertisers are increasingly employing covert arguments in their ads, often using more and more explicit and often violent imagery.

To use the purchase of consumer goods to compensate for evils experienced in the world is a questionable practice. That Ryka donates a percentage of its profits to end violence against women is admirable. They are, however, using an important social issue to create an ad that preys upon women's worries about violence for the purpose of selling a consumer good. The author has labelled this an unethical ad.

Emotional Unethically Deceptive Ad: Jordache Clothing

In an ad for Jordache clothing at the May company, we see a full-page black-and-white picture of a man shaking his finger in a scolding manner at a woman who is grasping his coat, thrusting her body toward him. Her long hair flows down her back, her eyes are cast down, and her mouth gapes in what could not possibly be labelled a smile. The stance of the chastising male is threatening, the evoked emotion is frightening, and it is being used to sell women's clothing. Giving the advertiser the benefit of a great deal of doubt, one might construct the following First Figure, AAA Mood syllogism for a logical argument in this ad:

All dresses that are pretty are good for attracting men.
Jordache dresses are dresses that are pretty.
Therefore Jordache dresses are good for attracting men.

We may accept the premises as true and the inferences as acceptable, making the syllogism sound. Examining only the logical mode of argument could cause us to say the ad is non-deceptive. One might question, however, if the person judging the ad's ethics had done enough. Is it a fair argument? Is it a decent ad to put in a magazine young impressionable girls will see? To answer questions like these, which flirt with asking, "Is it ethical?" we need to look beyond just the logical argument.

It would be unfair to the advertiser to construct a logically flawed syllogism for the emotions in this ad or one that had as its conclusion something negative about the company or the product because the advertiser would not have that as its conclusion. An argument exemplifying both these faults might look like this:

All women who wear skimpy dresses are asking for trouble.
Men prefer women who are submissive.
Therefore if you buy a Jordache dress you will be endangering yourself.

We can, however, create a First Figure AAA mode syllogism for the covert argument we have decided is the underlying message in an ad. This might be:

All dresses that attract powerful domineering men are good clothing for women.
Jordache dresses are dresses that attract powerful domineering men.
Therefore Jordache dresses are good clothing for women.

Although almost any advertiser's message ultimately will be "buy our product" (or "conform to our belief"), it is best to try to avoid having as the conclusion the simplistic statement that we should buy the advertiser's product. We need to look for something to imply WHY it is a good idea to buy the advertiser's product.

One major problem with analyzing emotional ads is the concept of trying to force such ads into the shape of a logical syllogism to view the emotional argument (All M are P, All S are M, Therefore all S are P.) Emotions do not necessarily work in logical ways. More work is needed on how to evaluate emotional arguments in ads.

Considering the argument in the emotional mode, even if using the logical structure, we find emotions appealed to and expressed which may be offensive to anyone concerned about relations between men and women. The author thus labelled this ad not only deceptive, but unethical.

Not everyone agrees, especially younger audiences, and one must always take age into account when considering the psychological mindset of a possible target audience. Younger students in university classroom presentations of this material have argued that the female in the picture is just playing with the guy, that she is coming on to him more than he is to her, that there is nothing offensive at all about the image portrayed here.

Visceral Unethically Deceptive Ad: Capri Cigarettes

Cigarette ads are one of the best examples of the misuse of the physical argument with ethically questionable deceptive methods. In an ad for Capri cigarettes, we see an elegant blond-haired woman sitting at a sunny table, a light shawl draped around her shoulders, the blue of the sea extending beyond her balcony, flowers blooming on the ledge, a picture of beauty. She is smoking a cigarette and the copy reads, "She's gone to Capri and she's not coming back". The other half (not shown) of this two-page ad extends the view of the sea and the patio and includes the United States Surgeon General's warning about the health hazards of smoking.

Trying to find a valid syllogism in First Figure, AAA Mode, we can construct this one:

All things associated with Capri are things that will make you beautiful.
Capri cigarettes are things that are associated with Capri.
Therefore Capri cigarettes are things that will make you beautiful.

Taking each premise separately, we can judge they are both true, if we ignore the equivocation and take *Capri* with a separate meaning in each sentence. In the first premise,

Capri refers to the beautiful isle of Capri in the Mediterranean Sea. Anyone might imagine the relaxation and ease brought about by a visit there could make one beautiful. *Capri* in the second premise refers to Capri cigarettes, and we must accept the truth of that tautological statement. If we accept each premise as true and recognize the syllogism as First Figure, Mood AAA, we would have to say that the argument is non-deceptive.

Even ignoring the equivocation, however, we must examine the visceral or physical argument made by this ad. There is nothing in the use of a cigarette that brings fresh sea air or beauty to the user. Thus the ad uses as its argument something that not only is unrelated to the product but is destroyed by its use. Instead of showing cigarette smoke which would cloud the view of fresh sea air, or a wrinkled face and stained teeth on the smoker, the physical arguments presented relate to the beauty of the scene and of the smoker. The author thus labelled this ad unethically deceptive for its attempt to sell an addictive drug with physical images of things it will damage. This tendency to use images of physical beauty appears often in cigarette ads, from the rugged Marlboro cowboy to the spring green scenes of Kool.

Kisceral Unethically Deceptive Ad: The National Rifle Association

The wedding ring and smiling face of balding bespectacled uniformed Police Sergeant Richard Beckman in a picture that covers more than half the page of an ad for the National Rifle Association suggests to the viewer a family man, a pillar of his community.

In the copy at the bottom of the page, he invites us to make the intuitive leap from police weapons training to the private ownership of guns as endorsed by the NRA. The story tells how Officer Beckman managed, through his NRA training, to save the lives of his partner and a seventeen-year-old boy who was tending the store when an armed ex-con took him hostage. The last paragraph of the officer's statement concludes, "I also believe in the National Rifle Association because I believe every law-abiding American citizen has a right to own a firearm. Armed citizens deter crime". Trying to fit a First Figure, AAA Mood syllogism, we can suggest:

All things that produce well-trained police officers are things that are worthwhile.
The National Rifle Association is a thing that produces well-trained police officers.
Therefore the National Rifle Association is a worthwhile thing.

The first premise can be labelled true. To give the benefit of doubt to the advertiser, the second premise also might be taken as true. If the NRA provides additional expertise in crime-fighting activities, it may be a worthwhile thing for police officers. Even if we were to accept the syllogism as valid in examining the ad in the logical mode, however, the overall effect of the ad is to bamboozle the reader with intuitive leaps of faith and connection that simply are not justified. The overall effect of this ad is to argue that if the police think it is a good thing, the NRA must be a good thing. Even if we believe Officer Beckman's unlikely contention that he learned to shoot with the National Rifle Association rather than in his police training, he is promoting not the training of police officers but the ownership of guns by private citizens.

The psychological make-up of the target market is an issue here. This ad would not be an effective means of persuading the reader of the need for private gun ownership if it were run in a magazine like Women's Day. Run in a sporting or hunting magazine, however, its arguments would be well received by most readers. For its abuse of intuitive arguments to promote ownership of weapons for killing, the author labelled this ad unethical.

The ultimate decision about the ethics of this ad does not depend upon which side of the firearms issue one supports. This is one of the advantages of the Gilbert model – it enables ethical decision-making in areas which otherwise tend to be black-and-white issues with many people.

CONCLUSION

To a large extent, what makes an ad ethical depends on how it presents its argument. Advertisers may use logical, emotional, physical, or intuitive reasoning, and most ads employ a combination of all of these modes. We accept that ads use some fallacy in making their argument; we expect some exaggeration; we laugh warmly when it is done openly and in fun. But when an ad uses argumentation that is based in unfair, damaging, dangerous fallacy, we may question the ethics of that ad. Gilbert's model of Multi-Modal Argumentation provides a method for examining more than just the formal logic involved in the argument presented by an ad, and thereby provides a better chance of identifying unethical elements in an ad. Future research should examine how we determine the validity of an emotional, physical, or intuitive argument.

REFERENCES

Armstrong, G., Kotler, P., Cunningham, P., Buchwitz, L.A. (2010). *Marketing: An introduction* (3rd ed.). Toronto: Pearson Canada.

Balthorp, B. (1980). Argument as linguistic opportunity: A search for form and function. In J. Rhodes and S. Newell (Eds.). (1980). *Proceedings of the Summer Conference on Argumentation,* 1979. Annandale, Virginia: Speech Communication Association.

Carozza, L. (2002). Visual argumentation: Traditional argumentation broadened (Masters dissertation, University of Windsor, 2001, 30-56.

Duran, C. (2009). Revisiting emotional arguments in the context of Western culture. Forthcoming Proceedings from the Ontario Society for the Study of Argumentation 2009, Windsor, Ontario.

Elkyam, D. (2003). Classroom presentation in Philosophical and Ethical Issues in the Mass Media, Professors Claudio Duran and Louise Ripley,: York University, Fall/Winter.

Engel, M. (2000). *The chain of logic.* Englewood Cliffs, New Jersey: Prentice Hall.

Gilbert, M.A. (2004). Emotion, argumentation and informal logic. *Informal Logic* 24:3, 245-264.

Gilbert, M.A. (1994). Multi-modal argumentation. *Philosophy of the Social Sciences,* 24(2), 159-177.

Gilbert, M.A. (1995). Emotional argumentation, or why do argumentation theorists quarrel with their mates? In F.H. van Eemeren, R. Grootendorst, J.A. Blair, and C.A. Willard, C.A. (Eds.). *Analysis and Evaluation: Proceedings of the Third ISSA Conference on Argumentation. Volume II,* Amsterdam, 3-12.

Gilbert, M.A. (1997). *Coalescent argumentation.* Mahwah, New Jersey: Lawrence Erlbaum Associates.

Hegel, G.W.F. (1977). *Phenomenology of spirit.* Oxford: Oxford University Press.

Holbrook, M. (1987). Mirror mirror on the wall: What's unfair in the reflections on advertising. *Journal of Marketing* (July), 95 -103.

Johnson, R.H. (2007). *Manifest rationality: A pragmatic theory of argument.* Mahwah, New Jersey: Lawrence Erlbaum Associates, Publishers.

O'Keefe, D. J. (1982). The concepts of argument and arguing. In J. R. Cox and C. A. Willard (Eds.). *Advances in argumentation: Theory and research* (pp. 3 -23). Carbondale: Southern Illinois University Press.

Packard, V. (195 8). *The hidden persuaders.* New York: Pocket Books.

Pollay, R. (1987). The distorted mirror: Reflection on the unintended consequences of advertising. *Journal of Marketing* (July), 104-10.

Ripley, M.L. (2009). Refraining Emotional Arguments in Ads in the Culture of Informal Logic. Forthcoming Proceedings from the Ontario Society for the Study of Argumentation 2009, Windsor, Ontario.

University of South Carolina (Greensboro) Department of Philosophy (2009). On validity. Retrieved June 2009 from: http://www.uncg. edu/phi /phi115/validity.htm.

van Eemeren, F.H. and Grootendorst, R. (1989). Rationale for a pragma-dialectic perspective. Amsterdam: *Argumentation* 2, 271-92.

Willard, C.A. (1983). *Argumentation and the social grounds of knowledge.* Tuscaloosa: University of Alabama Press.

Willard, C.A. (1989). *A Theory of argumentation.* Tuscaloosa: University of Alabama Press.

In: Psychology of Persuasion
Editor: J. Csapó and A. Magyar, pp. 171-182

ISBN: 978-1-60876-590-4
© 2010 Nova Science Publishers, Inc.

Short Communication

INTERACTION WITH A MIRROR THAT FACILITATES REFLECTION ON DAILY WALKING EXERCISE

Kaori Fujinami[*]
Department of Computer, Information and Communication Sciences,
Tokyo University of Agriculture and Technology, Japan

Abstract

The advancement of technologies has brought us numerous advantages in our daily lives, however, at the same time, a sedentary lifestyle has caused lack of physical activity and lifestyle-related disease, which is becoming a social problem. We propose to utilize a mirror as a medium that increases awareness of daily walking by facilitating reflection, where motivational elements are embedded into not only presented information, but also its presence. A mirror acts as a self-focusing stimulus, which facilitates *objective self-awareness*, a state in which an individual is ready for evaluating her current self-conception against an internal standard of correctness. Furthermore, the *objective self-awareness* is enhanced by super-imposing motivational information with the appearance of a person staying in front of a mirror.

In this article, we design an augmented mirror with four strategies to reflect on daily walking: 1) pleasurable interaction with information obtained through daily activity, 2) supporting reflection on each day's walking, 3) avoiding negative feelings while providing negative feedback and 4) facilitating inter-personal encouragement. Then, in-house experiments are conducted with 8 participants for 3 to 6 months. A comparative study with other display objects, a digital photo frame and wall, is done to see the effect of a mirror. The result implies that our proposed system supported reflection on a person's daily walking. Positive effects of the four strategies have also been found.

[*]E-mail address: fujinami@cc.tuat.ac.jp

1   Introduction

Today, the advancement of technologies has brought us environments where people can do many things without going out of the home, or they do not need to do anything because of automation. At the same time, it has led to a lack of physical activity and to lifestyle-related disease, which is becoming a social problem [15, 18]. A pedometer is a device that counts steps per day in an unobtrusive manner, which is utilized to increase not only awareness of daily activity but also a person's levels of physical activity [1, 22].

The technology advancement also allows a pedometer to evolve in two areas: network connectivity [19, 11] and integration into a mobile phone [17]. By connecting to one's PC or a portable gaming terminal with wired or wireless communication, data can be stored, shared, analyzed, and presented in more persuasive ways than mere numbers. A service is basically provided with a graph of a recent trend, diagnostic messages based on the data, or the states of other persons to encourage each other [19]. A service is otherwise provided as a gaming function[11]. However, people need to intentionally run such applications, transfer data, interpret complex presentation; when they are busy or in a low motivational period, it may become a barrier to restart *using* the system afterward.

Integration into a mobile phone would increase awareness of activity due to its "always-with" characteristic if presented on the background screen of a mobile phone, e.g. [17]. Actually, as Consolvo, et al. reported [3], a *glanceable display* with a stylized, aesthetic representation of physical activities and goal attainment successfully keeps a user focused on self-monitoring and her commitment to fitness. Although such a mobile phone-based service may provide instant access to information, it might not be effective for those who rarely utilize mobile phones and thus do not always carry them with them, e.g., putting it on a dining table all day, and those who have weak motivation to purposely check them whenever they put them on. We consider it important for them to provide a chance to reflect on themselves forcibly yet naturally.

Our design principle to address the above issues in usability and lack of chance of reflection is to embed motivational elements not only into the presented information itself but also into a medium. So, we propose to augment a mirror as a medium to increase awareness of daily walking exercise by facilitating reflection, where the information is super-imposed with the appearance of a person staying in front of a mirror. People usually become inquisitive about their physical appearance by looking at a mirror. Here, a mirror acts as a self-focusing stimulus and then facilitates objective self-awareness [7]. Objective self-awareness is a state in which an individual's conscious is directed toward the self, and the individual comes to evaluate her current self-conception against an internal standard of correctness; she feels tension and discomfort when there is a clear negative discrepancy, and tries to either avoid self-focusing stimuli or to reduce the discrepancy through changing attitude or action. On the other hand, when she perceives a positive discrepancy, she feels pleasure and happiness and tries to pursue the stimuli.

In addition to such an original effect of a mirror, we consider that super-imposing would enhance objective self-awareness. As suggested by Pinhanez, et al. [20] based on a psychological phenomenon known as "functional fixedness" [6], presenting information on or close to an object enhances the relationship between the information and the object when the information is naturally connected to the object. Here, the super-imposed information that represents one's activity would be quite naturally linked to the appearance reflected on the surface of a mirror, and thus facilitates objective self-awareness. In these ways, people are neither required to perform any additional action to get information nor is it necessary to change their patterns of mobile phone usage. Their daily activity is an input to a mirror (or a system), and a mirror affects activities of people through its presence augmented with motivational information. This is an interaction with a mirror, which is naturally embedded into our daily living.

In this article, we describe an initial case study to demonstrate the feasibility of our approach, where the design rationale of the system and the result of in-house evaluation with 8 people for 3-6 months are presented. We have also conducted a comparative study among other visually intensive daily objects that surround us: a digital photo frame and a wall (projection), which is intended to confirm the effect of a mirror. In section 2, designing motivational information presentation is described as well as a prototype implementation. In-house experiments are presented in section 3 followed by discussion. Finally, section 4 concludes the paper.

2   Ambient Walking Persuasion with an Augmented Mirror

2.1   Designing Motivational Expression

We have specified four strategies for walking promotion in an ambient manner that keeps original usage of a mirror intact: 1) pleasurable interaction with information obtained through daily activity, 2) supporting reflection on each day's walking, 3) avoiding negative feeling while providing negative feedback and 4) facilitating inter-personal encouragement.

People continue to interact with things if they find something pleasure as well as effective for the original purpose [16]. Based on our earlier work [9], we consider an appropriate level of unpredictability is a source of pleasure, which attracts people to the display and thus becomes a trigger to become aware of their health.

Secondly, we consider that not only an accumulated history, but also day-by-day one is helpful for a person to increase the awareness. An accumulated history means that the presentation reflects the result in a specific period of time, e.g. growing fish [13], [14] or a tree [12]. On the other hand, day-by-day history is shown in a manner that a person can identify everyday achievement at a glance, i.e. a feedback to walking activity of a day. Here, three types of day-by-day history indication are introduced: 1) the actual number of steps per day, 2) an accomplishment flag against a fixed number of steps and 3) comparison between consecutive days. The first feedback is straightforward that just presents the achievement of a day, while the second one indicates whether a user walked beyond the goal of the day, e.g. 10,000 steps, or not. The number for a daily goal is set to more than 8,000 based on each participant's preference. Although more than 10,000 steps per day is recommended to maintain health, it is not easy to reach through routine daily activities [2]. In this study, we stress commitment to a goal and its attainability to maintain motivation. With the third feedback, a user would feel satisfied at a minimal degree even though the goal was not achieved if the day's result was better than the nearest preceding day. On the other hand, a bad result should make her recall the day's activity compared with the day before. We believe that such a daily result contributes to remind a user of the activity of a day, by which she can develop a strategy to get a better result on an upcoming day more concretely.

To realize the first two strategies, we have utilized a flock of life-like characters that represent day-by-day history of walking of a week or more. Here, a character corresponds to the achievement of a day, and moves autonomously in the screen following the Boids algorithm [21]. As a result of local decision-making based on the neighboring view, a wide variety of flock forms emerge, i.e. unpredictable behavior. Furthermore, we have introduced instant interaction with the mirror, where a mouse click acts as "a stone thrown into a pond". A user can interfere the flock and observe the process of re-organization. This would also contribute a person to reflect on herself with a fun.

Regarding the third strategy, although Consolvo, et al. suggested "positive reinforce-ment" [4], we have decided to apply both positive and negative reinforcement based on the *objective self-awareness* that suggests a negative discrepancy is also effective in changing attitude or action as described in section 1. Drawing a realistic character, e.g. bird, might allow people to have intimate feelings and become more aware of the states. However, people with low motivations tend to refuse the system when characters do not grow or die, rather than watch their unhappy appearance [13]. So, we have decided to provide a char-acter with an abstract form of appearance. The parameters of a boid, i.e. the figure/size of the body, the neighboring view, and the velocity, are controlled by a daily achievement, and eventually the behavior of a flock is formed, whose detail is described in section 2.2.

Fogg states that a technology allowing other people to be virtually present is able to motivate its users to perform a target behavior [8] based on the social facilitation theory [25]. Inter-personal encouragement has been realized in a way that flocks for a group of users are presented in the same display, and members in different flocks try to avoid collision when they come to close. Here, a group is identified by color. Additionally, a characteristic that a mirror is basically a public object that is shared with others facilitates inter-personal encouragement. Here, mere chatting about the presented information on-site or off-site would motivate users to walk more.

2.2   Mapping Daily Walking into the appearance and the behavior of a Boid

Mapping a person's level of activity of a day into a boid is the most relevant task for making the information comprehensive, credible, and thus persuasive. However, we designed so that the presentation does not allow rapid understanding for a person, but gives her a time to think seriously. This sounds inconsistent with a previous requirement, *comprehension*, since it would pose multiple interpretations. However, as Sengers, et al. argues [23], posing ambiguity while supporting a space of interpretation around a topic, e.g. healthy lifestyle, encourages a person to relate the presentation to her life, which would support reflection.

The appearance, i.e. the shape, size, and the behavior of an individual character have been designed to reflect the healthiness of one's body, which are controlled by the ratio of the number of a day to the nearest preceding day. With this metaphor, we have tried to represent an appearance and a capability of a person who is doing more exercise, *walking*, and thus active; more walking makes a person thinner, and it allows her to move more quickly and have a broader outlook. This is what people generally wish to become, and we consider it easy for them to accept the mapping rule.

A triangle shape is utilized to clearly indicate the moving direction, and it is more likely a creature than a rectangle or a circle (ellipse). The width of a triangle varies according to the ratio of a day to the day before. The more a person walks compared to the nearest preceding day, the sharper the shape becomes. Figure 1 illustrates three types of boids with (a) lower, (b) equal and (c) higher ratio, where the neighboring view of a boid is also shown (the dark fan-like area). The definitions of the controlling parameters are shown in (d). Additionally, Figure 2 presents an illustrative example snapshot of boids that represents a person's walking results for one week. Here, the date is put near the body in order to help a person recall the activity of the day. The ratios of "yesterday" and "the day before yesterday" are presented in a relative manner like "kinou" and "ototoi" (indicating the two dates in Japanese), rather than a direct date expression. This helps a person find the latest results quickly. The feedback for the goal achievement of a day is provided by the blinking color of the body. (See boids for 23, 24 and 25 April in Figure 2.)

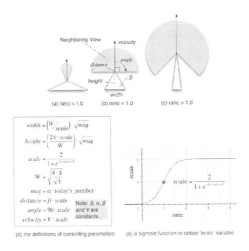

Figure 1: The shape and the neighboring view of a Boid with controlling parameters.

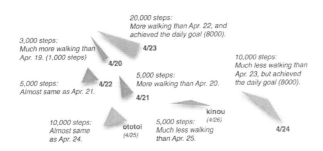

Figure 2: An example snapshot of boids for one person. Note that only triangles and their date annotations are drawn in an actual presentation. The numbers and the interpretations are just for explanation.

As can be seen in (d), the width and the height of a triangle are actually controlled by the *scale* variable that is represented by a sigmoid function (e). The reason for applying a sigmoid function is that 1) it can specify the lower and the upper bounds by saturation with a single function and 2) it can emphasize the difference around 1.0. The upper bound is especially required to avoid too tall triangle that is difficult to draw in a limited display area. The emphasis around 1.0 would be effective to give a noticeable feedback to those who did a little more/less than the nearest preceding day. Especially, a person who walked a bit more would feel happy with such a small but steady achievement.

The variable *mag* that appears in the definition of *width* and *height* indicates the magnification ratio of the body of a boid. This has been introduced to meet pilot users' requests; they wanted to see the absolute result as well as the relative one because they had felt "unreturned" to see a flat triangle when they could not walk more than the day before but the number of steps actually had been large, e.g. 20,000. Hence, the number of steps is reflected on the size of the body, where a large body is built as a result of a large number of steps. For example, the shape of a boid for April 24 in Figure 2 is an obtuse triangle that means the number of steps in April 24 is less than April 23 (ratio < 1), but the actual number is large, i.e. 10,000.

The neighboring view of a boid is also a function of the ratio. The behavior of a boid is determined by perception of a small neighborhood. Here, the view defined by *distance* and range (*angle*) gets longer and wider when the ratio is high. So, such a boid can find members in the same group to approach as well as an obstacle, i.e. other group members, to avoid earlier (See boids for 20 to 23 and 25 April in Figure 2). Meanwhile, a boid with short and narrow view tends to be isolated (See boids for 24 and 26) Finally, the *velocity* is proportional to the ratio, which allows a boid with high exercise ratio to move faster.

2.3 Prototype Implementation

An augmented mirror has been developed by attaching a glass two-way mirror board on an ordinary computer monitor, where bright color behind is seen through while an object in front of the board is reflected in dark colored area as realized in our previous project [10]. Boids' positions are updated every 100 msec. Figure 3 shows a scene of using the display. A 19-inch ordinal LCD display is connected to a controlling PC. As mentioned in section 2.1, we have introduced an interaction mechanism with a mirror through physical world events, where a computer mouse is utilized. Once a user clicks at any position on the screen, flocks of boids are broken and soon they start organizing.

3 Experiments

In-house experiments have been conducted for three to six months to investigate the acceptance of the concept.

3.1 Methodologies

Totally, eight people (four males and four females; four students, two house wives and two self-employed individuals) from three sites (Home1, Home2 and Laboratory) participated to the experiment. The age ranges from 22 to 72 years old with 30's as the most frequent range of the age. A participant who lives in Home1 is a member of family living in Home2.

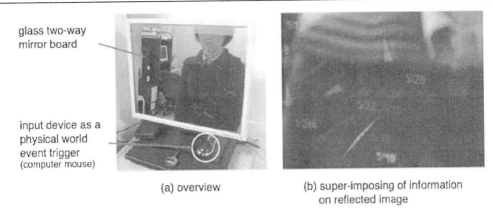

glass two-way
mirror board

input device as a
physical world
event trigger
(computer mouse)

(a) overview

(b) super-imposing of information
on reflected image

Figure 3: Appearance of a prototype of an augmented mirror for promoting daily walking exercise.

So, the data obtained from both sites are shared for remote inter-personal encouragement. The participants were asked to wear a commercial pedometer (TANITA FB720[24]) all the day (except for during sleeping) and manually report the number of steps of a day by e-mail from their mobile phone or PC. They just wore pedometers in the first week to get familiar with a pedometer itself, and then started utilizing our system. The mirrors were actually installed outside the lavatory to avoid damaging machines by dew condensation although it seems reasonable to install an augmented mirror into the lavatory because we usually spend time when we brush teeth, wash face, make up, etc. The alternative placement has been decided based on the preferences of the participants. They were 1) on the shoe cupboard in the entrance, 2) on a drawer in the living room, and 3) on the fridge in the laboratory.

Furthermore, we have tested the effect of a mirror with two different types of visual-intensive daily objects in an office (four people) for a week: 1) a digital photo frame and 2) wall. A version with boids that are super-imposed on a photo image (Figure 4-(a)) was utilized as an extension of a digital photo frame. A digital photo frame is getting popular, which could be another medium for information presentation in the future. A wide variety of digital images were tested to capture the participants' preferences, which includes a world map, landscape, food, buildings, and abstract pattern. The other version is boids projected on the wall (b), where information is directly presented on surrounding environment like the frameless display [20]. Although direct projection on a physical object is not so popular expression in our daily living, wall itself is very familiar object. These two versions were expected not only the familiarity of these objects but also the novelty of the combinations; the combination of artificially generated information, *boids*, and a photo image (or a physical object) might provide a curious scene that attracts a person, which would also be a pleasurable experience.

Note that the evaluation was conducted through an interview, rather than comparing the number. We consider it difficult to show the net result of the approach in a quantitative manner; various factors affect people's motivation besides our system, e.g. TV advertisement, organizational dietary campaign, etc. Additionally, as Rooney, et al. shows, just wearing a pedometer increases awareness of daily activity and leads to increased physical activity [22]. So, we should extract elements related to our system through the analysis of the interview. Further exploration of the evaluation methodology is subject to future work.

(a) super-imposed boids on a photo image   (b) projected boids on the wall
e.g. christmas showpiece

Figure 4: Example snapshots of boids on different surfaces: a) super-imposed on a photo image as an extension of a digital photo frame and b) projected on the wall.

3.2   Results from Participants' Interview and Reflection on Design

As foreseen from [22], all the eight participants have become aware of their walking activity level. An interesting thing is that one participant (P5) turned into the most active participant; she had not been interested in the walking exercise at all before the experiment. She sometimes spent long time with the mouse clicking interaction, where she enjoyed destroying the flocks and watching the re-organization process many times. According to her, she talked with herself in a mirror and checked her appearance against the movement of her flock. At the same time, she thought about her health as well as other things that were too embarrassed to tell other people. This is the very effect of a mirror. She likes to be a person with prompt action and self-organized. So, she disliked the disordered flock with flat and isolated boids, e.g. labeled with "4/24" in Figure 2, because it did not look so for her. Then, she intentionally walked more than or equal to the day before to generate or maintain "beautiful" flock.

We have confirmed the effect of pleasurable interaction, day-by-day comparison, and inter-personal encouragement through interviews. Emergent behaviors of boids like chasing and skirmish (or chatting) pleased them; the participants actually named these patterns and looked to forward to seeing new ones. Participants generally liked to see what happens next especially on the day they had walked a lot, and some participants intentionally walked more; the participants at Home2 (P2-P4) went further when they took a dog for walk. They were pleased when they saw the blinking boid, i.e. the daily goal was achieved, and even a sharp boid that was not blinking. A housewife participant (P3) liked the expression based on the ratio of two consecutive days. She was satisfied with the increasing number even though the number itself is small, e.g. 600, because she was aware of shortage of exercise and even slight increasing meant the progress for her. Finally, regarding inter-personal encouragement strategy, the participants enjoyed talking about their achievement in both good and bad cases, where they explained what made a boid so sharp (flat) and/or large (small). Through the explanation, they remembered past activities, which should have increased awareness of walking. We did not see a competition-like behavior among the participants in the achievement; they knew it was useless, instead, they, some active participants, attempted to overcome themselves like P5 mentioned above. However, a participant (P7) who often forgot to report the daily number preferred an idea of gaming with participants, where the right to change the background of the screen is given to a *winner* determined in any way.

Major negative comments on the system were 1) inappropriate installation of the display and 2) inaccurate sensing of activity. For the first comment, the participant at Home1 (P1) complained that the placement of a mirror-based display in the entrance did not provide sufficient time to reflect on herself. This is because of the situation where people stay at the entrance; the place is usually a passing point to the outside or inside, and they just do "final checking" of their appearance in going outside. This implies the presentation should take into account the characteristics of the place to install the system to work persuasion effectively. The second issue was obtained from P7 who mainly utilize a bike as transportation. Since a pedometer is basically to count steps, the actual number differed from what he had perceived as activity. Even though he rode a bike for five hours, the number of steps is not so large. This issue has also been pointed out by Consolvo, et al. [4] as a design strategy for increasing credibility, where they have adopted a manual entry (also edit and delete) mechanism. The advancement of an experience sampling method (ESM) [5] as well as activity sensing technologies would address this issue.

A side effect of the display is that a participant (P6) took an action that made him totally healthy, e.g. avoiding sweets, even though he was too busy to have enough time to walk more than a specific goal. This is because he notified of the small number of steps in a recent week at a glance of the display. Considering the final goal of walking exercise, *healthiness*, the system was successful for him. Another interesting effect is that a family at Home2 (P2-P4) wished to buy a pedometer for their dog and present "his" own boids on the same surface. They wished to share time and space even in a cyber world, which would contribute to make them mentally healthy.

Regarding the media to present information, a mirror-based one was actually not the most preferred one, although all the participants (P5-P8) accepted the suitability in a daily environment. The major reason for the negative feeling was the difficulty in seeing boids through a two-way mirror board. If a part of a reflected image has bright color, e.g. light-blue shirt or white wall, super-imposed information behind the panel could be drawn on the same area. This makes the information difficult to recognize. The color should be carefully selected so that it could be seen through. P5 preferred the photo frame-version when she saw particular background images: a christmas showpiece (Figure 4-(a)) and a landscape of a lake with mountain range far away. She told that she had enjoyed making stories using boids and the backgrounds. On the other hand, she was not interested in the other background like food, building and abstract pattern. Some participants found a world map image interesting because they felt they were flying on the earth. This suggests that the combination of artificially generated information and a photo image attracts people if they could find relationship with them. This could be explained by the notion of "functional fixedness" [6] as described in section 1. A projection-based presentation (Figure 4-(b)) was not successful in providing a curious scene that attracts people because of invisibility of projected information in a bright room. We also consider that the failure came from disconnectedness of the information to the objects on the wall. However, the tangibility of information was preferred by P5.

4   Conclusion

In this article, we have described our approach towards increasing awareness of daily activity, *walking*, and thus level of the activity. The design principle to address the issues in usability and lack of chance of reflection in advanced pedometers is to embed a motivational element not only into the presented information but also into a medium. So, we have proposed to augment a mirror as such a medium, where the history of daily walking results is super-imposed with a reflected appearance of a person staying in front of a mirror. Also, to maintain attentions of people, we have introduced a fun aspect where animation of life-like characters is presented to emerge unexpected behavior.

In-house experiments have been conducted to investigate the acceptance on the concept. Other types of visual media that exist in our daily lives have also been compared. The experimental results imply that the presentation can provide a person with an opportunity to increase their awareness of walking exercise. Especially, the reflective characteristic of a mirror suggests a potential to allow a person to watch herself from a third person's perspective, which would be helpful to notice her current habit of exercise and improve if not desired. We need to investigate the difference in the effect of walking persuasion between a mobile phone-based and a stationary object (mirror)-based approaches. We will further explore the value of *ambiguity* in reflecting on a person's activity and changing attitude/activity, which is currently realized by a flock of life-like characters and abstract forms of their bodies.

Acknowledgments

The work has been supported by Foundation for the Fusion of Science and Technology.

References

[1] D. M. Bravata, C. Smith-Spangler, V. Sundaram, A. L. Gienger, N. Lin, R. Lewis, C. D. Stave, I. Olkin, and J. R. Sirard. Using Pedometers to Increase Physical Activity and Improve Health: A Systematic Review. *JAMA*, 298(19):2296–2304, November 2007.

[2] B. Choi, A. Pak, and J. Choi. Daily step goal of 10,000 steps: A literature review. *Clinical & Investigative Medicine*, 30(3), 2007.

[3] S. Consolvo, P. Klasnja, D. W. McDonald, D. Avrahami, J. Froehlich, L. LeGrand, R. Libby, K. Mosher, and J. A. Landay. Flowers or a robot army?: encouraging

awareness & activity with personal, mobile displays. In *Proceedings of the 10th international conference on Ubiquitous computing (UbiComp2008)* , pages 54–63, New York, NY, USA, 2008. ACM.

[4] S. Consolvo, D. W. McDonald, and J. A. Landay. Theory-driven design strategies for technologies that support behavior change in everyday life. In *Proceedings of the 27th international conference on Human factors in computing systems (CHI '09)* , pages 405–414, New York, NY, USA, 2009. ACM.

[5] S. Consolvo and M. Walker. Using the experience sampling method to evaluate ubicomp applications. *IEEE Pervasive Computing*, 2(2):24–31, 2003.

[6] K. Duncker. *On Problem Solving*. Psychological Monographs No. 270, 1945.

[7] T. S. Duval and R. A. Wicklund. *A theory of objective self-awareness*. Academic press, 1972.

[8] B. J. Fogg. *Persuasive Technology: Using Computers to Change What we Think and Do*. Morgan Kaufmann Publishers, 2003.

[9] K. Fujinami and F. Kawsar. An experience with augmenting a mirror as a personal ambient display. In *Proceedings of the 8th Asia-Pacific conference on Computer-Human Interaction (APCHI'08)*, pages 183–192, Berlin, Heidelberg, 2008. Springer-Verlag.

[10] K. Fujinami, F. Kawsar, and T. Nakajima. AwareMirror: A Personalized Display using a Mirror. In *Proceedings of International Conference on Pervasive Computing, Pervasive2005, LNCS 3468*, pages 315–332, May 2005.

[11] Hudsonsoft, Inc. Tekuteku-Angel. *http://tekutekuangel.jp/index.html* (accessed 19 June, 2009).

[12] J.-C. Ko, Y.-P. Hung, and H. hua Chu. Mug-tree: A playful mug to encourage healthy habit of drinking fluid regularly. In *Adjunct Proceedings of the 9th International Conference on Ubiquitous Computing (Ubicomp2007)* , pages 220–223, September 2007.

[13] J. J. Lin, L. Mamykina, S. Lindtner, G. Delajoux, and H. B. Strub. Fish'n'Steps: Encouraging Physical Activity with an Interactive Computer Game. In *Proceedings of the 8th International Conference on Ubiquitous Computing, UbiComp2006* , pages 261–278, September 2006.

[14] T. Nakajima, V. Lehdonvirta, E. Tokunaga, and H. Kimura. Reflecting Human Behavior to Motivate Desirable Lifestyles. In *Proceedings of the 7th ACM Conference on Designing Interactive Systems (DIS'08)*, pages 405–414, 2008.

[15] National Institute of Health and Nutrition, Japan. Exercise and Physical Activity Reference for Health Promotion 2006 (EPAR2006). *http://www.nih.go.jp/eiken/english/research/pdf/epar2006.pdf* (accessed 19 June, 2009).

[16] D. A. Norman. *Emotional Design: Why We Love (or Hate) Everyday Things*. Basic Books, 2004.

[17] NTT DOCOMO, Inc. FOMA SH706iw. *http://www.nttdocomo.co.jp/english/product/foma/706i/sh706iw/index.html* (accessed June 17 2009).

[18] C. L. Ogden, M. D. Carroll, L. R. Curtin, M. A. McDowell, C. J. Tabak, and K. M. Flegal. Prevalence of Overweight and Obesity in the United States, 1999-2004. *American Medical Association*, 295(13):1549–1555, 2006.

[19] Omron Healthcare Co., Ltd.   Walking style, a PC-linkable Pedometer. *http://www.healthcare.omron.co.jp* (accessed June 17 2009).

[20] C. Pinhanez and M. Podlaseck. To frame or not to frame: The role and design of frameless displays in ubiquitous applications. In *Proceedings of the 7th International Conference on Ubiquitous Computing (Ubicomp2005)*, pages 340–357, September 2005.

[21] C. W. Reynolds. Flocks, Herds, and Schools: A Distributed Behavioral Model. In *Proceedings of the 14th Annual Conference on Computer Graphics and Interactive Techniques (SIGGRAPH'87)*, pages 25–34, July 1987.

[22] B. Rooney, K. Smalley, J. Larson, and S. Havens. Is Knowing Enough? Increasing Physical Activity by Wearing a Pedometer. *Wisconsin Medical Journal*, 102(4):31–36, 2003.

[23] P. Sengers and B. Gaver. Staying open to interpretation: engaging multiple meanings in design and evaluation. In *Proceedings of the 6th conference on Designing Interactive systems (DIS'06)*, pages 99–108, New York, NY, USA, 2006. ACM.

[24] Tanita Co. 3-Axes Pedometer. *http://www.tanita.com* (accessed June 17 2009).

[25] R. B. Zajonc. Social Facilitation. *Science*, 149(3681):269–274, 1965.

INDEX

C

CAD, 42
CAM, 42
candidates, 54
case study, 126, 173
cast, 4, 20, 164
casting, 4
cell, 87
certifications, 54
charm, 161
cheating, 106
childhood, 157
children, 10, 12, 17, 29, 43, 130
Christians, 72
Chrysler, 158, 159, 162
cigarettes, 165, 166
citizens, 167
civil law, 17
classical, xi, 6, 25, 46, 50, 101, 110, 114, 117, 118
classification, 18, 25, 26, 27, 153, 162
classrooms, 162, 165
cluster analysis, 144
clusters, 138, 139, 140, 144
coaches, ix, xi, 121, 122, 123, 124, 125, 126, 127, 129, 131
coercion, 45, 57
cognition, 76, 77, 79, 81, 83, 84, 85, 92, 95
cognitive associations, 58
cognitive models, 37, 38, 40, 41, 42, 43, 53, 54
cognitive process, 37, 53, 122, 130
cognitive processing, 122
cognitive psychology, 40, 44
cognitive science, 40
coherence, 38, 47, 49, 52, 57, 67
cohesion, 128, 130
collaboration, 40
commerce, 50
commercials, 72
commodity, 12
communication, ix, x, xi, 1, 2, 21, 23, 36, 37, 38, 40, 42, 43, 44, 45, 46, 47, 49, 50, 51, 53, 54, 56, 57, 60, 71, 72, 92, 93, 101, 117, 135, 146, 150, 172
communicative intent, 21
communities, 41, 43, 50, 51, 60
community, x, 35, 36, 37, 38, 39, 45, 46, 47, 48, 49, 50, 51, 52, 54, 55, 56, 57, 58, 59, 60, 61, 63, 64, 68, 146, 162, 166
competence, 43, 49, 62, 114, 124, 125, 128, 130
competition, xi, 54, 121, 123, 124, 126, 179
competitive markets, 158
compilation, 37
complexity, 47

compliance, 110
components, x, 35, 37, 38, 43, 49, 60, 130, 153, 161
comprehension, 38, 39, 51, 94, 174
computer science, 40, 43, 44, 55, 58, 62
computer systems, 44
concealment, 56
conception, 4, 37, 125, 171, 172
conceptual model, 41
condensation, 177
conditioning, 58
confidence, 73, 74, 77, 79, 80, 81, 85, 87, 90, 92, 94, 97, 123, 125, 127
conflict, 3, 4, 5, 13, 15, 16, 18, 19, 23, 24, 25, 32, 102, 112, 117, 118
conformity, 52, 66, 67
confrontation, 20, 117
confusion, 63, 74
conjecture, 27, 28
connectivity, 172
conscious activity, 36
consciousness, 150
consent, 30, 105, 113, 118
conspiracy, 72
construction, x, 31, 36, 95, 98, 105
consumer choice, 94
consumer goods, 163
consumers, 150, 153, 160, 163
consumption, 163
context-sensitive, ix, 1
continuity, 102, 117
control, 59, 62, 63, 72, 124, 126, 128, 144
control condition, 72
control group, 144
convergence, 44
conviction, 108
correlation, 138
correlation coefficient, 138
courts, 18, 21
covering, 135
credibility, x, 15, 19, 35, 36, 37, 38, 40, 41, 43, 45, 47, 49, 50, 51, 52, 53, 54, 55, 57, 58, 59, 60, 64, 117, 122, 179
crime, 11, 13, 15, 17, 19, 25, 26, 27, 91, 167
critical thinking, 77, 86, 87, 91, 93
criticism, 39, 40, 53, 87, 90
cross examination, 13
crying, 157
cultural heritage, 56
culture, 76, 123, 145, 149, 168
curriculum, 49, 52, 54, 61

G

H

0 1341 1366596 9